THEY TOO WORE PINSTRIPES

ALSO BY BRENT P. KELLEY

*Voices from the Negro Leagues: Conversations with
52 Baseball Standouts of the Period 1924–1960* (1998)

*The Early All-Stars: Conversations with Standout
Baseball Players of the 1930s and 1940s* (1997)

*In the Shadow of the Babe: Interviews with Baseball
Players Who Played With or Against Babe Ruth* (1995)

*Baseball Stars of the 1950s: Interviews with
All-Stars of the Game's Golden Era* (1993)

*The Case For: Those Overlooked by
the Baseball Hall of Fame* (1992)

PUBLISHED BY MCFARLAND

THEY TOO WORE PINSTRIPES

*Interviews with
20 Glory-Days New York Yankees*

by BRENT P. KELLEY

McFarland & Company, Inc., Publishers
Jefferson, North Carolina, and London

On the cover (clockwise from top left):
Dooley Womack, Lou Clinton, Rip Coleman
(ALL COURTESY NEW YORK YANKEES)

British Library Cataloguing-in-Publication data are available

Library of Congress Cataloguing-in-Publication Data

Kelley, Brent P.
    They too wore pinstripes : interviews with 20 glory-days New York Yankees / by Brent P. Kelley
        p.   cm.
    Includes bibliographical references and index.
    ISBN 0-7864-0355-1 (sewn softcover : 50# alkaline paper) ∞
    1. New York Yankees (Baseball team)   Biography.   2. New York Yankees (Baseball team)—Interviews.   I. Title.
    GV865.A1K437   1998
    796.357'092'27471— dc21
    [B]   98-28112
                                                                       CIP

Manufactured in the United States of America

McFarland & Company, Inc., Publishers
  Box 611, Jefferson, North Carolina 28640

To Barbara and Jeff

ACKNOWLEDGMENTS

As usual, great appreciation goes to the men who took time away from their schedules so I could interview them. Some of them were kind enough to supply photos when the usual sources failed to have what was needed. The Yankees were a great help with photos, as were the ever-cooperative Tigers, the Reds, the National Pastime, and George Brace. Appreciation also goes to the editors of *Sports Collectors Digest, The Vintage and Classic Baseball Collector,* and *Ragtime Sports.* These interviews appeared originally in their pages, though they have been reworked for inclusion here.

CONTENTS

INTRODUCTION

No team has enjoyed the success that the New York Yankees have. The team has won more league titles and more World Championships than any team in any sport.

It has been done with some of the greatest stars to have ever played baseball. Babe Ruth, Lou Gehrig, Lefty Gomez, Joe DiMaggio, Mickey Mantle, and Yogi Berra are just a few. Other teams have Hall of Famers they can claim as theirs, but none can boast the number of stars as the Yankees.

Stars alone have not made the Yankees into this greatest of all franchises, though. Ruth and Gehrig were not out there on that field by themselves. Mantle and Berra had seven other players with them as they dominated the American League in the 1950s.

Volumes have been written by and about the great players, but they all had supporting casts about which little or nothing has been written. And very little is written *about* them in these pages. Instead, they tell their stories themselves. The "Big Three" Yankees of all time are easily Ruth, DiMaggio, and Mantle; teammates of all three talk about the days they played and the men with whom they played. Yankee history from the early 1920s into the 1970s is told here by the men who made it.

There are All-Stars and utility players in here, but they all have one thing in common: they were good enough to be Yankees.

LOU CLINTON
Hot

Yankees 1966–1967

*Best remembered as a member of the Boston Red Sox, "Ponca City Lou"
Clinton enjoyed a high level of popularity everywhere he played. In 1960, he
took over right field for the Bosox when Jackie Jensen retired for the first time.
Jensen had a morbid fear of flying and these were the days when teams began
to use planes regularly. When Jensen returned in 1961, Clinton asked to be
sent back to the minor leagues. He was accommodated and put together his
finest year with Seattle of the Pacific Coast League. In 1962 Jensen was gone
again and Clinton returned to Fenway Park's right field as a platoon player.*

*By late June he was playing every day, and he tore up the American League
for the rest of the season. Batting .096 at game time on June 29, he started
hitting and didn't stop.*

*On that day — June 29 — he hit two home runs, one a grand slam, against
the Kansas City Athletics in Boston. Five days later, in a July 4 doubleheader
versus the Twins, he had seven straight hits. The All-Star break didn't cool
him off; on July 13 in Kansas City, a game in which his father and brothers were seeing him play for the first time in the major leagues, he hit for the
cycle and threw in an extra single.*

*In his final 85 games of the season, he batted .326, the same average
teammate Pete Runnels had to lead the league. His season average was .294.
He also banged out 18 home runs and drove in 75 runs for the year in fewer
than 400 at bats. He finished third on the club in both categories to Frank
Malzone and rookie Carl Yastrzemski, each of whom had more than 600 at
bats.*

*He followed that with another productive season for the Red Sox, finish-
ing with 22 home runs and 77 RBIs, both second on the team to Dick Stuart.
He wreaked particular carnage on the Los Angeles Angels, who, in an act of
self-protection, traded for him in 1964.*

*In 1965, his teams began using him more as a pinch hitter and from then
until he retired in 1967, he batted .382 in that role. Since retiring, he was
successful in the oil business.*

You were a very popular player. Why?
Lou Clinton: In L.A.'s case, I hurt L.A. quite a bit in crucial situations
[while with Boston]. As a matter of fact, I heard that after July of '62, when
I had hit a home run out there to beat Bo Belinsky in the first game of a
doubleheader and in the nightcap I hit one with two out in the top of the
ninth to beat Dean Chance, they had a billboard out on the freeway with a
picture of tombstones with "L.A. Angels buried by Lou Clinton". It might
have been situations like that. I don't know what causes the reaction of the
fans. I enjoyed playing, I know that. I don't know whether that showed
through or not.
Did the Red Sox sign you originally?
Right, by Danny Doyle. I was 17.
*You spent that year [1955] in Bluefield [Appalachian League] and you should
have been up a little higher [17-76-.361 in 288 at bats].*

I got out of high school and they sent me up there for two months and then the last month they sent me up to [Class] B ball — the Carolina League [Greensboro].

You moved pretty quickly. You reached the majors in 1960 at the age of 22. On August 9, 1960, you literally booted a ball.

Vic Power was up, Bill Monbouquette was pitching, and Vic was just a little slap hitter. I wasn't playing particularly deep in right field, Vic being a righthanded hitter and he didn't have a whole lot of power. He hit a line drive over my head. I'm going back and on a line drive you've got to keep watching the ball. I'm going back and looking over my shoulder. We were ahead, four to two, at the time and there was a chain link fence out there and on top of the fence they always have a pipe go across there to protect you from hanging up on the fence.

I'm going back and running and the ball hit the top of that pipe on top of the fence and bounced back toward me and as I'm taking a step I just kicked it out of the ballpark. I went in and argued that it hit the ground first, which then it would've been a double, but the umpire didn't buy it, so they beat us five to four. (Laughs) My rookie year.

Did it hit the ground first?

Nah.

After a good year at Seattle in 1961, the first part of '62 you couldn't buy a base hit. What turned you around?

I don't know. Carroll Hardy got sick to begin with.

See, I asked to go down in '61. The manager didn't particularly care for me — Pinky Higgins — to set the stage. It was over something that wasn't even related to baseball. We had a party one night after a special camp was over; we were down there for a month. I was going home the next morning. We had a big party and we came in late — two of us. Everybody else stayed out all night and we were the two who got caught. Joe Cronin caught us coming in. He [Higgins] never got over that and he held it against me.

I went up in '60 after he got fired in August of '59. I went up with Billy Jurges as manager and I made the team in spring training and was playing. They fired Jurges and he [Higgins] came back and first thing he did was send me down and then I came back up a month later when [Gary] Geiger had a collapsed lung. I played the rest of '60. In '61, Jackie [Jensen] comes back and I asked to go down to force them to use up my last option so they couldn't use it some other time. I'm just taking a chance that I would have a good year and somebody else would trade for me.

I had a real good year and I thought I had the job sewed up the next year, to be honest, and should have. But most of the time, I'd play a game and Carroll would play two or three games, then I'd play a game and he'd play two or three games; that's the way it went through the end of June. He got the flu and I had to play and, actually, the first night I went like one for four but I knew that I was seeing the ball well and I knew that I would be hitting good. The next night I played and I hit a two-run homer and a grand slam homer and I was off. I hit .500 for about a month.

In a July 4 doubleheader versus the Twins, you had seven straight hits. Who were the pitchers?

One of them was [Ted] Sadowski and one of them was [Bill] Pleis. [Jim] Kaat always pitched. Kaat was good for at least a homer a game. He's the one that I hit better than any pitcher in the big leagues. As a matter of fact, *USA Today* had an article where they were interviewing Kaat and they asked him who were the toughest three hitters he ever faced and I was number one. He said in the article I hit .667 that year; well, I think it was pretty much every year. My first big league game was off him; I hit three for four and from then on that was just about the way it went. You keep hitting them and you know what they have to do then. You know what they've got to try to throw you next.

And, especially, you hit off the catchers a lot. The Yankees used to be in a rut. I used to hit the Yankees well. They'd get in a rut—hell, I could tell you by the count what they were going to throw. The Twins did that with [Earl] Battey; he would get in a rut. He'd pitch you the same way all the time. That's why you knew what they were gonna throw and that makes a difference. Now when Jerry Zimmerman caught for Minnesota, I couldn't hit them. Same pitchers, but I couldn't hit them. With Jerry, there was no consistency with what he was going to do. He would get you out one way and the next time you wouldn't even see that pitch. And I played with Jerry and he did the same thing in '58 in the minors during the [Junior] World Series and the playoffs. He caught and we won ten straight games. He was a great catcher, but he just couldn't hit. But he called a great game; he'd keep the hitters off balance. But Earl Battey was a .300 hitter. I doubt if they realized how set he was in the way he called a game.

As I said, the Yankees were notorious for that, throwing certain pitches on a certain count. They would never throw you a fastball up and in unless the count was two strikes, no balls or two strikes, one ball. Otherwise, you never got a fastball up and in. You would guarantee yourself that you were going to get it if that was the count. Other than that, they'd stay away from you with fastballs and breaking balls. I don't know if they pitched everybody that way, but that's the way they pitched me.

There were a lot of pitchers that gave their pitches away and you'd keep a book on them.

On July 13, 1962, your dad and brothers came to Kansas City to see you play and you hit for the cycle.

Ed Rakow was one of the pitchers. I got five hits that night and the next

Lou Clinton *(courtesy New York Yankees)*

night, I guess, I got five hits in the doubleheader, or something like that. I had just worn them out in Boston and came back after the All-Star break and wore them out in Kansas City.

You wore the whole league out from late June on in '62 and had another good year in '63. You really looked as if you were on your way. What happened?

I got traded to L.A. [Angels]. (Laughs) I drove in 77 runs in '63 and [Dick] Stuart hit right in front of me and drove in 120, so it was a good year from that standpoint. When I got traded to L.A. we had very few on base, number one, and number two, I got traded out there because I was hurting Dean Chance a lot. I was wearing Dean out; I hurt him in critical situations. I got out there, then [manager Bill] Rigney platooned me against lefthanders. Hell, I never saw lefthanders in Boston. I couldn't handle lefthanders. And L.A. certainly wasn't a hitters' ballpark. It was tough.

In 1965, you joined Kansas City for one game. What was the story?

That went back to Chicago, Labor Day. I was two for three the first game of a doubleheader and the bases were loaded and they brought in [Bob] Locker to pitch to me and Rigney took me out for Willie Smith. They'd bring in a righthander, he'd bring in Willie. He took me out and I went in the clubhouse and swung a chair and, as I was rounding the corner, I gashed my forehead open on a cement block. The trainer came in and said, "If we stitch it, Rigney'll see it. We'll just put a bandaid on it and go from there." I said, "Fine," and during the course of the conversation I said something to him about the fact that I wasn't too happy and I suspect that the trainer went and told Rigney.

In the second game of the doubleheader I came up. [Gary] Peters and [Tommy] John pitched those two games and I was two for three again and with the bases loaded again in the fifth inning, and he leaves me in. (Laughs) He didn't take me out, which meant to me right then that he became aware of what was said in the clubhouse. *Then* he took me out and put Smith in to play right field.

We got to Kansas City and we have the next day off. I come back the day after and he calls me, "I didn't know a thing about it, but you got traded." (Laughs) So I go to Kansas City and I go out there and Haywood Sullivan's down there — he played with the Red Sox and he's managing. He said, "Go ahead and suit up tonight. The trade's not all complete yet but go ahead and suit up."

That was the night that Bert Campaneris played all nine positions. I started and when he came to right field I went out. The next day I go to the ballpark and Tommy Ferguson, who was the traveling secretary for L.A., says, "You belong to Cleveland."

What happened was, when cutdown date and trading deadline would come, usually they would put everybody's name on the list so nobody knew who they were trying to get through on waivers. They'd put all 25 names on it. The rule was, if you went on the waiver list three times in one year it was irrevocable and they had to leave you on it, couldn't take you off. What would happen, they'd put you on the list and if somebody claimed you the first day, then they'd take you off. You had to be claimed two days in a row.

Well, the league office is supposed to denote it if it's irrevocable waivers and they didn't denote it when I went on the waiver list. Consequently, they called [Kansas City owner] Charlie Finley — Cleveland had claimed me the first day — and said, "Look, we made a mistake. If you want him, you can have him." He said, "Yeah, we want him." That's how I played with Kansas City. And Gabe Paul [Cleveland's general manager] contacted him and said, "I'm going to sue you. He belongs to me." And that's how I ended up with Cleveland. And Charlie Finley never paid me. (Laughs)

At the end of your career, you became a real good pinch hitter. Was it a tough adjustment, going from playing everyday to coming off the bench?

There's a mental adjustment, but when I went to New York I knew what my role was going to be. I went over there the day after they announced that [Mickey] Mantle had to have his arm operated on in January. They announced it one day and I went over there the next day. Well, I knew what my position was going to be, that was to play for Mickey when he was hurt or down and same thing for Roger [Maris]. So you go in with a different mentality. Now, if you were playing on a club where you think you ought to be playing every day, hell, it's tough because you're mad all the time. It's tough to do anything right. But there, I kept myself ready to do pinch hitting duties and stuff like that, and worked hard.

I think probably my concentration wasn't good for 600 at bats a year. The reason I drove in a lot of runs, in my opinion, was I did bear down more and I was a lot better hitter with men in scoring position. You know, I was a lot tougher out with men on base, so maybe that was part of it.

You played with and against some super ballplayers. Who was the best one?

I know who the best hitter was. He had one bad swing at 42 years old. (Laughs) There's no doubt who *that* was. He said he could hit .300 all of his life, it was just too much work. He had one bad swing against [Dick] Stigman, and that was it.

There's so many guys up there that had so much ability that it's hard to say [who was the best]. The guy that impressed me more than anyone else — and it didn't necessarily have to do with having the most ability, but it was leadership ability — would have been Mickey. A team can't win without leaders and he was a leader. They had [Joe] DiMaggio as a great leader and Mickey was a great leader and they had a tremendous amount of respect from all the players.

When you were with Mickey, he was a mere shadow of his younger days.

That's right. He would *always* play when he could. When they operated on his shoulder, he was supposed to be back at the end of June. I was expecting to play until he came back. He hadn't run a lap, he hadn't thrown a ball, he hadn't taken a swing when we broke camp and went north. We were going to play three games in Atlanta and go north to open the season. We go to Atlanta, he said, "I'm ready." He told me, "The fans come out to see me play and expect me to play, and I will any chance I can." That was his attitude. And the players liked it.

Who was the best pitcher?

If you had to win a game, it'd have to be Whitey [Ford]. Best pitcher for a year, there's no doubt, was Dean Chance. Unbelievable. He shut the Yankees out five times and the only run they scored on him, Mickey, in the seventh inning, hit a high fly ball to right-center and it hit the top of the fence and bounced out. That was the only run they scored in six games. 1.65 ERA. Unbelievable! He was 20 and 9, I think, for a team that couldn't score any runs. He could've been 29 and oh probably.

Who was the toughest on you?

Dick Hall. I couldn't *foul* a ball. I laughed at him one night. I foul ticked the ball and I laughed at him. (Laughs) He didn't even waste time on me; he'd throw three strikes and that was it. I knew what he threw, I just never could see him, pick him up.

When I first saw Dean Chance in spring training, I said, "Oh, my God! I don't want to hit off that guy!" He'd turn his back on you, he'd come wheeling from the side and threw hard as hell and good curveball, but the first time I faced him in my life was when I was in that hot streak. Consequently I saw him good and I saw him all my whole career. That's the way things go in baseball. If you pick them up, you can hit them.

And ballparks. You can hit in certain ballparks. I hit well in Minneapolis because I played in the minor leagues there — in '58 and '59. Now, when Jack Kralick was with Minnesota, I hit him well. Cleveland — I was a .250 hitter against Cleveland. One year I did hit nine home runs off them because they'd try to buzz me inside with a fastball. They had all those hard throwers over there. They traded Mudcat Grant to Minnesota for Kralick. Kralick goes to Cleveland, I can't hit Kralick and start hitting Mudcat. Again, it's just the ballpark, plus the catcher.

Which games stand out the most?

Well, the best day, of course, would've been July the fourth — seven straight hits. And then the first couple homers I hit off of Kansas City when I got into that streak. In that streak, I remember getting two hits off of Pleis that day looking for a sinking fastball down and away and hitting it in the center field bleachers, and looking for a curveball down and away — trying to nick the corner — and I tripled into right-center. You know, hitting perfect pitches that a guy should never hit, but, like I say, at the time I was so hot they couldn't do anything else with me. They had to try the pitches I was looking for and I knew that and the guys were making perfect pitches.

Another time, when Sadowski was pitching, there was a man on first base or something and it was a semi-bunting situation. But I was hot and in Fenway and Sadowski was out there. He stepped off the mound real quick and broke his hands to see if I was gonna bunt or not. Well, I just instinctively squared around to bunt, make him think I was bunting. Then I knew where he was going to throw it — a fastball up and in on me — and I hit it off the wall for a double. Things like that just happened and you *know* what they've got to try to do. As soon as I squared around, I knew he thought I was going to bunt and he was going to throw me a fastball up and in and I hit a line drive off the left-center field wall. I remember [Sam] Mele came out to pull him out and Sadowski was cussing me out there, you know. (Laughs)

There are so many games that you look back on. Your first game — that was the one time that I think I really had a thrill or chill. The fact that you go out in your first big league game and get three base hits. That was meaningful to me. Having those hits with my family in the stands, getting in a hot streak like that. They're important.

I thought Gene Mauch was the best manager I ever played for. Absolutely loved the man. Very tough and I hung on every word he said. If I'd played for him, I'd have been in the Hall of Fame because he'd have gotten that much more out of me than anybody else did. Hell, he got me playing hard and doing roll-blocks into the second baseman or shortstop in double plays. I was doing anything for the man. Today's ballplayers, they can't play for him because he's too tough. Mauch was my first real good manager, and like I said I just especially thought he was as good as anybody that's ever managed. I absolutely loved him.

He had three wishes in his lifetime. He wanted to dance at his daughter's wedding and wanted to go to heaven and he wanted to play in a World Series. He said, "That's the three things I want in life." He came awfully close a couple of times.

He coached with Kansas City in 1995.

I was up there twice playing golf tournaments that year and I was hoping they'd be in town. I was going out and see him but they weren't in town either time. I think that was a great move on [Bob] Boone's part in hiring Mauch. That was brilliant. A lot of guys wouldn't have enough confidence in themselves to do that.

Do you still get fan mail?

Oh, yeah. I probably get two or three a week.

Any regrets from your career?

Oh, you always look back and say you wish you'd have done this or that or something. After I got through and started coaching kids, I had a better understanding of hitting and everything. Just as soon as I got out, we started using cameras to film the hitters with, studying them, and I learned more about hitting coaching the kids and watching the films. Had I known enough about it, I'd have been a better student of the game probably. I'd have been a lot better ballplayer. I thought I worked hard and everything. Maybe I was just too dumb. I don't know.

Would you do it again?

Oh. sure. And I'd recommend anybody do it. I loved it, but when I was ready to get out, I was ready to go and move on to something else. And I would never make a different decision than that.

It just seems like, from the background that I had, I can't believe that my life would work out the way it has. You know, getting into baseball and I've been very, very fortunate in everything I've done. A lot of people have helped me along the way and I think it's because of baseball — some of it. It opens some doors. I went to work with my uncle and he spent a lot of time in New York. He'd come to New York or Boston and watch us play and I ended up going to work with him and it made the rest of my life.

You're in oil now.

Yeah. It's like baseball. (Laughs) You know, if you're in a hot streak, it's fantastic. There's nothing worse than getting a dry hole or going oh for four. It's the same thing. And I absolutely love the oil business. I would have a rig running every day if it was up to me. Give me the investor with some money and I'd be out there. I love that part of it. I like competition and that's all a part of the competition.

LUCIEAN LOUIS (LOU) CLINTON
Born October 13, 1937, Ponca City, Oklahoma
Died December 6, 1997, Wichita, Kansas
Ht. 6'1"   Wt. 185   Batted and Threw Right

Year	Team	G	AB	R	H	2B	3B	HR	RBI	SB	BA	SA
1960	BosA	96	298	37	68	17	5	6	37	4	.226	.379
1961		17	51	4	13	2	1	0	3	0	.255	.333
1962		114	398	63	117	24	10	18	75	2	.294	.540
1963		148	560	71	130	23	7	22	77	0	.232	.416
1964	BosA	37	120	15	31	4	3	3	6	1	.258	.417
	LAA	91	306	30	76	18	0	9	38	3	.248	.395
1965	CalA	89	222	29	54	12	3	1	8	2	.243	.338
	KCA	1	1	0	0	0	0	0	0	0	.000	.000
	CleA	12	34	2	6	1	0	1	2	0	.176	.294
1966	**NYA**	80	159	18	35	10	2	5	21	0	.220	.403
1967		6	4	1	2	1	0	0	2	0	.500	.750
Yankee years		86	163	19	37	11	2	5	23	0	.227	.411
Career		691	2153	220	532	112	31	65	269	12	.247	.418

Courtesy New York Yankees

RIP COLEMAN

Pennant Insurance

Yankees 1955–1956

Once upon a time, there were only eight teams in each major league. There were no official divisions but unofficially the American League consisted of two—the Yankees and the other seven clubs. The reasons for the Yankee domination were basic: better hitting, better fielding, and better pitching. And a steady stream of talent coming up from the minor leagues.

In Casey Stengel's reign as New York's manager, he would regularly dip into his minor league pool to bring up pitching help in mid or late season as the doubleheaders and summer heat made it necessary to give a boost to his staff. And year after year it worked. Duane Pillette, Whitey Ford, Art Schallock, Bill Miller, Tom Gorman, Rip Coleman, Don Larsen, Ralph Terry, Al Cicotte, Zack Monroe were among those called up. Some of these young hurlers went on to greater glory and some didn't, but all of them gave the Yankees a much-needed lift in the stretch run of another pennant race.

Not coincidentally, the first year Stengel managed the Yankees in which the club did not win the pennant was also the first year in which late season pitching help was not forthcoming. The Kansas City Blues, their top farm club, had an uncharacteristically poor season in 1954 and there wasn't anyone available to help the parent club. Thus Cleveland bested the Yankees and set a new A.L. record for wins with 111.

In 1955, the Indians were again being pesky, as were the Chicago White Sox. Indeed, both of these clubs held the league lead at different points in September, Cleveland as late as ten games to play. New York did not clinch the flag until the next-to-last day and that probably would not have happened were it not for the pitching help summoned from AAA Denver, the Yankees' new top farm team.

First, in mid-summer Don Larsen was called up. Larsen had been acquired from Baltimore before the season, but he was sent down in training camp. When Bob Grim came up with a sore arm, Larsen was recalled and responded with nine wins.

Then at the end of July, veteran lefty Ed Lopat, the last of the "Big Three" of the early 1950s (Vic Raschi and Allie Reynolds were the other two), was traded. Many of the old Yankee fans were shocked by this—after all, it ended an era—but it created a roster spot for another southpaw. After Larsen's departure, Rip Coleman had become the ace of the Denver Bears. After a bad start, he had rebounded to have 12 wins and was overmatching most American Association batters.

In the last six weeks of the season, Coleman was used as a spot starter and occasionally in relief. He won two games and was credited with one save as New York edged Cleveland by three games. He may have been the difference.

Coleman's career never took off after that, though. He spent another year in New York, was traded to the Athletics, and was up and down for the rest of the decade. He retired from baseball in the early 1960s. Nowadays he does a lot of fishing.

Did the Yankees sign you originally?
Rip Coleman: Yes. The local scout was a guy named Tom Kane. He was

the bird-dog and he had Paul Krichell, who was their head scout, come up and he did the actual signing.

I was at Wake Forest. They scouted me all through high school and my father insisted I go to college so the Yankees made a deal with us that they would pay for college — board, room, books, the whole thing and some spending money. On the basis of that, when I graduated or when I came to sign, I gave them first crack. It didn't really work out that way because when it came time to sign I went around and worked out with various clubs. Although the agreement had stated if they [the Yankees] met any other club's bonus I would sign with them, they didn't. The Phillies offered me more money, but all of a sudden the Phillies, who were supposed to be in Albany to sign me on a Monday, called up on Friday and said, "We can't touch you."

Subsequent to that, we found out that Bob Carpenter, who owned the Phillies, had gone to the fights in New York with Dan Topping, who owned the Yankees, and Krichell. The next word we got was that the Phillies didn't want me at any price. The money was not what the Phillies had offered. In fact, they were about $25,000 shy. I got 30 plus the college and all that.

They sent you to Binghamton.

The Eastern League. It was probably the best [Class] A league in the country.

I had to stay in school until school was over. Wake Forest played very good baseball and also I'd been to spring training with Binghamton that year for about ten days — Orangeburg, South Carolina — so I really didn't have a great adjustment to make. About the only thing I needed to do was get the ball over the plate. I think the first game I started — in Hartford or someplace — I walked myself out of the ball game. That might have had something to do with nerves. Then after that, it was just a matter of throwing strikes. I really didn't have any problem at that point. I threw as hard as I ever did in my life and I also had an exceptionally good curveball.

They moved you all the way up to Triple A the next year.

K.C., yes. I didn't get there until the end of June because of school. That year we had a good team — played in the Little World Series. We had a very good team; we had Bob Cerv, Moose Skowron, Jim Brideweser — we had some good ballplayers. Billy Virdon, although he got sent out when I was sent there, which was a crime, but they didn't have any money tied up in him and they did in me.

I threw very hard. I had a very good fastball, so when all else failed you could just tell 'em you were throwing it and throw it and still get 'em out. And at that time, I still had a very good curveball. Although I might have been a little bit wild, I had the stuff to pitch my way out of it in most cases. I wasn't really learning anything about pitching; I was just getting by on whatever natural talent I had.

Rip Coleman *(courtesy New York Yankees)*

I never learned to pitch 'til ... pretty much until I was all through. I mean, I would say in Denver under Ralph Houk I learned to pitch somewhat. I was a better pitcher there then than I was my first two or three years. I think I maybe learned to pitch to a certain degree for the first time really the year I lost 16 games for Kansas City [1954]. We had a poor team and, hell, I pitched every damn day it seemed like. We were terrible. (Laughs) But still, in a situation like that, you tend to learn to pitch. You can't go out there and throw nothing but fastballs when you're pitching every third day all summer in that heat. And, therefore, I necessarily *had* to go to other stuff and try and change speeds more and that kind of thing.

You were very successful in Denver.

I started out very, very poorly. I was down to about 160 pounds from 190 'cause of the heat out there [in Kansas City]. They said, "You gotta put on weight over the winter," so I certainly did. I laid on my butt and drank beer and wound up about 210 when I went to Lake Wales [Florida], where spring training was, and I couldn't get out of my own way. When the season started, I think I lost my first five games.

But Ralph Houk was the manager — that was his first year managing — and he just told me, "I don't give a damn if you lose 20 games. You're gonna start every fourth day." So finally I pitched my way into shape — or got into shape — and once I got into shape I had no trouble at all.

You know, we never lost in Denver. We got acclimated to that atmosphere out there and the poor guys that came in from like Louisville and places like that, I mean their noses were bleeding after a couple of innings. You always had the idea if you just stayed in the ball game, you were gonna win. We never lost at home.

We had a great team out there. Great manager. It was a fun summer. Don Larsen came down. He didn't start the season there but he was there most of the year and he had a hell of a year and I had a hell of a year. He got called up about three weeks ahead of me, and he immediately started to win like crazy up there. Then they called me up.

Do you remember your first appearance for the Yankees [August 15, 1955]?

I think it was in Baltimore. I joined the club in Baltimore, I think on Saturday and pitched on Sunday in the second game of a doubleheader. I won. I think I pitched 6 2/3 [innings] and I remember I struck out 12 or 13 men.

You were one in a long line of young pitchers the Yankees would bring up late in a season to give them help down the stretch.

Which really hurt their minor league clubs on many occasions. Houk continued to win at Denver, but pulling Larsen and me out then could've put him in a very bad position.

You pitched in one game in the 1955 World Series.

Yes. I was terrible. Stengel had just got through saying in the meeting before the game, "We won't use any left-handers with these short walls [in Brooklyn]." I've never been so damn nervous in my life. I know I relieved Larsen and I think I only got about two outs.

It ranks high in the most nervous moments, but it's probably one of the most disappointing moments I've ever experienced in baseball. What the hell, it's the World Series! If you're gonna do good, do it there. And at that time, I'm kind of the fair-haired kid. As I remember, at the end of the summer the

Yankees put a list in the papers of the people who were expendable and most of 'em were. I happened to be one of the few that wasn't, so I was in their eyes, at least, a hot prospect at that time, and I particularly wanted to do well in the Series and I did anything *but* well.

You were still with the Yankees in 1956 and, even though you were three and five, you pitched well.

I wanted to be a starter and thought I would be after the year before. I had a very good spring and at the start of the season I was just spot starting. I was getting eight, nine, ten days between starts and I didn't like it and I showed my dislike for it, which is something you didn't do with the Yankees. It just seemed the games I did spot start that Tom Morgan came in to relieve me most times and *every* instance he blew the ball game.

Finally, being young and stupid, Stengel came out to get the ball from me one game — I'd thrown a hundred pitches or something but I was leading by two or three runs — and when I saw Morgan come out of the bullpen I just told him I wouldn't give him the ball. He told me I'd better, so I threw it into center field and I never pitched another game [for the Yankees], I don't think.

I was nothing but a starter in the minors, except like if they needed a left-hander to strike somebody out or something they might call you in the day after you pitched. And obviously I was so much more successful in the minors than I ever was in the majors, so you can say, in that context, I was much more successful as a starter than I was as a reliever.

However, when I got sent to Kansas City [A's], you have to remember I was in the rotation, along with [Ned] Garver and so forth; I was starting every fourth day. I lost seven ball games. Some I pitched well in, some I didn't pitch worth a damn, but that's certainly far from successful.

Then, of course, I was put in the bullpen. Quite frankly, when I was with Kansas City I felt I did pitch well out of the bullpen. I didn't get a lot of wins, that's for sure, but, let's face it, the club didn't get a lot of wins. I really pitched better than I did any other time in the major leagues in relief for Kansas City, yet I couldn't do a damn thing in Kansas City starting.

Hell, I went back and forth to Buffalo so many times I was dizzy, but the thing about it is they'd send you to Buffalo and you'd be down there for one game or two games, you'd win, they'd call you back, they'd start you immediately. If you lost they'd send you right back. There was a time there that summer when I got called back to Kansas City and I think I wasn't there ten days. I spent a lot of time going back and forth.

The thing is, I was usually the middle man. I was not the guy that was coming in and closing, which would show on the record because it would show saves. I was picking up in the fourth, fifth, sixth, seventh innings — something like that. But I really felt that I had pitched fairly well there, not nearly as well as I had hoped but certainly better than I did as a starter.

In 1957 you didn't win a game but you're credited with a shutout.

You know what it was, I think that was a five-inning ball game and rain and it was nothing-nothing.

In 1959 you were with both Kansas City and Baltimore.

I was in Kansas City most of the year and then at the end of the season, they [Baltimore] had a chance for the playoffs. They had Billy O'Dell as a left-hander and [Paul] Richards got me to help out, but I didn't pitch much.

Then I started the next season in Baltimore but about May I went to Toronto [International League] and had a real good year. Great place to play. You'd find a little extra check for a thousand dollars in your locker every time you pitched a good ball game. We had a payroll that was probably higher than a lot of the clubs in the American League because [Jack Kent] Cooke really paid, I mean, big-time! And we won. Nobody could touch us.

I played there that year and '61 and in '62 Cooke got United States citizenship and pulled out with his money. The first thing they did [the new owners] was try to cut the highest-paid players. I remember being called in. I was going badly that year; I was out of shape and I had just started to come around. They told me the Harbor Commission or something was taking over the ballclub and they were cutting my salary by 50 percent and I said, "Not hardly you aren't!" So I just quit. I wasn't gonna play for that kind of money.

I went up to my summer home and fished. Irv Noren at that time was managing Hawaii [PCL] so I got a call from Toronto saying that Hawaii would pick up my full salary that I was getting at Toronto. Irv tried to talk me into it and I've always regretted not going, but I turned it down. My daughter was getting older and we were a little sick of bouncing around, so I just bagged it. With what transpired after that — the expansion and so forth — I've always regretted to a certain extent that I quit right then. There were open spots and I could still throw.

I think the big difference between my career in the minors and the majors is that in the minors every guy that came up there I tried to strike out. It wasn't the thought, I hope they hit it here, I hope they hit it there. My thought was, I'm gonna strike this sucker out. When I got to the majors, I guess being overly impressed with the fact that they were in the majors, I was thinking on the context of, I hope I can get 'em out, and that's a big bad difference because all of a sudden you're not nearly as aggressive. I had realized that *at* the point I quit, really, that I would never make that mistake again. But coupled with that, somewhere and for some unknown reason about three years into my career, I lost my curveball entirely. I had a great one to start and suddenly it was gone and I never could get it back. I didn't hurt my arm. I have no explanation for you.

I used to have to improvise with sliders and forkballs and things like that, but there's nothing that answers the problem like a hell of a good curve behind a good fastball. I lost it and it made all the difference in the world. I went from a power pitcher that really had no fear of *any* hitter walking up there to a guy that said, "Uh-oh, I gotta be careful because they can lay on that fastball now." I had nothing else to show 'em that was nearly as good. I became a one-pitch pitcher. Had I kept the curve to keep 'em honest, I think it would've been a whole different situation. You know, all the coaches — nobody — could tell me. At least, if they were telling me right I couldn't do it.

It gets to be mental after a while.

Oh, it definitely does. You get in a spot where you gotta throw the fast-ball because you can't rely on anything else. You're thinking to yourself, I gotta be so *fine* with this, I gotta put it right on the black. And then, of course, you overthrow or you do something.

The other big thing about it, if I had an observation about playing pro-fessional baseball, the guys you find to be the most successful are not the thinkers. And that goes for the hitters as well as the pitchers. Self-analysis is bad, very bad. You wind up invariably out-thinking yourself. You're think-ing, I gotta be sure I let this go in front of me, that I pull it down just so. When you get in the game, you say, "Arm, do it!" You don't think about it.

When you start thinking about mechanics, you have no mechanics.

Absolutely. That's what you tend to do because if you're having trouble with a pitch, you're gonna say, "Now I must do it *just* right; I gotta let that ball go *just* right." Once you start doing that, you're done. You can't do it. *That* you may do on the side, but you sure as hell don't do it in a game.

Who was the best player you saw?

I'd say [Mickey] Mantle. Not the best hitter; [Ted] Williams was. Man-tle was the best all-around player. He could do more and God knows what he could've done if he'd been healthy. He made you feel like you were play-ing in one league, but he was playing in another one. I think he could've had many years like '56 if he hadn't been in pain all the time. Besides that, Mickey was so muscular that he was forever pulling muscles or getting charlie horses and things of that nature.

When he hit 'em, oh man! There was nobody that could touch off a ball like he could. (Laughs) It's like the difference between watching a good pro longball hitter on the golf course and a good weekend golfer.

What about the best pitcher?

I'd say [Whitey] Ford, day-in and day-out. And I say that for several rea-sons. Whitey always pitched against the other club's best pitcher. That's the only way he was happy and they tried to regulate his rotation that way, so when he won 18 games or whatever, he was winning against Billy Pierce or Bob Lemon or guys like that.

When Stengel left, Ford began pitching in regular rotation and began fac-ing the weaker teams. Then he started winning 20.

Yeah, that's true, but, then again, I wonder if that was advisable. If you could look at his sequence of starts that year and see whether the guy that *would've* pitched against him won. There's only one guy gonna win it. If he beats the top guy, you got a hell of an edge.

Also Ford's innings went up.

I'm not saying Stengel was wrong. Maybe he was right in Whitey's case simply because Whitey was perfectly capable of pitching every fourth day. He was strong. Still in all, he's beating the other guys' best pitchers every time. I think he could have prolonged his career because Whitey was fairly well along by the time Stengel left. Maybe adding another 75 innings was not the best thing to do at his stage.

Yes, he was the best *pitcher.* Not the best stuff. Not by *far.* He'd win for you. The best stuff I ever saw and the kid that, I think, would have revolutionized pitching and been so far above — he would've been to pitching what Mantle was to hitting in '56 — was Herb Score. The guys, they weren't even in the same league with him. Nobody was. He overmatched *every* hitter he faced. He was unbelievable!

He was in Indianapolis one year when I was at Kansas City [Blues]. We pitched against each other five times; he beat me five times. He shut me out three times. Every game was a complete game for both of us. I think I averaged 14 strikeouts and I think he averaged something like 18 and struck out 22 once. He was just unbelievable! He threw so hard you could not follow the ball. Forget about it.

But Cleveland in those days, they had four starters, for crying out loud, that all threw around a hundred [mph]. Now they talk 95 is incredible. They had [Early] Wynn, Lemon, [Mike] Garcia, and Score, and [Bob] Feller, although Feller was done but he wasn't throwing slow. Then they had Ray Narleski in the bullpen and he could fire. And they didn't win. We beat 'em every year. Our defense and hitting was better. Granted, we had to hit against those guys but everybody on our club was a good hitter, even the guys that weren't playing.

Do you get much fan mail today?

I get an awful lot of bubble gum cards. I don't know what's "much"; certainly not as much as guys that were stars. I send 'em to a place called *Sports Autographs.* They came along a few years back. It got to be a deluge. An awful lot of guys jumped on that.

Did you save souvenirs from your career?

I had a few. I had, like, World Series bats and things. I gave most of 'em to clients or kids of clients and things like that, so I really have nothing left. Baseball memorabilia wasn't anything in my day. I wish I had [saved things], don't get me wrong. I can remember Mantle burning carton after carton of his baseball cards because you had to get 'em out of the locker. You had so damn many of 'em you couldn't get dressed. Stop and think what that would be worth in his case. (Laughs)

If you were a kid now, would you be a ballplayer again?

For this kind of money? You bet your life! Hell yes, I would! The way it is now, with baseball as diluted as it is, with so many teams and the talent so diluted, I honestly think that anybody that was playing when they had 16 ball-clubs — stars, rinkeydinks, all of 'em — could sure find a place to make a lot of money right now. Even the guys that were mediocre in my time would be making a lot of money today.

WALTER GARY (RIP) COLEMAN
Born July 31, 1931, Troy, New York
Ht. 6'2" Wt. 185 Batted and Threw Left

Year	Team	G	IP	W	L	Pct	BB	SO	H	SHO	SV	ERA
1955	**NYA**	**10**	**29**	**2**	**1**	**.667**	**16**	**15**	**40**	**0**	**1**	**5.28**
1956		**29**	**88.1**	**3**	**5**	**.375**	**42**	**42**	**97**	**0**	**2**	**3.67**
1957	KCA	19	41	0	7	.000	25	15	53	1	0	5.93
1959	KCA	29	81	2	10	.167	34	54	86	0	2	4.56
	BalA	3	4	0	0	.000	2	4	4	0	0	0.00
1960	BalA	5	4	0	2	.000	5	0	8	0	0	11.25
Yankee years		**39**	**117.1**	**5**	**6**	**.455**	**58**	**57**	**137**	**0**	**3**	**4.07**
Career		95	247.1	7	25	.219	124	130	287	1	5	4.58
			World Series									
1955	**NYA**	**1**	**1**	**0**	**0**	**.000**	**0**	**1**	**5**	**0**	**0**	**9.00**

RUSS DERRY
Yankee Slammer

Yankees 1944–1945

Russ Derry was a ballplayer. He could run, hit, field, and throw. He led his minor league in home runs four times. He owns the single season and career home run records for Rochester (International League). He belted the first Opening Day grand slam in American League history. In 1945, he had the highest ratio of home runs to at bats (minimum 250) in the A.L. He has the highest percentage of grand slams from total home runs (minimum 10) in major league history. And each of his grand slams was the deciding blow in a Yankee victory.

He was a good fielding, good running center fielder with a right field arm whose time had come in the early 1940s; unfortunately, he was owned by the New York Yankees. The outfield in Yankee Stadium in those days was manned by Charlie Keller, Joe DiMaggio, and Tommy Henrich, so there was no room for a rookie.

If that trio was not enough to contend with, a back injury incurred on Labor Day 1942 while with Newark hampered him for the rest of his career — and still does today. That year the Bears won the International League pennant by ten games and Derry had the highest home run ratio in the league (22, all before his injury, in 329 at bats). He returned to Newark in 1943, but his back held him to only 40 games. Nonetheless, in '44, still slowed by the injury, he made the big club.

On August 13 of that season, he hit his first grand slam. It came in the third inning of a game against the Chicago White Sox and broke a 1–1 tie. The Yankees went on to win, 10–1.

Grand slam number two came on April 17, 1945, Opening Day, against the Boston Red Sox. Boston starter Rex Cecil entered the bottom of the seventh with a 4–1 lead over the Bronx Bombers; the one run had come on a third inning Derry homer. George Metkovich, the Red Sox first baseman, chose this inning to enter the record book — he made three errors (two on one play) and the score became 4–3 with the bases loaded. Derry took Cecil deep into the bullpen and the score was 7–4, New York. The final was 8–4.

On Sunday, April 29, Derry homered twice again, this time versus the Senators in a 13–4 Yankee win. His grand slam again put New York ahead to stay.

That year he homered 13 times in 253 at bats — a home run every 19.5 at bats. Returning soldier Hank Greenberg was number two in the league in this category, 20.8, while the league's home run leader, Vern Stephens, was third at 23.8. In a year when home run totals were down because the balls were made of materials not needed for the war, Derry's total of 13 was seventh best in the league.

Also in 1945, Derry finished third in the A.L. in RBI percentage (RBIs divided by at bats), trailing only Greenberg and Yankee teammate and RBI leader Nick Etten. And he had the highest ratio of RBIs to hits in the majors.

The future looked bright but Derry's back was still such a problem that he had to play in a corset. When the war ended the Yankees sold him and Tuck Stainback to the Philadelphia Athletics. Philadelphia had been the one city in major league baseball which was seemingly unaffected by World War II. Both the A's and the National League Phillies had fielded very bad teams before the war, fielded very bad teams during the war, and continued to field very bad teams after the war. (Much is to be said for consistency, of course, but not consistency of this sort.)

To put it bluntly, the A's of 1946 were horrible and Derry wanted out. After being traded to the Cardinals, he returned to Rochester in the International League where he set records that still stand.

Back in 1938, with Joplin in his second professional season, he led the Western Association with 24 home runs, then in 1939 he topped the Piedmont League (at Norfolk) with 40. At Rochester, he led the International League twice, with a franchise-record 42 in 1949 (and 122 RBIs, second in the league to teammate Steve Bilko's 125) and 30 in 1950 (with a league-leading 102 RBIs). All told, he spent a little over five years in Rochester and blasted 134 home runs, all with a bad back that caused him to miss several games each season. For his professional career, Derry belted 311 home runs and drove in 1,161 runs, five times exceeding the 100 RBI mark.

Unlike many sluggers who spent years in the minor leagues, Derry could also run and field. His time in baseball was not a running time, but five times he stole in double figures and had 111 when he retired.

And most years he was a center fielder, historically the spot where your best outfield glove plays. Toward the end, when a step had been lost, he played right field, where he led the I.L. in assists with 29 in 1950.

Today very few people, even diehard Yankee fans, have ever heard of Russ Derry, but he was a legitimate major league ballplayer and an outstanding minor leaguer. He deserves a little recognition.

There's a story that you learned to hit using a wagon tongue.

Russ Derry: No. There was some guy up here in the country where I live. He made some little bats out of dried hickory and I had one of them. It was narrower than a regular bat and you really had to watch the ball to hit it. I've thought I might have one like it made to practice with, but I never did.

The Yankees signed you originally and sent you to Joplin, where you had a really good first year [110 RBIs] and the next year you led the league in home runs there.

I think the power was always there, but they always stressed back then they wanted you to hit .300. Then, after I got to hittin' a few more home runs, why, the fans liked it and you got more publicity it seemed like, talked about more. I was a good RBI man all through my career.

In 1939, you left the Western Association and went to the Piedmont League and led in home runs again.

I had a good year there, but the Yankees had a lot of good ballplayers about then, you know.

I had a good start at Kansas City [American Association in 1940] and they had to send me out along about the first of July. I had quite a few home runs and I think I was leadin' the club in RBIs at that time and home runs both. I had to be sent out because they sent some guys down from the Yankees — Buster Mills and somebody else, I think. And they had two ex–big leaguers — [Frenchy] Bordagaray, and he's havin' a great year, and Nino Bongiovanni. He wasn't doin' nothin' but they had to keep him, you know, so they sent me out.

They wanted me to go up there and learn to drag bunt at Binghamton [Eastern League], so I tried that. I didn't do too good at Binghamton, I don't think, but we did, I think, win the playoffs or the pennant. I was at Kansas City in '41. I got hurt and then went to Binghamton up in the season and then I came back later.

Did you spend any time in the service?

No, I didn't. I was 4-F. Back. I hurt my back slidin' the first time I think about '41, and I broke a collarbone at Binghamton in '41 and that kept me out a while. Then I hurt my back again at Newark in '42 — real bad. I had to change from the collarbone operation to a different kid of a swing. It took me a while but I finally come out of it.

You made the big club in 1944.

I was tickled to death.

Do you recall any of your grand slams?

Yeah. I hit one on Opening Day, which I think was the first one that was ever hit by a Yankee or even by an American Leaguer on Opening Day. It was against Boston. Then I hit one the next Sunday. [Opening Day] was a packed house. Course, I suppose about a third of 'em were free passes, or half of 'em, from the army and navy. Everybody got in free then that was in the service.

We was playin' Boston and I forget what inning it was I hit the home run. Babe Ruth was in the stands and that's probably one time in years he'd been there. He was with the Postmaster General — Jim Farley I think it was, he always wore a top hat and a long black coat and he had a box, the first box behind the screen where he's protected there. Babe was with him that day.

When the game was over and I come joggin' in from the outfield, why the Babe stood up and hollered, "Hey, kid, come over here!" I went over there and shook hands with him, talked to him awhile. That one home run I hit back in the back part of the bullpen; I kinda golfed it and hit it high and seems like it took forever to get out. He said, "That's the way ol' Babe used to hit 'em."

It surprised me. I knew he was there, you know, but, 'course, [Joe] McCarthy was the manager and they didn't get along and he would never come in the dugout or the clubhouse. I think 'bout the only time he was on the field there was when he and Gehrig got together on that Gehrig Day. I think this had to be one of the very, very few times he was ever in the stadium.

In 1947, you were with the A's and in '48 with Rochester. Were you the Cardinals' property then?

Gee, I don't know. I went in the Eddie Joost deal. I was traded for him. Mr. [Connie] Mack called me in at the end of the [1946] season and he wanted me to take a thousand dollar cut and I'd be with 'em next year. I said, "Mr. Mack, I can't play on this kinda club." We'd just lose every day and he'd play you when you was hurt. I remember one time I had a big cyst in under my right arm — I mean, it was as big as a great big marble or almost a hen egg — and they wouldn't send me to a hospital in Cleveland and Detroit. I had to stay with 'em 'til we came back to home. I couldn't throw, I couldn't move that arm. I had to wait to come back home to be operated on.

The second day [after the operation] I was out at the ballpark and my name was in the lineup. (Laughs) He did a lot of things like that that year. He just wasn't all there. We had some terrible players.

I knew the [Pacific] Coast League wanted me because there was two scouts there, and then Earle Brucker [Sr.], he was a coach, and he told me how bad they wanted me in a couple of places. I said, "If I can't go back to the big leagues to some club where they got a decent park that will help me" — right field — "I wanna go to the Coast League." I told him that and I told Mr. Mack I didn't wanna come back and take a thousand cut. I said, "There's two clubs in the Coast League here after me. I'd like to go there." But he didn't send me there.

You really found a home in Rochester.

Yes. I wrote the business manager and told him I didn't wanna come there, but he came here in the wintertime and he talked to me two or three hours here at home and talked me into comin'. So I went there.

At the end of the 1949 season, the Cardinals called you up and the next spring you seemed to have made the roster. What happened?

They got waivers on me or something 'cause I was listed on the plane to go out the next morning and then when I went to the park the next morning, why I'd been sent to Rochester and another guy's name — a right-hand hitter — was on there.

You walked a lot.

I had over a hundred and some walks a couple of years there. I may have that record for the league or for Rochester. I don't know for sure. I was a guy that could break up the game, you know, and they just tried to get me to hit bad balls. 'Course they knew I just swang for the fence about every time and they tried to pitch me bad.

Rochester sold you to Columbus in the American Association in '52.

Yeah. I had trouble with Harry Walker. He was a pistol. He resented me bein' there and the fans in Rochester really wanted me to be the manager — that's what the papers said sometimes — and he wanted me outta there. He kept insistin' on me hitting to left field all spring training. He wanted me outta there, and at the start of the season he played somebody else, and then I played against left-handers. He come out in the paper there that I wasn't hittin' any home runs — I'd only played about four or five games — "The big boy ain't hittin' no long home runs or doin' what he should do."

'Bout the next game, some left-hander threw *behind* me and I straightened up and I stuck my left elbow back and it hit right on the elbow. (Laughs) That thing got as big as a goose egg right now, you know. I showed it to the trainer and he put ice on it, and 'course I went back to the outfield and he told Walker about it and Walker never asked me anything about it. I told Danny — Danny Wells, the trainer — I said, "I don't think I can swing the bat with this thing." I tried it there in the dugout and I couldn't, and he [Walker] told him to forget about it, and I had to go back [to bat] the rest of the game two or three times. I think I did get a base hit but I was just kinda swingin' one-handed.

Then he [Walker] said something to somebody, I think it was the next day. I said, "I've seen enough. I've gotta get outta here." I thought they'd trade me somewhere, you know send me out to the Coast League or something. I said, "I can't take it no more. He don't want me here and I don't wanna be here." So that's when I left.

Johnny Keane was at Columbus and he wanted me to come over there. I'd played for him for three or four years. Cedric Durst was my manager at Rochester when I started there.

When you went to Columbus, you tore the league up during the last half of the season (.318-18-55 in 223 at bats).

I did all right. I know the first game I played I think I hit a couple of home runs in Indianapolis, and they said it come out in the Rochester paper — headlines in the sporting pages. "Derry starts Columbus hot — two home runs first day." (Laughs) Or something like that. And the fans raised cain about it because I'd left.

You finished your career in the California League with Modesto in 1954.

We won the pennant and we needed one game to win the playoffs against San Jose. I don't think we were on the final game. My daughter was showin' calves in St. Jo at a 4-H show, and I had a plane ticket for one out of Frisco that night at a certain time and I said to one of the boys, "In order to make this plane to get to St. Jo to see that calf show, I've gotta hit a home run, so I think I'll jerk one out." And luckily I did. I think there was one man on.

Who was the toughest pitcher you saw?

Eddie Lopat was 'bout the toughest for me and, of course, there was some more left-handers there. Mickey Harris was there or in the minor leagues; he was really rough. And Mickey Haefner was one that was tough.

I faced [Hal] Newhouser. The first year I had good luck against him and

Russ Derry *(courtesy New York Yankees)*

then the second year, Paul Richards got to catchin' him and he'd take you down to three and two and throw you a change-up. And you'd just stand there and jump up and down. (Laughs) I mean, Paul Richards made him a pitcher because he taught him how to change-up and he would call for the change-up on three and two, you know. Nobody back in those days would ever do that. I'll say one thing, he turned out to be a good pitcher. I didn't do too good against him in '45.

I'll tell you, about the toughest man I'd ever seen — and I saw him when

I was with Kansas City and he was with Minneapolis — was Elon Hogsett. He's a big man and arms twice as long as anybody, and he'd step to first base and swing that arm around and you couldn't tell where he was goin' (laughs) — kinda underhanded and then sidearm. He was just finishin' his career when he was with Minneapolis, I think.

I remember we played one game [in 1940] and Bud Metheny and [Mike] Chartak and I was the 3-4-5 hitters and he struck them two guys out four times and me three. The next day Mickey Haefner pitched and he struck those two guys out three times and me three times. (Laughs) We won the pennant that year, I think, but that was the year I left 'em awhile.

But later on that season, we was playin' Minneapolis and Hogsett was pitchin' and Buster Mills had come down from the Yankees. He had played with him for two or three years — good friend of his — and they had us beat, I think, eight to nothin' in the ninth inning. I remember Buster goin' off the bench and I think there was one out or two out and he says, "I'm not gonna break up his no-hitter. I'm gonna hit down on the ball and hit the ball on the ground." Buster's a good right-handed hitter, you know. And he hit down on the ball and hit a line drive right over short. That really made Buster feel bad.

Who was the best overall player?

I suppose that one or two years there you'd have to pick Mickey Mantle and [Joe] DiMaggio would be the best everyday, long-term player by far, I think. [Ted] Williams hit more line drives than anybody else. I've seen him hit four line drives in a game and they'd catch three of 'em.

The Yankees didn't always treat you right.

Well, yeah. I had to come home for my brother's funeral. I was home here about a week, ten days. I was Joe DiMaggio's fill-in all spring training there and dressed right beside him all spring training and when we got ready to break camp I asked Joe [McCarthy] if I couldn't go over and play with the second team. I wasn't gettin' enough at bats. He said, "Sure," and he let me go over there and then I was goin' north with 'em.

We was in Norfolk, Virginia, and my brother was killed in a car wreck and so I came home. Then when I went back to New York I was at the hotel there and Parke Carroll called me from Newark and said I was comin' over there. I said, "When'd this happen?" He said, "Well, yesterday." I said, "It wasn't in the papers or anything. Nobody's called me."

So the next day I called Larry MacPhail and he said, "Yeah. We got rid of you. You're goin' over there." I was out to the clubhouse that day to get my stuff from my locker there and McCarthy and [Dan] Topping and [Del] Webb and MacPhail came through. Half the clubhouse wasn't finished yet — there was a new clubhouse that year — and Joe said to me, "Russ, it's gonna be hard and damp to dress in here, isn't it?" I said, "Joe, I don't know. I'm not supposed to dress here." He said, "How come?" I said, "Well, Parke Carroll called me, said I was supposed to come over to Newark." He said, "That's a hell of a note. When did this happen?" I said, "Yesterday, I guess."

And he asked MacPhail and he said, "Yeah, we sent him over there." And Del Webb and Dan Topping said, "That's news to us, too." That's how it happened.

McCarthy really liked me. I mean, I played with him, wore a corset on my back and I played the last half of the season there [in 1945] and did the best I could. He really appreciated it.

He called me up that time he flew the coop — you know, left the ball-club for about two weeks when they were goin' on a road trip — and he talked to me and told me things then. He said, "Russ, I think you can make it all right and I think you can be a good ballplayer. Don't get doin' like some of these guys around here."

I said, "Joe, I don't drink any. I drink a beer once in a while but that's it." He said, "I know. I'm just tellin' you." He said, "I made a mistake here and I'm goin' home and I don't know what's gonna happen. I may stay." So I bet Atley Donald ten dollars he wouldn't be back. (Laughs) He did come back. That was '45. He had eyes in the back of his head and he seen everything that went on and he could read people, too. He could read 'em.

Did you save anything?

I sent Cy Young's old bag that he carried with the Cleveland club to the Hall of Fame. He had a brother that lived here in this town that I did and he'd come visit here about every winter. He left this bag and some more stuff with his nephew and his nephew never wanted it. When he moved and sold the farm up here, why they give it to my wife's aunt, who was married to a half brother to his nephew. So she gave it to me and I wrote to 'em [the Hall of Fame] and asked 'em if they'd like to have it. Oh, they was tickled to death. It was one of then ol' rural bags, you know. It had his name printed on it and everything.

After Modesto what?

I went back to farmin'. Still doin' it.

ALVA RUSSELL (RUSS) DERRY
Born October 7, 1916, Princeton, Missouri
Ht. 6'1" Wt. 180 Batted Left and Threw Right

Year	Team	G	AB	R	H	2B	3B	HR	RBI	SB	BA	SA
1944	NYA	38	114	24	29	3	0	4	14	1	.254	.386
1945		78	253	37	57	6	2	13	45	1	.225	.419
1946	PhiA	69	184	17	38	8	5	0	14	0	.207	.304
1949	StLN	2	2	0	0	0	0	0	0	0	.000	.000

Year	Team	G	AB	R	H	2B	3B	HR	RBI	SB	BA	SA
Yankee years		**116**	**367**	**51**	**86**	**9**	**2**	**17**	**59**	**2**	**.234**	**.409**
Career		187	553	68	124	17	7	17	73	2	.224	.373

CHARLIE DEVENS
Hasty Pudding

Yankees 1932–1934

Harvard-educated Charlie Devens was born a member of the Massa-chusetts gentry, an unlikely combination for a major league ballplayer, but in addition to his studies in college he excelled in sports. He starred in both football and baseball for his alma mater.

His strong right arm attracted the interest of professional baseball and the New York Yankees offered him a contract almost unheard of at that time: a substantial bonus (reported by The Sporting News *years later as $20,000) and the contractual stipulation that he could not be sent to the minors that first year.*

That first year was 1932 and the 22 year old Devens joined a Yankee team that summer that consisted of 10 future Hall of Famers (including manager Joe McCarthy), three of them on the pitching staff—Lefty Gomez, Red Ruffing, and Herb Pennock. In addition to those three, the Yankees also had top-notch hurlers Johnny Allen, George Pipgras, and Danny MacFayden, stolen from the Red Sox in early June. Those six won 91 games for New York that year; the team won 107.

The club was also on a mission, trying to regain the American League title it had pretty much owned through most of the 1920s. Connie Mack's Philadelphia Athletics had taken over the AL driver's seat in 1929, however, and continued to hold the reins through '31. In 1932, McCarthy, in his second year at the Yankees' helm, was leading his club to a runaway and didn't want to risk any games by putting an untried college boy out there on the mound. There was little opportunity for a young, inexperienced pitcher under these conditions.

On September 13, the Yankees clinched the pennant, the earliest date since the 1927 Yankees also clinched on September 13. With the flag sewn up and his rotation for the World Series showdown with the Cubs set, manager McCarthy at last used "Hasty Pudding", as Devens was called by his team-mates, in a game on September 24. He went the distance, winning the game and allowing only two earned runs.

Devens enjoyed moderate success in 1933, splitting time between New York and Newark, but he became seriously ill before the 1934 season began. Appearing in only one game for the Yankees, he defeated Philadelphia in 11 innings, again allowing only two earned runs. It was his last game.

He got married after the 1934 season and felt professional baseball was not the place for a married man. He entered the banking business in Boston and today he is worth as much as many of today's major league stars.

The Yankees signed you out of Harvard for a reported $20,000 bonus.
Charlie Devens: Yes, but it was for less than that.

You were a highly regarded football player in college. Professional football was in its infancy then. Was there any temptation to play?

Yeah. Somebody asked me whether I'd be interested and I'd already gotten mixed up with the Yankees, so I said no.

Your Yankee contract called for you to spend your first season with the major league club. When did you join the team?

It was about the first of July.

You didn't play much.

Yeah. Batting practice and exhibition games and one game against the Red Sox. Everything was fine except one inning I got wild and walked four men and walked in a run. Aside from that, I got by all right.

The next year, 1933, you were sent down.

I pitched quite a lot. I had a good record down south [in spring training] and I pitched a no-hit, no-run game in an exhibition game against Yale. Naturally they wanted me to pitch and then McCarthy sent me over to Newark [International League] the next day. I was over there for a month or so and did all right, then they brought me up. I was a starting pitcher the rest of that year.

The two best games I pitched — one ended up an 18-inning tie and another one I walked the first guy up in the ninth inning and I was ahead, one to nothing, and they put in Herb Pennock. McCarhy said, "Here. Sit down here on the bench. You're makin' the game too hard." So I watched and the final score was Cleveland 7, New York 1.

Did you go the full 18 in the other game?

Oh no. The first nine. It was Pennock again; I walked the first guy up again and he scored. Pennock came in to pitch and he gave up the run. That meant it was a tie game as far as I was concerned. That was against the Chicago White Sox.

You were very sick over the 1933-34 winter.

I was sick that winter — peritonitis — and I finally ended up by pitching a bit over in Newark and came up to New York and I had to pitch an 11-inning game against Philadelphia. We won that game, four to two, in 11 innings. Should've only been nine innings, but a guy made a two-base error in the infield, so two runs scored and tied the game so we had to play a couple more innings.

That year—1934—was your last. What happened?

After that I got married. I told 'em when I started that I'd do it three years. I didn't think it was much of a life for a girl married to a ballplayer because they're away so much. I told 'em I wouldn't and they tried to get me to play and I said no.

So then I started at the State Street Bank and Trust Company, which is a bank, for the munificent sum of $15 a week. That went on for a year and a half before I finally got a raise.

You were decorated in World War II.

We were just under attack, that was all. Got hit by two or three kamikazes. The ship was on fire and one thing and another. Hell, I just did what anybody else would do. I didn't want to go swimming. We just put out fires — exploding ammunition and that sort of thing. I was in charge of the flight deck and I wanted to save that, no matter what. We couldn't operate after that 'cause we had a bunch of holes in the deck that the kamikazes had hit and bombs goin' off, et cetera. It wasn't much fun.

You played amateur tennis.

Oh, I really didn't play much amateur tennis. I played with a fella called Barry Wood, who was a partner of mine. I lived next door to him in Milton, Mass, when we were kids and he turned out to be a wonderful athlete. He was captain of the Harvard football team and I don't know how many letters he got — football, baseball, hockey, tennis. He was better than I was at tennis. When I stopped playing, which was when I was about 15, he was a little bit better and he went on and he didn't play much more, but he was at the medical school down at Johns Hopkins — he became a doctor — and he played for two weeks and then went into the Nationals and played against Johnny Doeg. Doeg won the championship that year and Wood took him five sets not having played at all, so he was pretty good. [Wood was first team All-American quarterback at Harvard in 1931.]

With the Yankees, you had some great teammates.

[Babe] Ruth was a hell of a good fella and a wonderful ballplayer. He used to drink a bit and liked the ladies. He was getting on; I think he only played a couple years after I got out and he played a year or half a year for the Boston Braves, which was a mistake. I think he felt very badly that [Yankees owner Jake] Ruppert didn't make him a manager, but Ruppert told him that if he couldn't watch after himself that he couldn't coach a ballclub, either.

[Lou] Gehrig was totally different — *wonderful* fella to have on your team. He wasn't half as much fun as Babe and he was much more serious, but a wonderful ballplayer.

And then [Tony] Lazzeri was one of the best ballplayers I ever saw. Had he played in Boston, I think he'd've hit about 70 home runs. He'd hit the ball all day long in Yankee Stadium to left field and I don't know what it was, something like 400-and-God-knows-how-many feet out in left field, so it was pretty hard to hit 'em into the stands there, but he still hit a few. Quite a few.

[Frank] Crosetti. He's still alive. I think he's the only one on that '32 championship team still alive, besides myself. He's a wonderful fella, awful nice.

Then, of course, Red Rolfe played third base and I played against him. He went to Dartmouth. Harvard and Dartmouth used to play baseball. And Joe Sewell, Bill Dickey — he died just recently — Ben Chapman, and Earle Combs.

[Lefty] Gomez. Gomez was a good pitcher. Sort of a nut. He was an eccentric kind of a fella, couldn't sit still, but a damned good pitcher. And [Red] Ruffing, of course, was a damned good pitcher.

Johnny Allen was a damned good pitcher, but he was a tough egg and I don't think he got on particularly well with McCarthy. After a year or so they shipped him off to Cleveland. Of course, then he won something like I don't know how many straight ball games.

I've heard Allen had a hard time getting along with anyone.

I don't know. He was a pretty tough boy and, anyway, he was a damned good pitcher, I'll say that for him. At least he had a lot of stuff and he had one wonderful year with Cleveland [15-1 in 1937]. How many games in a row did he win?

Fifteen. He missed tying the record by one.

Yeah. I think [Lefty[Grove missed the record by one. A fella who was with Newark — I can't remember his name — he was a fielder on the Athletics. He dropped a fly in the ninth inning and Grove got beaten when he was trying to win his seventeenth straight game. This fella said he hardly dared go into the clubhouse. [On August 23, 1931, Grove was going for a record 17th straight win against the St. Louis Browns. Jimmy Moore, playing left field instead of regular Al Simmons, misplayed a routine fly ball to allow the only run of the game as the Browns won, 1–0. Grove was furious with Simmons for not playing.]

Other than your teammates, who were the best players you saw?

[Al] Simmons, Jimmie Foxx, [Mickey] Cochrane — they were all good. That was that Athletics team. They won the pennant in '31, I guess it was, and the World Series for a couple of years. Who was it, let's see — Cochrane, Foxx, [Max] Bishop, [Jimmie] Dykes. I'm trying to think, who was the shortstop? Then there was Simmons and [Mule] Haas and [Bing] Miller in the outfield.

Was Eric McNair or Dib Williams the shortstop?

I don't remember. I thought McNair played on the Red Sox.

He did. Boston got him from Philadelphia.

That Philadelphia team of '29-'30-'31 was the best they ever had, but I don't remember the shortstop.

We should be able to figure out who it was. It wasn't [Jack] Barry; he had been gone for years by then.

Berry? Wasn't he a catcher? Caught for the White Sox. I think he was an All-American football player. He beat me in a game — I remember him. He was a dead pull hitter so I pitched to him and he just scraped the ball along the right field foul line — he was a right-handed hitter — and, of course, Chapman was playing right field and he was playing practically in center field because this guy was supposed to be a dead left field hitter. He hit a double on the right field line — just a cheap hit but it beat me. [Charlie Berry had been a first team All-American end in 1924 at Lafayette. He played both professional football and baseball and in 1925 led the NFL in scoring. After his playing careers, he became both a major league umpire and an NFL referee. His father, also Charlie Berry, had played major league baseball back in 1884.]

Did you save souvenirs from your baseball days?

No, not really. Gosh, I had a watch and it was stolen — for the World Series. I guess it was for the World Series; I don't remember whether it was the World Series or the fact that we won the American League pennant [in 1932]. I've got a baseball, autographed. Except for a few pictures, that's all.

I've got these darned cards. Megacards. Does that sound right?

The Conlon Collection?

I think that's it.

I guess that's the only card you appeared on. They didn't have much in the way of baseball cards back then.

No. And they only produced this one a year ago about. For a while, these collectors — I don't know what they paid for 'em — sent 'em to me to sign. I think I heard that Shoeless Joe Jackson's card went for over $200,000. Think that one over.

How much fan mail do you receive now?

Oh gosh. I suppose it averages out about a letter a day. I think it's all on account of this card.

It tells on the back if the player is living or dead. I guess if collectors see the guy is living, they write for an autograph.

Well, they better hurry.

Would you go back and play baseball again out of college?

Oh yeah. I enjoyed it. I liked it very much. I was scared half to death. If I do say so, I had as much stuff as anybody around there *but* I didn't have too good control. I used to walk four or five people a game, but it was getting better. It comes with confidence.

The years you were there, the Yankees were in pennant races. It's very difficult for a manager to put an untried young ballplayer in under those conditions.

Oh sure! Hell, he was winning the pennant when I joined 'em and he didn't want to fuss around with me except to pitch exhibition games and things like that. I think it was the last game of the season, or next to last game of the season, he started me against the Red Sox and we beat them all right.

I think he was a damned good manager. He didn't get on too well with Ruth. I don't think Ruth liked him and I think mainly because Ruth wanted McCarthy's job and he couldn't get it. I don't know whether Babe would have been a good manager or not, but he was a good fella — a very generous man. If it hadn't been for him, everybody would have been working for far less money in those days.

What was the average major league salary when you joined the Yankees?

I would guess that the average was between five and ten thousand dollars. What the hell, what are they now? In the millions! It makes me sick.

It's enough to make a man want to try a comeback.
Yeah. (Laughs)

CHARLES DEVENS
Born January 1, 1910, Milton, Massachusetts
Ht. 6'1"   Wt. 180   Batted and Threw Right

Year	Team	G	IP	W	L	Pct	BB	SO	H	SHO	SV	ERA
1932	NYA	1	9	1	0	1.000	7	4	6	0	0	2.00
1933		14	62	3	3	.500	50	23	59	0	0	4.35
1934		1	11	1	0	1.000	5	4	9	0	0	1.64
Career		16	82	5	3	.625	62	31	74	0	0	3.73

RYNE DUREN
Back on Track

Yankees 1958–1961

The St. Louis Browns languished in despair for most of the club's existence. They eventually fled the city and became the Baltimore Orioles, where things weren't much better on the field for several more years.

Off the field, however, the situation improved. The new owners had money, a commodity which had been in very short supply in St. Louis, and the new city had fans, also something the team had sorely lacked before the move.

But maybe, if Bill Veeck, the last owner of the Browns, had slightly deeper pockets, the sale and move wouldn't have happened and, again maybe, some of the young hurlers the Brownies had in the minor leagues could have pitched them to respectability. The potential was certainly there, for moving through their farm system in the late 1940s and early 1950s were some outstanding young arms.

One belonged to Eddie Albrecht. He won 32 games in 1949 for Pine Bluff (Cotton States League) in the Brownies' system, then one-hit the White Sox in a rain-shortened game on the last day of the season.

Albrecht's arm went bad, but there were others who survived and prospered at the big league level, although not for the Browns or the Orioles. Three right-handers who signed with St. Louis in the 1940s were Bob Turtley, Don Larsen, and Ryne Duren. One way or another, all three gained fame as Yankees.

Duren was signed in 1949 by scout Eddie Dancesak after one year at the University of Illinois. Over the next few years, he averaged nearly 11 strikeouts a game while yielding fewer than six hits per nine innings. Unfortunately, he was also walking six or seven men a game and actually hit Billy Hunter in the on-deck circle in a Texas League game. Finally, in 1956 with Vancouver (PCL), he found some control and became a pitcher.

He was traded to Kansas City following that season and made the big club in 1957, but in one of the infamous deals between the A's and the Yankees he was dealt to New York on June 15. He was sent down to Denver (American Association), where he went 13-2 in the last half of the season.

In '58, Casey Stengel made him a reliever. He led the American League with 20 saves and was named The Sporting News' *Rookie Pitcher of the Year. He followed in '59 with 14 saves, and at one time went 18 games (36 innings) without allowing a run. It was shortly after this streak ended that Mr. and Mrs. Sandberg of Spokane, Washington, had a baby boy, whom they named Ryne Dee (for Duren). This young man later became an All-Star second baseman for the Cubs.*

Duren was overwhelming when he was at his peak. Of all pitchers who ever pitched at least 500 innings, he ranks third in strikeouts per game (9.62) and fifth in fewest hits per game (6.77).

Somewhere along the line, he became a drinker and it became a real problem. Even with all his ability, his career began slipping. He was traded to the expansion Angels in 1961 and bounced around both leagues through 1965, when the end came.

As an alcoholic ex-jock, he found life pretty rough for a few years, but he licked the adversity and everything is going great for him now.

*You pitched well in the minor leagues and the Browns weren't going any-
where. Why did they never call you up?*

Ryne Duren: I was still pretty wild and there was a whole raft of good
pitchers in the minor leagues: Turley, Larsen, a guy by the name of Eddie
Albrecht that they did bring up. And my control was the issue, but one time
they did send a scout — in '53 — to interview me. I had a good streak going
and he came down to Tulsa to take a look at me [Duren was with San Anto-
nio] and they sat right behind home plate — he and his wife. I got wild and
threw a ball that went through the screen in back of home plate and hit his
wife right on a big buckle right in the center. (Laughs) I didn't go.

*You were walking a lot of men, but you were striking out a lot, too. You led
three minor leagues in strikeouts and were second two other times. Were other teams
trying to get you?*

No. In our organization, for instance, there were ten guys, I think, that
could throw about as hard as I could. A guy by the name of Bill Pilgrim, a
guy by the name of Bob Harrison, Jim Upchurch, Bob Nordgren, and there
were a lot of others that had decent, probably 90 mile-an-hour stuff. The
minor leagues were a lot different then and every organization had tremendous depth and then there were only 16 teams at the top. You were damn lucky
to get there at all, I guess, but the thing that held me back was the control.
There's no doubt about that. I finally became a pitcher in the [Pacific] Coast
League.

When the A's acquired you, were you given an opportunity?

Well, I made the ballclub and it wasn't a matter of me not getting the
opportunity or belonging there. The Yankees wanted me. That was the way
it was. Lou Boudreau told me the night I was traded, he said, "Hell, you're
the best pitcher on my staff. I think more of you than anyone else. I had nothing to do with this, Ryne."

My first start in the big leagues was against the Yankees and they beat
me, two to one, and the only run we got I drove it in myself with a two-out,
two-strike drag bunt.

What was the highlight of your rookie year with the Yankees?

I think just being there. Oddly enough, the first game I saved I saved
with my glove. Ralph [Houk] and I were out there early and he was hittin'
shots back at me on the mound. Somehow or another I happened to be in
that game and I think it was Jim Marshall hit a ball back to me and one-hopped
on the mound and stuck in my glove and I went second to first. I think there
was a man on first and third at the time, tying run on third.

How was Casey Stengel to play for?

He was great for me. He managed the New York press more than the
ballclub. He'd blow smoke at me because he just knew that I needed it, I
guess. He sensed that. I thought the world of him. He'd get me aside once in

Ryne Duren *(courtesy New York Yankees)*

a while and tell me how much he appreciated what I was doing and he'd see me by myself and he'd grab me and say, "Come on, we're gonna have dinner together," and that kinda stuff. He was always good for a laugh. He was interesting and he loved to talk and he loved to put on a show.

He took you to the All-Star game that first year.

I was there twice in '58. One of the things that I always say at the old-timers golf tournaments we go to when they introduce me and say I made the

All-Star team three times and I keep telling 'em I made it five times in three years. (Laughs) [When Duren was selected in 1958 and 1959, there were two All-Star games played each year.]

You pitched three strong innings in one of the 1959 games.

In Pittsburgh. I don't remember much of it, just that they had me in the game. I know that somebody — I think it was [Willie] Mays — I knocked him down three and two. I didn't try to, but that's what happened. [A fellow] in the commissioner's office — I think [Orlando] Cepeda was on deck — and you'll have to excuse me but these were the words he said, "That's the whitest I ever saw a black man." (Laughs)

You were in two World Series—1958 and 1960. In '58, you had a win, a loss, and a save.

I won the sixth game. I think the third game I had a save. I think it was Larsen's game. And then in the fifth game I was a loser. Billy Bruton hit a ball up the alley off me.

In '61, you were traded to the expansion Los Angeles Angels and you became a starter for the first time in several years.

We didn't have much of a ballclub out there. One start, when the Yankees came back to L.A. after they traded me, I started the game and I drove in the go-ahead run with two out and two strikes and the bases loaded in the bottom of the sixth inning. Actually, it was kind of a pinch-hit situation except that I was pitching good, so he [manager Bill Rigney] left me in. I got the hit off of Turley. Houk always said that Turley was never the same after that. (Laughs)

How was Rigney as a manager?

I liked him. I never played for anybody I didn't like. I was very, very lucky.

You pitched a shutout with the Angels.

In Cleveland at the end of the year. I'll never forget that particular day. I think it was traveling day; we were going back to L.A. Pee Wee Reese and Dizzy [Dean] were up in the booth. Diz told me that if this game wasn't over in two hours they couldn't catch their airplane. He said, "Just get that ball and *thow* it!" He didn't say "throw," he said "thow." I did. It may have been a one-hitter. It was one hour, 58 or 59 minutes. I pointed to the clock for Diz as I left the field. (Laughs)

You left the majors after the 1965 season. What then?

When I got out, I was in the throes of alcoholism and I tried to find some kind of a job down in San Antonio and I couldn't. I ended up that fall at the state hospital down there for alcoholism and I was in there for almost 90 days.

I got out and I started a service station. I was clean for six, eight months, something like that. I started drinking again and then I took the geographic escape back to Wisconsin and stopped drinking for a short while. Then after

I get a job up here in the trucking business, I started drinking again. I wrecked a truck, then I ended up in a rehabilitation hospital up here.

When I got out, I worked with delinquent kids for four years and then I opened a treatment hospital and ran that for ten years and kinda worked in the field of alcoholism in different areas — education and awareness — all over the country.

When did you become aware that drinking had become a problem?

I knew that there was something really wrong with me. I didn't know that it was the drinking; I thought that there was just something wrong with me in this life, that I was misunderstood and all the other things. There's a certain amount of truth to all of that in that here I was a has-been without education and without skills — these are the thoughts I had — and I didn't care about living anymore. But I wasn't courageous enough or whatever it takes to take your life — smart enough or dumb enough — but finally, after I got well, I realized that I finally got out of adolescence, that finally that was probably what it was all about.

Then I took some courses in child care and psychology, and when I had the opportunity I started that program in the hospital. When I worked with delinquent kids, I realized I was one of 'em in just an older body. So after we put all that together, I was able to do something with my life and my sick experiences. Some people turn those around, they can become pluses.

Back to your career. Is there one game that stands out?

I think that night I beat the Yankees out there. I think the score ended up 5–3; Mickey [Mantle] hit a home run off me later. I didn't lose the game by it. I pitched eight innings, I struck out 12 and gave up three hits, and I think Mantle had two of 'em.

Those '61 Yankees were tough.

Supposedly the toughest lineup ever. That was the year the catching department hit 72 home runs and Maris hit 61 and Mantle hit 50-something.

Who was the best player you saw?

I think Maris. Mickey was the most talented obviously; I think Maris was the best ballplayer for a year or so. That year before [1960] I think he was MVP then. He just did everything and did everything right and had a great attitude. He played outfield great, he threw the ball well, he ran the bases well. He was a pretty amazing guy. He was a good solid player, a good *strong* player. I think his demise, in spite of what people say, was when he hurt his wrist.

Best pitcher?

Oh, I don't know. God, [Sandy] Koufax was good! A guy with his ability you'd have to go with, but [Whitey] Ford was so good, so clever, such a psychologist, it's be hard not to give him a nod. In his own evaluation of himself, he was so good. He used to call the bullpen and ask me how I felt. Sometimes he'd talk to the bullpen catcher, too. He'd take himself out of the game.

He'd say, "I think I've had it." He had a tremendous amount of confidence, but I know one time he took himself out of a one to nothing and had me come in in the seventh or eighth inning.

It's a smart man who knows his own limitations.

It certainly is. Not only is that the mark of a smart man, but also of a team man.

Several players of your era have said the best *pitcher was Koufax, but if they wanted to win a game, they'd probably go with Ford.*

Yeah, he was great, but it'd kinda depend upon who you were gonna pitch against. He had a couple nemeses. A guy by the name of Jim Lemon just wore him out. (Laughs)

Did you save souvenirs along the way?

Not much. I've got a few old autographed balls that you can hardly read from them. That's about it. I don't have gloves — I've got one from when I played, but that's it. I don't have any caps. You had to be damned careful what you took outta the clubhouse in those days, other than baseballs. If the Yankees caught you takin' a jacket or something like that, your ass had had it. (Laughs) It was a different era, you know.

The clubhouse man in New York gives me stuff now anytime I want it. He's pretty good to me. I always offer to pay him something and usually I do, but he hates to take money from guys of that era.

What was your top salary?

Seventeen-five, but I think my big league salary average was around 13-something.

Do you receive much fan mail today?

Probably it's down to about ten pieces a week, but sometimes maybe it's more than that, up to 20. At one point — '59, when I put that streak together — I probably got more fan mail than anyone else in the clubhouse, save Mantle, maybe. There was a tremendous amount of strikeouts in there somewhere, like 16 out of 17 guys. [In 1959, Duren averaged 12 Ks per game.]

Any regrets?

Not really. The situation with drinking, of course; I'm sorry about that. My best friends — two of 'em, I don't think I wanna mention their names — died of it. They were the two guys I was closest to in baseball. But that aside, what regrets could a guy have that's still living and has had a good life? I look around and the quality of my life is so much better than so many of the guys who made a lot more money than I did, for that matter.

Yes, it would've been nice if I had been able to get into that career with my ability. Sure, I had Hall of Fame ability — there's no doubt about that — so maybe that's where I might have been, but I'll trade some quality years and longevity for the Hall of Fame. (Laughs) Right now, just one smile from my latest grandkid is worth so much.

Would you go back and be a ballplayer again?

Oh, yeah. I could handle that. The only thing that I feel about it is that education is a very important thing in the alcohol and drug aspect of it. Then I think they oughta have some in-house program to help these guys deal with the stress that they're under. That oughta be mandated by the commissioner's office. I think a good strong commissioner that could represent the integrity of the game and the American public's interest in it, rather than the owners, would be a great thing and I'd like to see a program run out of that office that dealt with a lot of the issues that seem to be hitting the press all the time. I'm talking about prevention, not just picking up the pieces.

RINOLD GEORGE (RYNE) DUREN
Born February 22, 1929, Cazenovia, Wisconsin
Ht. 6'2"   Wt. 190   Batted and Threw Right

Year	Team	G	IP	W	L	Pct	BB	SO	H	SHO	SV	ERA
1954	BalA	1	2	0	0	.000	1	2	3	0	0	9.00
1957	KCA	14	42.2	0	3	.000	30	37	37	0	1	5.27
1958	**NYA**	**44**	**75.2**	**6**	**4**	**.600**	**43**	**87**	**40**	**0**	***20**	**2.02**
1959		**41**	**76.2**	**3**	**6**	**.333**	**43**	**96**	**49**	**0**	**14**	**1.88**
1960		**42**	**49**	**3**	**4**	**.429**	**49**	**67**	**27**	**0**	**9**	**4.96**
1961	**NYA**	**4**	**5**	**0**	**1**	**.000**	**4**	**7**	**2**	**0**	**0**	**5.40**
	LAA	40	99	6	12	.333	75	108	87	1	2	5.18
1962	LAA	42	71.1	2	9	.182	57	74	53	0	8	4.42
1963	PhiN	33	87.1	6	2	.750	52	84	65	0	2	3.30
1964	PhiN	2	3	0	0	.000	1	5	5	0	0	6.00
	CinN	26	43.2	0	2	.000	15	39	41	0	1	2.89
1965	PhiN	6	11	0	0	.000	4	6	10	0	0	3.27
	WasA	16	23	1	1	.500	18	18	24	0	0	6.65
Yankee years		**131**	**206.1**	**12**	**15**	**.444**	**139**	**257**	**118**	**0**	**43**	**2.75**
Career		**311**	**589.1**	**27**	**44**	**.380**	**392**	**630**	**443**	**1**	**57**	**3.83**

Led league

World Series

Year	Team	G	IP	W	L	Pct	BB	SO	H	SHO	SV	ERA
1958	**NYA**	**3**	**9.1**	**1**	**1**	**.500**	**6**	**14**	**7**	**0**	**1**	**1.93**
1960		**2**	**4**	**0**	**0**	**.000**	**1**	**5**	**2**	**0**	**0**	**2.25**
2 years		**5**	**13.1**	**1**	**1**	**.500**	**7**	**19**	**9**	**0**	**1**	**2.03**

ALLEN GETTEL

Two-Gun Cowboy

Yankees 1945–1946

Tall, rangy, and good-looking, Allen Gettel looked like a cowboy. His Virginia drawl made him sound like a cowboy. And he loved horses. As arguably the best pitcher in the Pacific Coast League during the first half of the 1950s, he maintained a high profile, made even higher by leading parades astride his palomino stallion while dressed in western gear and toting a pair of six-shooters on his hips.

He never found his niche in the major leagues, although today it's difficult to understand why. After nine years in the minors, where he compiled a 93-63 record, he joined the New York Yankees in 1945 as the fourth or fifth man in their rotation, won nine games, and completed nine of seventeen starts. In 1946 he was shuffled aside when Bill Dickey took over as manager a few weeks into the season, but still posted a 2.97 ERA and won six games while completing five of his eleven starts.

It was apparent he was not in the Yankees' plans and he was traded to Cleveland, where in 1947 he was second to Bob Feller on the Indians' staff in wins (11), complete games (9), and ERA (3.20). He was then traded six weeks into the '48 season to the cellar-dwelling White Sox, where he again was a staff leader, topping the club in complete games and having the second most wins and second best ERA on the team.

After spending most of 1949 between the bad White Sox and the worse Washington Senators, he joined the Oakland Oaks of the PCL late that year and blossomed. Twice he won 20 and twice he was acquired by major league clubs—the New York Giants in '51 and the St. Louis Cardinals in '55—only to rejoin Oakland each time. In his four full years with the Oaks, he won 23, 17, 27, and 17 games and in 1955 had 12 wins when he went to the Cardinals in August. Used both as a starter and a reliever, he led the PCL in innings pitched three straight years.

The 1950s were the heyday of Western movies and television shows, and Gettel's cowboy persona eventually attracted the attention of Hollywood, where he won roles in several films. But he was a Virginia farm boy at heart and when his baseball days ended after the 1956 season, he returned to his roots. In 21 years as a professional pitcher, he won 235 games and hurled 3,698 innings. Not a bad career.

Who signed you originally?

The fella found me when I was in school, my last year in high school, and we played the Suffolk ballclub in Suffolk and he was at the ball game. His name was Gene McCann; he was a Yankee scout. He came to me after we played the ball game — we won, one to nothin' or two to nothin' — and he asked me had I ever thought about playin' professional baseball. 'Course I've always been tall and I said, "Heck, no. I was raised on a farm. Only thing I know is farmin' — horses and stuff like that." He says, "I'll tell you what I want you to do. When you go back home, you tell your daddy to take you out to old Tarr Park," which was here in Norfolk, over there by the Sunlight Laundry

Previous page: Allen Gettel with Oakland of the PCL, 1954.

then. And he says, "You go over and get your daddy to take you over there," 'cause I wasn't drivin' then, "and see if they won't let you work out." He says, "I'll tell you what. If you know what day you're gonna be there, I'll be there and make sure you get a chance to work out." And, by golly, he was there! Ol' Gene was there when I got there. In fact, he was there a day ahead of me.

I worked out and Johnny Neun was the manager of the ballclub then. I believe it was on a Saturday morning I worked out with 'em, worked out the whole three hours or four hours that they worked out and I pitched a little battin' practice for 'em and they said, "Can you come back to the park this comin' Monday? I want to see you pitch some more." This was the manager and the business manager of the ballclub.

So I says, "Well, I'll see if my father can get me back over here." So, sure enough, Dad took me back and I pitched. Before I left the ballpark after the workout was over, they had me on a contract. I think I was 18 or 19.

You had several good seasons, yet the Yankees didn't call you up.

One reason why they didn't call me up was because one of the managers — I think it was Johnny Neun — told me, "The reason we're holding you down is because you need a little more experience." I was very glad that they did because when I really got through the ten years of bein' in the minors, when I went up to the Yankees in '45, I was ready 'cause I could fire!

It surprised me. 'Course, I enjoyed it. I loved to play the baseball game anyway. I played all through school and I played in sandlot and I played in the city league here in Norfolk. I played a little bit of everywhere.

After two years in the majors, the Yankees traded you.

I never could figure that out myself, but they traded me. I tried to find out from [Larry] MacPhail and I tried to find out from Bill Dickey, who was the manager then. [Joe] McCarthy had quit and Bill Dickey was takin' over. After he took over, I didn't get a chance to work very much. I don't know what the story was. I kinda felt like that there was somethin' in the wind but no one would give me an answer, yes or no.

The year you were traded, your ERA was less than three.

Yeah, two point somethin'. Bein' a young fella, I did pretty good there but I never could understand why in '46 they got rid of me. Some of the people around there give me a story that they wanted the guy that they traded me to Cleveland for — Sherman Lollar. And they had an outfielder, too, a right fielder. I can't remember his name.

That's somethin' I couldn't understand. I was in the Yankee organization ten years and then all together I figure that I had done pretty good. I always figured that any time a young ballplayer can start on the bottom like I did in Class D and work himself up to get to the major leagues, I think that's an accomplishment all of its own.

You just missed a World Series three times in your career. The Yankees went in 1947 after you were traded, the Indians went in '48 after you were traded, and the Giants went in '51 after you were sent back to Oakland. That must have been frustrating.

Well, it was in a way, but when I was with the Giants — they sent me back to Oakland — they gave me a cut in that World Series. You know, that's done by the ballplayers, they vote and if you've been there a certain length of time, the ballplayers vote you in that you should have some. I was back home, up in Urbana, Virginia, livin' up there, and it come through the news that all the ballplayers recommended that I get a piece of the purse. It wasn't only me, there was four or five other ballplayers.

Just before you went up to the Yankees, your ERAs were so small you had to have a microscope to see them: 1.38 in 1943 and 1.81 in 1944.

(Laughs) Yeah, that was durin' the War. That was when they wouldn't take me in the service. I had arthritis in my spine and I tried to get in the service. All my buddies had gone and they told me they didn't want me. I was pitchin' up here in Norfolk until they found out that I was farmin'—I was farmin' with my wife's father — and they froze me on the farm. So durin' that year with Norfolk, I pitched night baseball and worked all day on the farm. I did that for a whole year until the man down at the courthouse here in Princess Anne County told me, "Gettel, I'm gonna put you in 4-F. Go on and play ball." His name was Traft, I think, R. F. Traft, and I told him I wanted to go [in the service] and he sent me to Camp Lee for ten days. And after I came back they sent him a report and I was the only one that had arthritis and they turned me down. So that's when I went up to the Yankees.

Your back sure didn't affect your arm.

No, no. I tell you, the first year with the Yankees, though, and comin' up in spring training, I wore a motorcycle belt — you know, like we used to wear years ago — a big wide belt that was narrow in the front but it was wide in the back, it had a little kind of a groove in it to where it would fit right in between your two back muscles, and it helped support me. After I got with the Yankees that second year, ol' Doctor Painter — that was the trainer there — he told me, he said, "Son, does your back bother you a whole lot?" I said, "Doc, not everyday or all the time. It just comes in spurts." And he said, "Well, I'm gonna tell you somethin' and I hope you do the right thing." He says, "I want you to take that motorcycle belt off and throw it away."

I said, "Yeah, but how am I gonna support myself?" He said, "That's all in your head. You get out there and take that motorcycle belt off and you run around that ballpark a couple times." You know, we had to do that, and he says, "If it hurts you when you come back in the clubhouse, I want to know 'bout it." So I went out there and took it off and went like he said. I got a little tired, but my back never bothered me at all from runnin' and chasin' fly balls and stuff like that. I had to grit my teeth a lotta times but I kept on goin'.

I left the Yankees and went to Cleveland, then to the Chicago White Sox, and then I left there and went to Washington. They sold me to Oakland and the reason I got sold out there was because of Charlie Dressen. Remember him? Charlie Dressen told Brick Laws, the owner of the Oakland ballclub — he told me this — he said, "You want a guy that can pitch out here in this league, but just don't pay attention to what he's doin' because it might make you mad 'cause you never know what he's gonna do from one day to the next." (Laughs)

I went out there — I think it was the last seven weeks of '49 — from the majors and then I came back home and I went out there until 1951 when I went to the Giants. Leo Durocher wanted me. I stayed with Leo part of that year, and then they sent me back to Oakland again. Then the St. Louis Cardinals bought me [in 1955] and I got tired of this travelin' back and forth and back and forth, so I went back to Oakland again and then I found out that in 1955 Brick Laws and his son sold the ballclub to a Canadian town — Vancouver — and they wanted me to go to Vancouver. Well, I had played out there [in Canada] and I didn't care too much about it when I was in the International League — before I went with the Yankees, when I was with Newark — and I didn't care too much for Canada. It was a nice place, but I mean it just didn't suit me. I said I just can't go to Canada and play up there, so I was gettin' myself all packed up and everything and I was stayin' at the hotel.

You remember Ralph Kiner? He was the business manager of the San Diego Padres and he called me on the phone and wanted to know if I would like to finish out another year in the Pacific Coast League. He didn't tell me who he was right at first. He says, "I'm gonna offer you a good salary, what you made at Oakland; I'm not gonna cut it a bit. If you help the ballclub I might give you a little more." So then he told me who he was and I said, "Ralph, you old rascal you!" (Laughs) "Why the heck didn't you tell me who you were before?!" He said, "At first I called Brick Laws to find out if you wasn't gonna go to Canada, that you was gonna retire and go home. And I figured that you could go a little bit longer and we needed a pitcher like you." So I went out there and finished that season of '56, and I just got tired of travelin' and doin' this and doin' the other, bein' away from home, so I just retired.

You were a good hitter.

Oh yeah. I had a couple home runs out there. I think I batted .354 one year, if I'm not mistaken.

Who were the best players you saw?

With the Yankees, I would say [Joe] DiMaggio, Phil Rizzuto, Crosetti. Frankie Crosetti was always a competitor. I mean, he was hard to get out and

Allen Gettel on Del Rey *(courtesy Allen Gettel)*

the reason I know that, after the Yankees sold me to Cleveland I had to face them boys I had been with all of my life, comin' up the chain. Frank Crosetti was one of the most aggravatin' guys at the plate ever pitched to. I never had any trouble with DiMaggio, Rizzuto , or any of 'em. 'Course, Phil was so dog-gone short I walked him more than I struck him out. (Laughs)

After I left there and went to Cleveland there was Jim Hegan, the catcher; he was great. And the fellow who played first base then — Eddie Robinson. 'Course, Cleveland had a pretty good ballclub. I didn't have no trouble with [Lou] Boudreau; he was the manager. 'Course, he got his base hits. Another one who I had a problem with with that club — he played in the outfield — was Dale Mitchell.

'Course, Ted Williams, he was a friend of mine. We got along fine together even though we were on opposite ballclubs. I never will forget the first time I faced Ted Williams. I had two strikes and three balls on him and I threw a ball down low and he golfed that thing and I think it's still goin'. (Laughs) I never had any problems with Ted after I found out he was strictly a low-ball hitter. I used to throw him a lotta junk up there and he'd get real mad at me. He'd squeeze that bat, boy, and you could see the sawdust fall out.

After I left Chicago and went to the Washington Senators, I had to face this cotton-pickin' Luke Appling. First, I'll have to go back to Cleveland when I first joined the Cleveland ballclub. We were playin' Chicago *in* Chicago and — holy cow! — he fouled off 16 pitches! I couldn't get the sucker out! So I just threw a wild pitch and let him go on base, give him a walk. He could foul 'em off any time he wanted to. While I was playin' in Chicago we got along fine but then when I had to go to Washington, I told him one day, "I hate leavin' here 'cause I got to face you again." (Laughs) I think Luke was about 36 or 37 years old. I think he played 'til he was 42 years old.

You played with Willie Mays when he was a rookie.

Oh yeah. Willie and I got along fine. I'll tell you a little story about Willie. I was with the Giants when they brought him up from Minneapolis and we was all in the clubhouse after a ball game. I noticed Willie was kind of sniffin'. I thought probably he had a cold or somethin', but I didn't say nothin' to him. I only dressed about three lockers away from him. I just kept an eye on him and I come to find out he was crying. I walked over to him, I said, "What's the matter, pardner? You havin' problems or you don't feel good or what?"

He says, "I can't get a daggone hit!" He'd already gone about 0 for 20-some, or somethin' like that. I said, "Lemme tell you somethin'. If you stay in this game a long time, you'll understand what I say. You've got to respect that pitcher out there on that mound." He never forgot that. He was one of the best. He could cover more ground than any one ballplayer I ever seen.

Ol' Monte Irvin was a good one, too. He hit a home run in Cincinnati and won me a ball game, one to nothin'.

Do you remember Joe Brovia?

Sure, I remember Joe. I played with him in Oakland. I got along good with Joe. I can tell you one thing, he could swing that bat! He used to make that fence in Oakland look like pine splinters out there.

Who was the best pitcher?

Oh, you're goin' through a whole bunch of 'em. There was several, but the one that was outstandin' to me was when I was with Cleveland. (Laughs) Ol' Bobby [Feller].

'Course, we had some good pitchers on the Yankees when I was there. There was Red Ruffin' and Joe Page. Old [Johnny] Murphy. Everybody looked for Murphy. Bullpen Murphy. (Laughs) There was a lotta good ballplayers.

The quality of play in the Coast League was very close to the major leagues when you were having those great years with Oakland.

Oh sure. We had eight ballplayers on the field that were ex–major league ballplayers. (Laughs)

You pitched a game that went 20 or 22 innings when you were with the Oaks.

I'll never forget it. I pitched three seven-inning ball games. 21 innings. I pitched 21 innings in four hours and 52 minutes. Of course, the pitcher that was pitchin' for Hollywood at the time — we were doin' this in Hollywood — Bob Hall went the full route, too. Jimmy Marshall, our first baseman, hit a triple with two men on and won the ball game. I think the score ended up 5–1 or somethin' like that. That was somethin' that I'll *never* forget.

I was listening to that game on the radio. I was about 12 or 13, I think, and I made it to about the fourteenth inning and my parents made me turn it off and go to bed.

A lot of the movie stars used to come out to the ballpark at Hollywood when Oakland was in town. For some reason or other, they just liked our ball-club. George Raft, Bing Crosby, and what was that old dancer — Bojangles [Robinson]? They all used to come to the ballpark, not only them but lots of the others and half of 'em had to go home that night because they couldn't stay up. (Laughs) They had to go to work the next morning.

We started the last inning at, I think, 1:45 and it lasted until right at two o'clock [curfew time]. Once you start an inning they let you finish it.

After all the pitchin' that I have gone through, I have *never* had a sore arm. I'd like to find out how many innings I did from 1936 to 1956.

You had three nicknames. Bill Dickey called you High Pockets because you were 6'3" tall, but on the Coast you were called Cowboy and Two-Gun. How did you get those?

I don't remember what year it was now, but I think I'd been out there two or three years. I've loved horses all my life and I used to go up to the stable there back of Berkeley. I used to go back and forth 'til I got a horse up there. I found one up there I liked — his name was Del Rey, a palomino stallion. He belonged to a fella there in Oakland and he let me have the saddle, bridle, horse, and all to do whatever I wanted to with him. I used to lead parades at the openin' of the baseball season out there.

Ol' Del was somethin' else. He'd do 'bout eight tricks. I'd stand where he could see me and all I had to do was use the different motions with the ridin' crop and he'd do exactly like what I said. He was trained like that before I got him.

The sergeant out there in the mounted police made me an honorary member of his group. There was 12 of us in the group and we used to ride up in the parks up there in the edge of the mountains where the kids used to park. We'd go up there with the horses — we rode in pairs all the time — and we'd go up there and run the kids outta these parkin' lots up there with their automobiles.

So then, after that, I was at the ball game one day and the sheriff of Oakland — his name was Gleason — made me an honorary sheriff of Alameda County and he gave me a star. In fact, I still have it. I went and bought myself a pair of western .44s. They were made by Colt, had stag handles and everything, and I had a fella to make me a pair of holsters for 'em and I used to wear them out there all the time. And I wore western clothes practically all the time out there; very seldom you'd see me without a western shirt or pants on. In fact, I've still got the boots now.

I led one parade out there one time and I never will forget it. It was when they brought the rodeo into Oakland with Dick West and his pardner, Jock Mahoney [from *The Range Rider* television series]. I was gonna lead the parade and this fella Kennedy — Douglas Kennedy was a movie star — he was the Grand Marshall and that's how I came to meet him. We had an enjoyable time.

This Two-Gun thing, how I got named that — a fella in Hollywood was gonna be my agent to get me into some of the movies and he's the one that put that "Two-Gun" bit on me because I wore that pair of .44s all the time. I was in two or three [movies]. I was in one with Douglas Kennedy, a television series, I was in a couple with Clint Walker — you remember him, don't you? [Walker was *Cheyenne*.] And, of course, I didn't have no big parts now, don't get me wrong. I was just in the picture. And he also got me into a picture called *The Tin Star* with Henry Fonda. I enjoyed that; it took almost two-and-a-half months to make that picture. They made it out there in the hills of Hollywood.

I enjoyed all that — all the people I met in the studios and the other people that was in there workin' just like me. You just don't forget those kinda people.

I played all over the country, I played in Canada, played in Puerto Rico, played in Cuba. I've enjoyed just the idea of bein' a major league baseball player. That's somethin', after I got started, I was determined to do it one way or the other. And I made it.

It's been very nice to be able to be remembered by a lot of people like I get fan mail from. I've been gettin' it ever since I've been out of baseball. I get at least two a week. They send me these reprints that the bubble gum company and the cookie company have reproduced.

You know, there's not very many people that still recognize the old ballplayers. It's great to have people that have loved baseball back in my time and the young people that are picking up on this card thing now. It makes you feel pretty good, you know? A lot of people today charge for their autographs and I've been signin' autographs since I was up to the majors and I've never charged a dime to nobody. I feel that if they still remember me, why should I charge 'em?

I'll tell you somethin'. If I had it to do all over again I'd do the same cotton-pickin' thing because I loved the game. I like to watch football, but football's not in my category. I played baseball so long. I was playin' when I was in the seventh grade for the high school team, so I played five years in school. Then I just kept goin'. I liked it so doggone much I just kept advancin', but I had no idea of goin' into the majors or goin' into professional baseball 'til that Gene McCann found me and that was it. That started the whole thing and I loved it all.

ALLEN JONES (COWBOY, TWO-GUN, HIGH POCKETS) GETTEL
Born September 17, 1917, Norfolk, Virginia
Ht. 6'3½"   Wt. 200   Batted and Threw Right

Year	Team	G	IP	W	L	Pct	BB	SO	H	SHO	SV	ERA
1945	**NYA**	**27**	**154.2**	**9**	**8**	**.529**	**53**	**67**	**141**	**0**	**3**	**3.90**
1946		**26**	**103**	**6**	**7**	**.462**	**40**	**54**	**89**	**2**	**0**	**2.97**
1947	CleA	31	149	11	10	.510	62	64	122	2	0	3.20
1948	CleA	5	7.2	0	1	.000	10	4	15	0	0	17.61
	ChiA	22	148	8	10	.444	60	49	154	0	1	4.01
1949	ChiA	19	63	2	5	.286	26	22	69	1	1	6.43
	WasA	16	34.2	0	2	.000	24	7	43	0	1	5.45
1951	NYN	30	57.1	1	2	.333	25	36	52	0	0	4.87
1955	StLN	8	17	1	0	1.000	10	7	26	0	0	9.00
Yankee years		**53**	**257.2**	**15**	**15**	**.500**	**93**	**121**	**230**	**2**	**3**	**3.53**
Career		184	734.1	38	45	.458	310	310	711	5	6	4.28

STEVE HAMILTON
Specialist

Yankees 1963–1970

What do Norm Cash, Jim Gentile, Don Mincher, Tony Oliva, Boog Powell, Leon Wagner, and Carl Yastrzemski have in common?

There are at least six areas of common ground:

1. *They were left-handed batters.*
2. *They played all or most of their careers in the American League.*
3. *They were not Yankees.*
4. *They were all important parts of their teams' offenses.*
5. *They played in the mid–1960s.*
6. *When their teams played the Yankees and they were up with the game on the line, they usually had to hit against Steve Hamilton.*

Hamilton had been a baseball and basketball star at Morehead State University in Kentucky, then a professional in both sports. The road to the major leagues was not without incident, but he finally made it in 1961.

He joined the Yankees shortly after the start of the 1963 season and stayed with them for nearly eight years. There were World Series checks his first two years there, but this was basically a rough time for that proud franchise. Even though the Yankees as a team failed more often than not, Steve specialized and did his specialty well. His specialty was to get the opposition's big left-handed batters out in crucial situations.

Steve Hamilton returned to his alma mater as the head baseball coach of the school's successful college team, then became the athletic director.

You were a successful starter in the minor leagues, winning 52 games in four years.

Steve Hamilton: When I first came into professional baseball I didn't understand relief pitching. In college here at Morehead and in summer ball most of the time we pitched the whole game. Even if you got beat, 10 to 9, you still pitched the whole game.

Throughout the minor leagues, I probably relieved in maybe six games. One of those was in the playoffs my first year. So I had a starter's attitude even though I didn't throw a lot of different pitches. I threw fastballs mainly and a curveball; I didn't have much of a change-up. I got by very well as a starter. I played basketball in the winter and baseball in the summer, so I had no problem pitching nine innings. I was strong enough. It was totally different to become a relief pitcher.

Did they teach you to be a relief pitcher?

Well, what happens, when you're a starter, you need to have about three pitches. If you've got two *good* ones, you're in good shape, but you need three. By the time you've gone around the order, unless you're a really good pitcher, they'll key in on you.

Like me, being tall, left-handed, I got left-handers out very well, but I was sort of a liability with some right-handers. I threw three-quarters to sidearm, so the second time around the right-handers would tune in on me pretty well. I didn't throw that hard, so it was really a matter of necessity to become a relief pitcher. It was Ralph Houk who was the man who explained all this to me and got me set up in it well. He told me the second time around I was less effective. I didn't believe him until the end of my career. But, mainly, I had one good pitch and it was a breaking pitch to a left-handed hitter, so I became a short relief pitcher getting out left-handed hitters. I thought I was better than that but he [Houk] probably had better judgment than I did.

Back when I started, in 1958, relief pitchers just sort of evolved. Now a lot of kids start off being relief pitchers. If you've got one really good pitch, you can be a relief pitcher today. Back when I began, if you couldn't make it as a starter you might become a relief pitcher.

I think it's [relief pitching] a lot harder on the hitters. The batting averages are lower, the home runs are down. And with reason! You bring in a Rob Dibble, throwing a hundred miles per hour, then a [John] Franco with that good sinker ball, well, the last two innings you're dead. It used to be, years ago, in the last two innings you could pound somebody. The goal was to pitch a complete game, but it's not relevant anymore.

Now, starting pitchers go five or six innings. Then they get to the two short relief men and everybody's got two of them. A complete game is just not as important anymore. Even if you're going well and have a chance at a complete game, they'll bring in Franco or Mark Davis and shut the door. It makes sense. A big difference from my time is this short relief man and the trick pitches they throw. Most of them are legal and there are a few that aren't legal. But all that's had a great impact on hitting.

Back when you pitched, the idea of a closer was maybe just beginning to form. Would you have been a closer?

Only against left-handed hitters. Ralph Houk started this before some of the others. I became totally a specialist on left-handers. If it happened that the last hitter or two was left-handed, then I'd be a closer, but I wouldn't be considered a closer. A closer is a guy like [Steve] Bedrosian or Davis. [Dennis] Eckersley is used in a way in which he can be used a lot — only warms up if he's going in a ball game.

A guy I pitched with, Lindy McDaniel, was the first one I ever knew who kept statistics that were meaningful. Each time he went into a game he'd determine how many outs there were, the men on base, and write all that stuff down. Day game, night game, home or away — all of this. I started doing it, too. And a true indication of how effective you are is *not* your earned run average, it's not your saves — it's how many runs score while you're pitching. When you come in, for example, with runners on second and third and one out and nobody scores, then you've really been effective. Or runners on first and second and nobody out.

Those stats are important. And another stat I kept from the beginning of my career to the end of it was how many times I warmed up. It will shock you when you start keeping track. It's not just how many times you got up, it's how many times you actually threw enough to get warm enough to go into the game. It was like almost 300 innings a year in the bullpen. I'd warm up as many as five times before I got into a game sometimes.

Al Lopez with the White Sox, a catcher in his playing days but a great pitching coach, never warmed up a relief pitcher more than three times. If he didn't get him into the game by then, he'd sit him down. When you warm up it takes a lot out of you. I'd warm up five times a game three days in a row — 15 times — and still not get into a game. Consequently, when I did get in maybe in the fourth game I wouldn't have real good stuff. It would be like a starting pitcher throwing maybe two or three innings maybe three days in a row. After three or four years, I learned how to warm up, how to prepare, how to save myself a little bit, and when you know the manager and the situation you pretty much know when you're going in.

Bur sometimes I'd turn myself up, thinking I was going in, and somebody would make a play — a double play or something — and we'd get out of the inning. This might happen two or three times in a game and each time you reached that peak of ready to go into the game, it's like you already pitched an inning. After a while the arm would maybe get a little sore and I'd have to go to Houk and tell him I needed a night off, unless maybe there was one batter he needed me for or something where I could get ready in a hurry. But when I could warm up gradually — when I knew I would go in next inning because of a pinch hitter or something — those were easy.

When I played with the Cubs my last year, my manager was Leo Durocher — fabulous Leo — who had been a good manager. But one night in Pittsburgh I was sitting in the pen and Willie Stargell came on deck to pinch hit. Leo called the bullpen for me to start throwing when Stargell was in the *on-deck circle!* I came into the game and I'd thrown five pitches in the pen! I got him out, but he popped up — missed a pitch he should've hit five miles. But when you don't get loose you're just not effective.

You only started a few games in the major leagues and one of them was a shutout.

It was in Cleveland, in the mid-'60s — the second game of a double-header, and I had flown back with another pitcher from Anaheim. We were playing a night game there, so they flew the two of us in the day before so we would be rested. But we didn't get any sleep. But I pitched that game; I threw 101 pitches, gave up five hits, faced 30 batters, two double plays, three strikeouts, no walks. I remember it well. I felt good about that game. Cleveland wasn't the greatest team in the league at that time, but I hadn't started a game in quite some time. I think we won five to nothing. It was my last start.

Why didn't you start again?

This happened to me a couple of times. When I first joined the Yankees in 1963, I relieved in a couple of games and then I came in on one of those Saturday afternoons, playing in Baltimore, in a Game of the Week. Dizzy Dean and Pee Wee Reese did the games then. The Orioles had a good team.

I came in in the first inning. The starter, Stan Williams, was wild and we were down two to nothing. They brought me in with two outs and I think there were a couple of men on. I faced Boog Powell and struck him out. I pitched eight and a third innings that day, gave up two hits, had 11 strikeouts, no walks, hit a triple with two men on — I mean, I did it all! I thought, man, I'm in good shape now. I'm going to get a start! But nah. Houk just kind of grinned. He thought I was more valuable in the bullpen.

At that time, I did some long relieving and probably could have started; later on I had a sore elbow and was out for about a month and a half in 1964. I had seven wins before the All-Star break, seven and oh, and then I was seven and two for the year and had a save in the World Series against the Cardinals. But Houk always told me he needed me more out in the bullpen.

Right after that, the Yankees stock dropped drastically and one reason, it seems, was the starting pitching.

The starting pitching didn't do well. Ralph Terry started to have problems, Whitey Ford's arm was bothering him, Jim Bouton hurt his arm and was never effective again.

But the biggest thing that hurt us was we didn't have a shortstop. Tony Kubek had had shoulder and back problems and he found it stemmed from a fractured vertebra that occurred when he was in the service. We never really had a solidified infield after that. Kubek was the guy who made the Yankees go. We tried Phil Linz, but Kubek was the glue. We still had Bobby Richardson; we still had Joe Pepitone, who was a little shaky but was a good ballplayer; and Clete Boyer was at third. But we missed Kubek.

Also at that time, Roger Maris was about ready to leave. He was very upset with the New York people, but he was a great player. Yogi had retired. We started dropping off.

One thing that happened was CBS bought the Yankees. For CBS, buying the Yankees in 1965 was strictly a business deal. They bought the Yankees for $15 million and did a short-term amortization and wrote off the entire $15 million over a five-year period.

In the meantime, they cut a lot of the minor league operations, got rid of some of the scouts, tried to bring in a lot of their own people to run the show. It wasn't a good baseball operation at that point. Our farm system went down the tubes.

They sold the team five years later for $14 million and they actually pocketed $14 million because of the tax laws and the way they did it. They really hurt us. They brought a guy in named Mike Burke, a nice guy but he'd been running a circus. He ended up as the team president. He was a fine man, but he wasn't a baseball man. It took the Yankees a long time to rebuild from that.

You had a pitcher who won a lot of games for an awfully bad bunch of teams — Mel Stottlemyre. What would he have done if he'd been there a decade earlier?

Stottlemyre would have been a Cy Young candidate. He was not a spectacular pitcher, but he pitched as well as anybody in the big leagues. He threw a lot of sinker balls; he was a very smart pitcher, a great competitor. He's a good friend of mine.

Mel came up and really won the 1964 pennant. Ford wasn't throwing well and we had other problems. Mel was a great gamer, but he was unspectacular, didn't strike out a lot of people, but they'd hit ground ball after ground ball off of him. Today he'd be worth a whole lot of money. He had a torn rotator cuff, but had he not hurt his shoulder he'd have been there a long time.

The only game I've ever been to in New York was Stottlemyre's first start. He beat the White Sox, 7 to 2, I believe. Does that sound right?

Yeah, sure does. It had to be around August. He was called up from Richmond. He'd been there in spring training, but we really didn't know him. I knew he had a funny name that was difficult to spell; it's still misspelled frequently. I knew it took him longer to write his name on a ball than anyone on the team. I told him to change his name to "Stott" and forget all those other letters.

He pitched in pressure situations — tough ball games — as a rookie. I had a lot of respect for him.

Hall of Fame?

Probably, if he had played longer. He played on some bad teams. In 1965 we went from first place to fifth or sixth that year.

Who was the best pitcher you saw?

Sandy Koufax. He was the best pitcher I've seen in my lifetime. There have been some great pitching *performances*. Whitey Ford was one of the best pressure pitchers. You could put him out there in a pressure situation and win a ball game. But Sandy Koufax could walk out and throw a no-hitter any time. He had a great fastball, everybody talked about that, but he had a great curve that went straight down, and he had a fantastic change. And he was very durable. It's unfortunate he had that arthritic elbow. Bob Gibson was an excellent pitcher, but he didn't have the tools that Koufax had.

And Koufax enjoyed the game. He didn't go out and sweat things. As a matter of fact, he was kind of a practical joker. He'd mess around in the clubhouse. And when he pitched, he never went out and gritted his teeth — you know, really tense. It was just a nice day on the mound.

I first saw Sandy when I was a freshman or sophomore here at Morehead.

He went to the University of Cincinnati and we'd play them in those days. He pitched against us one day. I played center field — I wasn't a pitcher then — and this guy's out there pitching, throwing the ball a hundred miles per hour! And he doesn't have a clue where the ball's going! An 18-year-old kid. The first time I go up to bat he throws the ball behind me! Well, that ended my hitting for the day. All I did was go up there and try to stay out of the way. And he's out there laughing, having a good time.

He spent over five years in the majors being ineffective because he couldn't throw strikes. I asked him once how he became a control pitcher with the same stuff he couldn't control for all those years. He said he had a change of mind. One day he went out to pitch a "B" game and his catcher told him to just throw batting practice. Lay every pitch in there, let them knock it as far as they can. He did, and he threw a one-hitter. He finally discovered he didn't have to strike everybody out. Let them hit the ball. A "perfect" game's 27 pitches, where everybody hits the first pitch and makes an out. When his attitude changed, he actually struck out more and his control was great.

Who was the best hitter you saw and who was the toughest on you?

The toughest batter I ever faced was Al Kaline. I got hitters out who tried to pull the ball, but Kaline went with the pitch. If I threw the sinker ball outside, he'd go to right field; if I brought the slider coming in, he'd pull it to left. I went three years without getting him out. Finally he hit a ground ball to Phil Linz and I said, "All right!", and Linz threw it into the seats. But finally I got him to fly out.

The first time I ever faced him I struck him out — started a slider outside and caught the outside of the plate for strike three. The next time I threw that same pitch to him, he hit a line drive to right field. He catalogued it.

The best left-handed hitter I ever faced was Tony Oliva of the Twins. A messed-up batting style, but great hand-eye coordination, a good natural hitter. He had real bad knees all the time, but what a hitter! Left-handers did not hit me. They just didn't hit my slider. I'd strike them out. I couldn't wait to face Oliva, the rookie sensation. This guy's killing everybody. I wanted to face him. I threw him my best slider that nobody ever hit! He threw the bat at the ball and hit a line drive over shortstop. From then on he hit me. But Al Kaline was the toughest I ever faced.

The best hitter I ever saw, that's difficult. The best ballplayer I ever saw, and that includes hitting, too, was Mickey Mantle. Mickey didn't take care of himself. If he had good habits, nobody would have been a better ballplayer. But he didn't take care of himself. He got hurt when he was young, when he played right field — tore up a knee. But he didn't rehab at all. He had such great natural ability. And in the clutch, he was a real tough hitter.

This will surprise a lot of people, but another real great hitter I saw was Bobby Richardson. He was the guy everyone liked to see come up with the game on the line. He'd get a hit to win it. He never struck out, didn't try to hit the ball out. But that whole Yankee team hit well.

In 1964, Roger Maris drove in the winning run in something like 21 of the last 28 games. He got hot, but nobody thought he did well because his home runs were down after he hit those 61 a few years before. Nobody appreciated him. He wasn't a great hitter, but he was a great clutch hitter.

But Mickey Mantle was the greatest player. Right-handed he was the best hitter I ever saw. Left-handed he'd hit a long way but he wasn't a great hitter. You could pitch to him left-handed. He had a real bad right knee and he really couldn't rotate well from the left side. If you pitched him out and down a little bit he'd hit it five miles, but if you pitched him inside he couldn't hit it. But right-handed he just killed the ball.

Mantle had a shoulder operation, maybe in '66 or so, and they sent him to the Mayo Clinic to have it done. While he was there, they put him on a physical therapy program with his knees and back and all and he came back that year running better and throwing better. He said, "I'm in great shape!"

What did he do? Did he continue doing his exercises? Nah. He quit. It was the first time I'd ever seen him run well. He could fly! But he quit his exercises and about a month or so later he pulled a hamstring. Out for two, three weeks. He kept doing that.

Mickey liked to go out and have a drink or two and that didn't help his career a bit. As a matter of fact, he made a statement often, "If I knew I was going to live this long, I'd have taken better care of myself." And he really meant that. His dad, his uncles, had all died before they were 40—they worked in the mines down there in Oklahoma—and he was convinced he would, too. He had a very fatalistic attitude.

What is the major change in the game in the years since you turned pro?

Artificial turf. As a pitcher I didn't like it. It hurt me; I was a ground ball pitcher and more of the balls get through. Conversely, the ball gets to the fielders quicker and there's no bad hops so they can get the double play faster.

I liked the grass much better as a player, but as a coach, and one who had to work on baseball fields, the turf has been great. When it first came in, though, in the Astrodome, it was hard as a rock. The Astros' pitchers would go outside on grass to run rather than hurt themselves on the turf.

In the daytime in St. Louis, before we got turf shoes, the spikes would actually burn red spots on your feet because it would get so hot. Maybe 130 degrees. But the turf today is much better—better padded—and the players have turf shoes.

And the bounces used to be terrible. The balls would rebound 15, 20 feet back then. An outfielder had to make a decision whether to stop or try to catch it, because if he missed it it would go for an inside-the-park home run. It's not as bad now.

In '71, when I played for San Francisco, we had turf. It would change the type of player you could put in the infield. We had [second baseman] Ron Hunt, who went to Montreal later, but he didn't have a lot of range. On the turf you had to have good speed, good range.

Another change is the emphasis on relief pitching and another is the designated hitter. I personally like the DH. If I was still playing I wouldn't like it. That was the one out I could be sure of, when that pitcher came up.

But even with the changes, guys who played 35 years ago could come back and play today. Football guys who played 30 years ago couldn't play today. And in basketball, guys who played *20* years ago couldn't come back and play today. It's a different game today. But baseball has stayed pretty much the same. Our equipment's better, the guys are bigger, they're probably a little faster overall. I'm not sure the desire's any more, but it's not any less.

I hope they don't take away the designated hitter rule. To my knowledge, the only league in the world that doesn't use the DH is the National League. Amateur or pro. As a pitcher, I liked it because you could stay in the game. You didn't have to worry about being lifted for a pinch hitter. It's easier on the manager, too. He doesn't have to worry about pinch hitting. The only time he has to take a pitcher out is when he's ineffective.

You mentioned Whitey Ford earlier. Talk about him.

I learned a lot from Whitey. I learned you didn't have to throw your glove or kick the bench or get all mad every time something went wrong. Once I saw him have a really bad first inning, gave up three or four runs. Mantle would break bats or kill water coolers, but Ford just came in, put his jacket on, got a drink, sat down for a minute, and then went out and shut them out the rest of the way. He won the game something like six to four.

When someone would boot the ball behind Whitey, he wouldn't get upset. He'd just bear down and get the next couple of guys out. His teammates liked him for that. Gaylord Perry was bad about that. When he pitched, you'd better play well or he'd get on you. It didn't help matters.

Did you come back here to Morehead after you left professional ball?

I'd been coming back here every year. I played professional baseball and basketball and after my second year of basketball I came back here to get my master's degree and help coach basketball. And each year I'd do that and teach a little and I'd work with the basketball team and later with the baseball team. So I'd really been here all along. When I left pro ball, I first worked in insurance here, but in 1976 I came here as baseball coach. In '75 I'd been the Tigers' pitching coach but I've been here since.

[College] recruiting is tough. But it doesn't take a smart guy to know someone is going to be good. Drew Hall, for instance, never had any success before he came down here. People said, "Boy, you did a great job with him!" No, not really. Drew did it himself. He'd never been in a program where he

orked on pitching, but this kid threw the ball 93, 94 miles per hour
lot of movement. Once he got his mind set, he was a first-round draft
p___ 3ut you see that kind of talent, you try to sign that kid.

But you've got to have good character. You're not trying to run a Boys
Town. And they've got to make it academically. I wouldn't bring a kid here
just to win a ball game. He's got to get something out of it, a degree, because
so few ever make it in pro ball.

Who's the best—or most successful—player you've turned out?

Most successful would be Walt Terrell. He had some good years with
Detroit and the Mets. He's one of only two pitchers I've had here that I let
hit. He played in the outfield some. But Walt was a good athlete — point guard
in basketball, a safety and tight end, an unusual combination, in football. He
was a good competitor.

We had a guy here named Jody Hamilton. He was probably the greatest
hitter I ever had here. He played about one and a half years in the Yankee
organization, but he didn't have great foot speed.

Did you save souvenirs from your career?

Not a lot. I have some baseballs signed by all the teams I played with.
Those balls are probably valuable on the memorabilia market today. I've got
a ball from the '63 Yankees with Berra and Mantle and Howard and all those
on it. And I've got World Series programs; some are autographed.

I wish I'd saved all those cards Topps used to give us, but I would give
them to neighborhood kids and they'd just eat the gum and throw the cards
away. They'd give us boxes of that stuff.

Do you get much fan mail?

Depends on what "much" means. I get a couple a week. We got a lot
when I played.

Do you sign?

Oh, yeah. Always have. They wanted me to get involved in a card show
here, where they charge for autographs, but I didn't want to do that. Sometimes someone will send six or seven cards. These guys are dealers. I'll sign a
couple and send the rest back.

Do you have your cards?

Most of them. I didn't appear on one my first year in Cleveland and my
second year I was traded to the Senators and didn't come up until about two
weeks into the season, so I didn't have one then, either. My rookie card was
in 1963 with the Yankees. Back then in the minor leagues, the guy from Topps
would come around and have you sign and give you $5. We figured we'd never
get to the majors so we'd sign and get an easy five and it was a lifetime contract! For $5. But they did give us nice gifts. Then Marvin Miller came in as
player association director and it's worked around to where the players not
only got a $250 gift a year but also a percentage over a certain amount of sales.

Back to your playing days. Do you remember Emmett Ashford, the first black umpire in the major leagues?

Yes. I liked Emmett. He wasn't the best umpire. I played at Salt Lake City when Emmett was in the [Pacific] Coast League. You wanted the batter to take the first pitch if it was a strike if Emmett was behind the plate. If you think Dutch Rennert lets you know it's a strike, you should have seen Emmett! He'd jump up in the air and swing his arms and scream, "Strike One!" We'd try to get the hitter to take the first pitch just to watch Emmett jump up and down.

He was a nice man and enjoyed what he did. But in the big leagues, Elston Howard didn't like him at all. Emmett was the first black ump. Ellie got on Emmett a lot because he thought Emmett was a little bit of a clown. Players would get on him, but he wouldn't fuss back. He had a great attitude. The players liked him for the most part. I never knew anyone who made a racial slur toward him. There weren't any black umps. I played in the Southern Association in 1960 and there weren't any black players, much less black umps.

Would you do it again?

Yeah, oh yeah. I worked very hard at it and I was very fortunate to be there. I got some breaks.

I didn't have a lot of pressure. I didn't *have* to make it. I was one of the few players to play in the big leagues who had a college degree. I had something to fall back on.

But in 1962, when I was sent back to Jacksonville, I wondered a little. Cleveland needed left-handed pitching. Dick Stigman went down with a sore elbow in spring training and they really needed pitchers and they sent me out anyway. I'd had a pretty good year the year before and had a good spring.

So I wrote Gabe Paul, the general manager, a letter. I told him the letter was not a threat in any way, but this winter I'm going to finish my master's degree and if I can't get to the big leagues this summer I'll retire and get a job. If I can get to the big leagues I'll keep playing. I told him to try to get somebody for me they could use. And two weeks later, I was traded to the Washington Senators for Willie Tasby. The Senators were an expansion team, so I was barely in the big leagues, but I was there. I wrote Gabe a note thanking him and we had a good relationship for years. I really appreciated it.

I was three and eight there. I pitched pretty good, but we were a *bad* team. We had Claude Osteen and Chuck Hinton, our only two bona fide players. We had guys like Dan O'Connell; he was a crazy man, he couldn't play. And John Schaive playing third. And Harry Bright was not a good player. We had Jimmy King, who had been a good player but wasn't anymore. And Jimmy Piersall in center field. We were a misfit bunch.

The next season I had pitched poorly and got a loss and two weeks later

I was traded to the Yankees. I greeted that with mixed emotions. On one side I was glad — I was going to the best. But on the other side, if I didn't pitch well I would be back in the minor leagues in no time. I'm not ashamed to admit there was a little ambivalence. I'd gone from the worst to the best in one day and there was a little fear of failure.

[I was traded for] Jim Coates. When Houk first saw me, he said, "Well, we've gained two inches in height but nothing in looks. The reason we traded for you was you were the only guy who could fit Coates' uniform." He was tall and skinny, too. That was the first thing Houk said to me.

Coates was as nasty as they come.

Everybody on the team came in and greeted me and said how glad they were to have me. Whitey said, "Even if you can't pitch a lick, that's a good trade." No one liked him; he got them into a lot of fights. He'd throw at hitters for no reason. They didn't want to come to his defense. Maybe there's a time to throw at someone, but we didn't do it often. Mantle couldn't get out of the way very well, so we were vulnerable. To stop someone from throwing at you, just drill their best player.

It just doesn't help to throw at some guys anyhow. Roger Maris was 50 to a hundred points better if you threw at him. Joe Pepitone — let him lay, let him do his hot-dog stuff. If you threw at him he was a whole lot better hitter. I never saw a guy respond the way he did.

But back to the original question. I'd do it again.

STEVE ABSHER HAMILTON
Born November 30, 1935, Columbia, Kentucky
Died December 4, 1997, Morehead, Kentucky
Ht. 6'6"   Wt. 190   Batted and Threw Left

Year	Team	G	IP	W	L	Pct	BB	SO	H	SHO	SV	ERA
1961	CleA	2	3.1	0	0	.000	3	4	2	0	0	2.70
1962	WasA	41	107.1	3	8	.273	39	83	103	0	2	3.77
1963	WasA	3	2	0	1	.000	2	1	5	0	0	13.50
	NYA	34	62.2	5	1	.833	24	63	49	0	5	2.60
1964		30	60.1	7	2	.778	15	49	55	0	3	3.28
1965		46	58.1	3	1	.750	16	51	47	0	5	1.39
1966		44	90	8	3	.727	22	57	69	1	3	3.00
1967		44	62	2	4	.333	23	55	57	0	4	3.48
1968		40	50.2	2	2	.500	13	42	37	0	11	2.13
1969		38	57	3	4	.429	21	39	39	0	2	3.32
1970	NYA	35	45.1	4	3	.571	16	33	36	0	3	2.78
	ChiA	3	3	0	0	.000	1	3	4	0	0	6.00
1971	SFN	39	45	2	2	.500	11	38	29	0	4	3.02
1972	ChiN	22	17	1	0	1.000	8	13	24	0	0	4.76

Year	Team	G	IP	W	L	Pct	BB	SO	H	SHO	SV	ERA
Yankee years		**311**	**486**	**34**	**20**	**.630**	**150**	**389**	**389**	**1**	**36**	**2.78**
Career		421	663.2	40	31	.563	214	531	556	1	42	3.05
League Championship Series												
1971	SFN	1	1	0	0	.000	0	3	1	0	0	9.00
World Series												
1963	**NYA**	**1**	**1**	**0**	**0**	**.000**	**0**	**1**	**0**	**0**	**0**	**0.00**
1964		**2**	**2**	**0**	**0**	**.000**	**0**	**2**	**3**	**0**	**1**	**4.50**
2 years		**3**	**3**	**0**	**0**	**.000**	**0**	**3**	**3**	**0**	**1**	**3.00**

BILLY HUNTER
All-Star Rookie

Yankees 1955–1956

In the last several years of their existence, the St. Louis Browns were on the edge of bankruptcy. They were doomed to the bottom of the American League standings because anyone who became a solid player was dealt away. There were two reasons for this: (1) they couldn't afford to pay their better players what they were worth, and (2) they could get much-needed cash in addition to minor leaguers in return for players who had shown they could play.

A typical Browns trade in the late 1940s and early '50s consisted of a proven or promising Brownie for two or three warm bodies and cash. Stress the cash. From 1947 through 1953, the team's last year in St. Louis, the club made 79 deals. Forty-one of them involved cash coming in (more than $1.5 million) and only 24 involved cash going out (less than $300,000). It was the only way the team could stay in business.

Imagine, then, baseball's surprise when, after the 1952 season, the Browns sent three players on their major league roster plus $95,000 (roughly one-third of their total cash outlay of the previous six years) to the Brooklyn Dodgers for minor league shortstop Billy Hunter.

Hunter wasn't just any minor league shortstop, however. In 1952 at Fort Worth, he had been the Texas League's Most Valuable Player. And the only reason he'd been in Double A then, instead of in Triple A or Brooklyn, was the logjam behind Pee Wee Reese. Dodger minor league shortstops during the late 1940s and early 1950s included Chico Carrasquel, Don Zimmer, Bobby Morgan, Rocky Bridges, Chico Fernandez, and Stan Rojek, as well as Hunter, and all of them became regular major league shortstops when they finally got out of Reese's shadow. There were also Jim Pendleton, Eddie Miksis, Tommy Brown, and Mike Rose; being a minor league shortstop in the Brooklyn organization was a very frustrating experience.

The Browns really did not have a shortstop in 1952. Joe DeMaestri played 77 games there, manager Marty Marion 63, and Freddie Marsh 60. DeMaestri and Marsh were traded and Marion retired as a player. The job was then handed to Hunter, who was in the lineup every day in 1953. He was batting .252 at mid-season and was chosen for the All-Star game. Chances are he would have won a Gold Glove if that award had been given then; he led AL shortstops in assists, total chances per game, and errors, and was second in putouts and third in double plays and fielding average.

He accompanied the franchise to Baltimore in 1954 and became the Orioles' first shortstop. He was part of the team's gigantic trade with the Yankees in 1955 and played regularly for New York and later for Kansas City. After his playing days, he eventually became Baltimore's third base coach, where he was baseball's most energetic traffic cop.

Later he managed the Texas Rangers and still holds the team record for career winning percentage. When he left professional baseball after the 1978 season, he began a successful career as baseball coach and then athletic director at Towson State University near Baltimore.

Previous page: Billy Hunter as a rookie with the St. Louis Browns.

Were you signed out of college?

Billy Hunter: Yes. Really, I went to the Dodger camp as a free agent. My father grew up with Mike Ryba, who spent a whole lot of time with Mr. [Branch] Rickey in the Cardinals organization and then went to the Red Sox as a manager in their minor league system. After the '46 World Series, he called and expressed interest and that was the year I graduated from high school.

I took a Penn State football-baseball scholarship out of high school. My freshman year in '47, Penn State did not take any freshmen on campus because of all the returning servicemen, so I went to Indiana State Teachers College in Indiana, Pennsylvania, as a Penn State freshman. The rest of the Penn State freshman football squad went to California State Teachers College in California, Pennsylvania, and we happened to play them when I was on the Indiana State team in that Pennsylvania State Conference.

I played football, basketball, and baseball as a freshman and went up to [Penn] State as a sophomore for spring football practice. They used a single wing and I was a T quarterback and it looked like I was gonna be about third-string running back on the '48 team. I told [coach Bob] Higgins that I was going to go back to Indiana because I wanted to play another year of football before I signed a professional baseball contract. Joe Bedink was the line coach and the baseball coach at Penn State at the time and he said, "Bill, forget football. We'll give you a full scholarship in baseball." And I said, "No, you don't understand. I wanna play football another year." So I went back there and I ended up being the quarterback on the IUP team my freshman and sophomore years. My freshman year I was an 18-year-old kid and most of the other players on the team were 26, 27 coming back from the service. I grew up in a hurry.

I only went that one semester [as a sophomore], still waiting to hear from the Red Sox. The Dodgers said, "Well, why don't you come to Vero Beach and if you like what you see, maybe you'll sign with us."

Mike Ryba was the manager of the Scranton club, and they were training in Cocoa Beach, which was right up the road from Vero. Well, I kept waiting to hear from them and I was there about ten days. They [the Dodgers] wanted to sign me, so I told my dad I was going to sign. And the next day we played Scranton in an exhibition game and Mike Ryba called me aside after the first inning. He said, "Are you from Indiana, Pennsylvania?" I said, "I sure am, Mr. Ryba." He said, "I've been waiting for you for three weeks." And I said, "I've been waiting to hear from you."

He said, "Have you signed?" and I said, "I signed last night." He said, "You know what this organization's [the Dodgers] like. They have 21 farm clubs." I said, "Well, if I have it, I'll get there. If I don't have it, it wouldn't make any difference whether I was in the Red Sox camp or in the Dodger camp." That's how I ended up with the Dodgers.

They offered me my choice of $2,000 however I wanted it. I could take it up front and work for nothing or I could take it a thousand and $200 a month, so I ended up doing that. I wish I'd have taken none and gone $400 a month because each year they gave you a little $50 a month increase and it took me four years to get to that $400 a month.

I spent five years in their minor league system and the last two of those five in Vero Beach I roomed with Don Zimmer, both of us heir apparent to Pee Wee Reese's job.

Major league baseball from the late '40s through the late '50s had Dodger "heir apparent" shortstops everywhere.

That was our problem. Carrasquel was called up a couple years before I went. The Dodgers sold him. They were stacked up. We had Pendelton and Bobby Morgan and Mike Rose and Don Zimmer and Stan Rojek and Rocky Bridges and Tommy Brown. Both Zimmer and I had Triple A contracts for a couple of years but played in Double A. He was at Mobile and I was at Fort Worth and I went back to Fort Worth for the second year. My second year at Fort Worth I was the Most Valuable Player in the Texas League and that's when I was sold to the Browns.

The Browns were always on the verge of bankruptcy. They paid a whole lot more for you than it seemed they could possibly afford.

They did. I was playing in Puerto Rico. In fact, I was supposed to go with Bobby Bragan to Alimendares in Cuba and the Dodgers wouldn't let me go with Bragan because they wanted me to go to Santurce in Puerto Rico and play alongside Junior Gilliam. I was the only white guy on the club. (Laughs) We had two pitchers, but I'm talking about when they weren't pitching. We had Billy Bruton in center field and Gilliam at second base and Willard Brown and Bob Thurman. Buster Clarkson was our manager and third baseman. Valmy Thomas was our catcher and we had an 18-year-old kid in left field by the name of Roberto Clemente. (Laughs)

That sounds like a doggone good team.

It was! We won the thing ... well, *they* won the thing. [Bill] Veeck called me in December and this is a story in itself.

We stayed right across the street from the Candada Beach Hotel in San Juan and my wife was pregnant with our first child and had morning sickness all the time. We'd go across to the Candada Beach for breakfast and the only place she felt comfortable was standing in the swimming pool. Evidently it took some of the pressure off and right after breakfast we would get in our swimsuits and go across and she'd stand in the pool and I would play volleyball with the ever-revolving Pan American Airlines personnel that stayed there at the hotel. After about a week of that, you wouldn't know I was the only white guy on the field. (Laughs)

Anyway, in the morning at breakfast it was a ritual that I'd buy the *New*

York Times and the small paper that always had the sports on the back — *Daily News*, I guess it was. The one I used to pick up first because it was easier to read at the breakfast table was the *Daily News*. It said, "Hunter Sold to the Browns for 95,000 and 3 Players." I said to my wife, "Let me see the *New York Times*." Really, I thought the guy at the newsstand was doing a number on me.

You know, in the *Times* you have to go through the paper a little bit to find the sports page and it was headlines there, too. I said, "Well, we better get back to the apartment because I think the phone is probably ringing." And it was.

When we went in the apartment, Veeck was on the line and he wanted me to come home. I said, "Bill, I can't come home." This was somewhere around the tenth or twelfth of December, I guess — it was just before Christmas — and I had been there two months and I was making 1200 a month down there. I said, "I can't afford to come home, Bill." He said, "I'll give you an extra thousand in your contract." I said, "Well, that's not gonna take care of us for the rest of the winter. It's a long time until the season starts."

And he said, "I'll give you a thousand when you get here *and* an extra thousand in your contract." I said, "I have an obligation to the people here." He said, "I've already talked to the owner of the club and he understands."

So it was the next day when we got out of Puerto Rico. I had my car stored in Miami and we flew there and I put my wife on a plane to Pittsburgh, Pennsylvania, and drove my car to St. Louis. She wasn't going to be able to travel when it was time to go to spring training. That's how it all came about.

When you joined the Browns, they put you in the lineup and you didn't come out for anything.

That's exactly right. I enjoyed it. I think that probably the best thing that ever happened to me was my five years' experience [in the Dodger organization]; I would rather it had been three or four, but I think I learned more baseball those five years than I would have anyplace else.

I'll tell you, it was a rude awakening the first day I reported to Vero Beach. Growing up in western Pennsylvania, being an all-state basketball and football player, I thought I was the best athlete that ever put on a pair of shoes until I got down to Vero Beach and saw 500 guys *under contract*— 21 farm clubs — and to be quite honest with you, there were a lot of people that were overawed and just turned and went home. It's an eye-opener.

You were an All-Star as a rookie. Shortstop in the American League in 1953 was tough — eight teams and five were chosen for the All-Star team.

Stengel took a lot of heat for that as far as the selection went. "Why did you have five shortstops?" Of those that went, I was one of the fellas that didn't even take a bat because I didn't expect to play, but I got in the game as a pinch runner. Of all the people, I ran for Mickey Mantle.

Billy Hunter *(courtesy New York Yankees)*

I think it was the eighth inning—I know it was late in the ball game; it was probably Mickey's last at bat anyway—and we were down. When I went out to first base there were two men out and Jim Turner was the first base coach and he said, "Bill, your run doesn't mean anything." I think we were behind, four to one, and he said, "Don't take any chances."

The next pitch, Yogi [Berra] hit a line drive to right field and I took off and rounded second, slid into third with a bang-bang play. Slaughter had taken the ball on one hop in right field and Turner's over there with his hands up. (Laughs) He's asking what am I doing and I just gave him the sign, you know, as the umpire does, "Safe." What he was telling me was there wasn't any need to go to third base on that play and had I been out I would've really been reamed out, but I wasn't out. I'm not sure who the following hitter was, but he flied out to make the third out and I didn't score.

It must have been a pretty exciting experience.

Oh, yes! It certainly was. I think the All-Star gift at that time was a silver service. You had your selection of a couple things, but I chose the silver tray and teapot and I still have that. That's one of the things that's in the closet at home that we'll cherish.

That year you hit one home run and it was the last one ever hit by a Brown.

I roomed with Jim Dyck and Dyck had a bet with about half the guys on the club that I would hit a home run. As it turned out, it wasn't the last game of the season; I think it was the next-to-last but it *was* the last home run of the Browns. Connie Johnson was pitching for the White Sox and it was down the left field line in Sportsman's Park and just made it, but it put me in the record book, I guess. Dyck went around collecting all his bets. (Laughs)

That's a record that will not be broken, one of the few safe ones.

That's right. I think Jim Pisoni, who was called up late in the season, had hit one either earlier in the game or the day before, but mine was the last one and my first one.

Funny thing about that year, I got started off *very* good with the bat I think the first of June I was among the top ten hitters in the American League and it just kind of nose-dived after that and I ended up hitting .219, I think, but I was over .300 for the first couple of months of the season.

You know, Harvey Kuenn was probably the best hitting shortstop of the bunch and he and I were kind of battling it out for the Rookie of the Year thing. I remember Veeck calling me in and he said, "Bill, don't be discouraged about the way the team's playing. You continue to do your thing." I don't know whether it was the fact that I played 161 games before [in 1952 with Fort Worth] and played a little in Puerto Rico and then in every game that the Browns played. In fact, I played in 155; we had a tie game that we had to play over again. Through about a month of that season I played with a broken finger; I played with a cast on but I hit very well with that thing on there. It wasn't the middle finger; it was the finger next to the pinkie because I could throw the ball and that cast was okay because it was on the side of the ball and it wasn't one of the ones that you threw the ball with.

I remember Bob Bowman, our trainer. He took it off and I think I went oh for 12 or something like that and I went back in in a couple of days and I asked him if he would put that damn thing back on my finger. (Laughs) He just laughed at me.

You got Jimmy Piersall with a hidden ball.

(Laughs) We were playing in Boston and Duane Pillette was pitching for us and Johnny Groth was our center fielder and there was one man out. There was a fly ball to Groth and he threw the ball in to me and I walked in toward Pillette on the mound at Fenway Park. He walked off the back of the mound and I didn't give him the ball; I just took it back out with me. Eddie Rommel was the umpire at second base and I made him aware that I still had the ball, then I went over to Piersall and I said, "Clean that base off!" This is when Jimmy was going through some of his difficulties and he stepped off and I had the ball up against him when he stepped off the base and Rommel called him out for the third out. This was the last year you still left your gloves on the field and I just tossed my glove back of the shortstop area and ran in. I turned around at the top of the third base dugout at Fenway, which is very close to the field, you know, and he's just standing there staring at me.

We come to bat. I think I was either the leadoff or the second hitter and I ended up on second base and there was one man out. In Fenway Park it's very difficult to score from second base on a base hit to left field. They had given me the green light to steal third if I could do it, so I'm getting a lead. Johnny Lipon and Sid Hudson were the shortstop and pitcher for the Red Sox and he [Hudson] picked me off second base. Well, Piersall's in right field and he's doing cartwheels! I think Clint Courtney was our batter—this is while they're pitching to Courtney—and if he had hit one to right field he would have had an inside-the-park home run 'cause Piersall's so elated out there that he wouldn't have seen the ball.

You were very high in all shortstop fielding categories that year. You probably would have won the Gold Glove if it had been awarded then.

I played deep. I could come in on ground balls very well and playing deep gave me more range, so I had a lot of assists. I made a lot of errors that I shouldn't have.

We went into Cleveland and I don't know if you're aware but Cleveland's infield is cut very deep and I'm playing at my usual spot. Fuzzy Smith hits a ground ball to me—just an ordinary two-hopper—and I come up and throw to first and he's already beyond first. Later on, Jim Hegan did the same thing. Hegan, for a catcher, ran decent, unlike most catchers. What, in essence, I was doing was playing too deep in order to field an ordinary ground ball and throw a guy out at first. That was a learning experience for me because I really didn't realize that that infield was cut about 20 feet deeper than the rest of the infields in the league, so I had to station myself midway on that infield rather than back on the outfield grass.

When the club moved to Baltimore in 1954, you didn't play every day and raised your batting average 24 points.

I was very unhappy in Baltimore. Jimmy Dykes was our manager there.

Jimmy Brideweser signed with us shortly after the season started, and they kind of felt like they needed more bat in the lineup and felt that he could do that. I had never played anyplace that I didn't play all the time.

I recall one game in Shibe Park in Philadelphia. Jimmy [Dykes] came to me and he says, "I'm not sure Brideweser can play. His little finger's bothering him." I didn't have a hell of a lot of sympathy for that. He put me in the game in the last inning. We're ahead by one run and he put me in in the ninth inning and all three balls were hit to me. We got all three guys out but I guess I howdy-dooed a couple of them and he jumped all over me after the game was over. "You're too good a player to do that!" And I said, "I don't know how the hell *you* would know that. I'm not playing." He says, "Well, I can send you to San Antonio where you can play every day," and I said, "No. I can play every day here. I was the Most Valuable Player in that league." From that point on, I played a little more than what I had played after Brideweser joined the club. As you know, at the end of that season I was involved in that 17-player deal [with the Yankees].

You went from the bottom to the top very quickly and you were essentially the Yankees' regular shortstop.

Phil [Rizzuto] was at the end of his career and I played 98 games with them in '55. We make a western road trip in August — late July and August — and on that trip I was 14 for 28 and I come back and the first game in Yankee Stadium — we were playing Cleveland and Herb Score was pitching — Casey took me out for a pinch hitter in the sixth inning. When I came out, he took me right into the locker room and he said, "I'm sending you to Denver." I said, "No, you're not," and he said, "Yeah. We just got Enos Slaughter from the Cardinals so he would be eligible for the World Series and I only have two players with options." He said, "I have you and Elston Howard." Elston was our only black player and he said, "I can't send out Elston Howard," even though Elston was playing very sparingly and, as I said, I had played 98 games and was doing well.

Casey said, "You're going to be my shortstop next year and you're going to come back and you won't be eligible for the Series but you'll share in everything that we're sharing in." I said, "I'm not going!" and I came home to Baltimore for four days.

Ralph Houk was the manager out in Denver and Ralph and I were good friends and he called me and told me how much he needed me in Denver. He says, "Bill, I understand how you feel," and so forth, "but I really need you." So I went out. I joined 'em, I think, in Indianapolis and then we went back to Denver and we had a homestand and in the final game of the homestand I broke my leg — badly.

It was the first inning of the ball game. Herbie Plews had led off with a base hit and on a hit-and-run play I singled to right. On the throw to third

I tried to go to second and I was out by about 12 feet. I tried a slide that I had never tried in my life — throwing my feet away and going in with my hands — and my front spike on my left foot caught and I just slid right over my foot. It broke it in three places; it broke on the inside of the ankle and two places on the outside of the leg. My toes were coming out where my heel is — you know, completely dislocated. I still have a screw in that inside ankle bone that was put in when that happened.

It took me quite a while in the spring of the following year. I went to early training with the Yankees and it seemed fine. Then all of a sudden I tried to get out of bed one morning and almost fell down. So I'm on the disabled list until just before the trading deadline early in the season.

Irv Noren was on the disabled list as well — he had had both knees cut on — and Casey said, "I'm gonna take one of you off and the way we're gonna do it is we're gonna have a foot race from the left field foul pole to the visiting dugout on the third base side." I beat Noren by about 20 yards, I think, so I came off the disabled list and they traded my roommate, Eddie Robinson, to Kansas City.

I was playing pretty regularly and hitting well. We're on the train going to Boston one day and Casey and I are having dinner in the dining car with Hank Bauer and Gil McDougald and he said, "Bill, I want you to pick the pitchers you want. You're gonna hit .300 this year." I think at the time I was hitting about .380. I said, "Casey, I gotta play every day." He said, "No, I'm gonna make sure you hit .300 this year." Well, I talked him into playing every day and I ended up hitting .280.

When I broke my leg at Denver, [Tony] Kubek was called up and played shortstop for Denver for the rest of the year. Then we went to the next year and while I'm on the disabled list McDougald was playing some shortstop. They just found that they had that position covered and that's when they traded me to Kansas City. Seven people this time.

You hit eight home runs with Kansas City in 1957, half of your career total.

I was kind of used early to open the season. DeMaestri was slated to be their shortstop and they didn't know if I was gonna play second base. They had a young fella by the name of Mike Baxes that they wanted to try out there and Hector Lopez was on third base and I ended up opening the season [at shortstop] because DeMaestri had food poisoning for a couple days. He and I and Tom Morgan shared an apartment together and they accused me of poisoning him so I could start. (Laughs)

I got started off well. I hit two home runs in the first couple of games and had five or six RBIs. Then as soon as DeMaestri was well, why he went into shortstop and they were using me at second base and late in the ball game at third base when Lopez had had his last at bat. It was the beginning of my utility program, I guess, and something that I didn't really care for. As I said, anybody who has been active in sports wants to play; they don't want to sit on the bench.

A lot of [the games I was in] was utility-type stuff. You may remember Tommy Brown used to keep batting practice home runs in the clubhouse. He had over 60 one year. We used to do that in batting practice. Gus Zernial was on that club. I was hitting the ball out of the park with regularity then, but most of it was batting practice.

In 1958, you were traded to Cleveland for Chico Carrsaquel.

[Bobby] Bragan was the manager at Cleveland at the time and I had played my last two years in the Dodgers organization for him at Fort Worth. The day of the trade, Kansas City was playing in Yankee Stadium a day-night doubleheader and I played the first game, the afternoon game, in New York. In fact, it was against Whitcy Ford and I went three for four in that game. Harry Craft [Kansas City's manager] called me in between games and said, "Bill, we've traded you to Cleveland. You can't play tonight." And I said, "Isn't Carrasquel playing tonight?" Cleveland was in Baltimore. He says, "Yeah, but they've asked me not to have you play the night game," so I left before the game got underway, took a train from New York to Baltimore, and got to Memorial Stadium before their game was over. Cleveland was going to Washington after the game was over and they allowed me to stay here at home that night.

Funny thing about it, Frank Lane [Cleveland's general manager] called me at home that night — this was just before the trading deadline — and I have an unlisted number at home and he couldn't get through and the chief of police called me and told me that Frank Lane was trying to reach me and was it all right to give my number out. I said, "No, it's not all right, and especially not to Frank Lane." I was just kidding and, of course, I talked to him and he said, "Bill, I have an opportunity to make another trade with Kansas City," and he says, "I can get Vic Power."

And I said, "Well, get him!" I said, "He's the best first baseman in the league." "Well, why do they want to trade him?" I said, "They want to trade him because he's running around with a white girl out there and the Kansas City police are after him all the time." (Laughs) Then I said, "But if you're talking about playing baseball, he's the best first baseman in the league."

He said, "Would you trade Preston Ward for Vic Power?" and I said, "In a minute!" And my roommate was supposed to be Preston Ward. He says, "They also would like to have one of our pitchers — [Dick] Tomanek or somebody;" he says, "I want Bill Tuttle." I said, "Why not Woodie Held?" And he says, "Why do you say that?" And I said, "Woodie Held is three years younger, gonna hit more home runs for you." So he ended up making that trade and Woodie Held was part of it, but in order to do it, he put Roger Maris in it. Now Roger Maris was never a part of our conversation, you know, and I didn't know much about Roger at the time, anyway. Preston Ward never became my roommate. Frank Lane would trade anybody.

In spring training the following year, when we were out in Tucson, I had shin splints and I could hardly walk, let alone run, and Lane sent me to San Diego [Pacific Coast League]. I got to Indio, California, and my shin splints disappeared in about two days. I don't know whether it was the dry heat or what. They sent Billy Moran and I both out there and they want Moran to play shortstop and me to play second base. It was okay as far as I was concerned and it ended up Moran wasn't even playing. Dick Smith ended up playing shortstop.

Midway through the season, Billy Martin gets hit in the face and they need to call somebody back up to Cleveland and they call up Billy Moran, who wasn't even playing. I ended up being the all-star second baseman in the league and led our club in about three or four offensive categories, hit eight home runs again, and I think I led our club in RBIs.

At the end of the season, they sold my contract to Toronto [International League]. Jack Kent Cooke owned the club and he called me and he said, "Danny [Menendez] tells me that you don't want to come to Toronto." I said, "No, I've asked them to put me on the voluntary retired list." I was 30 years old and I had just had as good a year as I could have in San Diego. I told him, "If I can't get back to the big leagues with that kind of a year at age 30, no sense in me coming to Toronto. I know I'm not gonna have a better year at age 31. The only way I'd come to Toronto is as player-manager." Cooke said, "I just hired a manager yesterday. We hired Mel McGaha." And I said, "Well, just put me on the voluntary retired list."

Then I had Cookie Lavagetto from Washington, Bob Elliott from Kansas City, and one other person call me about being their shortstop. I'm at home here in Baltimore and I said, "You have to talk to Frank Lane. I belong to Cleveland." Well, he wanted one of their regular players in return for me, and, of course, they didn't want to do that. So that's how I ended up being retired.

Hoot Evers became acting general manager [of Cleveland] then and he asked me if I'd do some scouting. He said, "Bill, I need a report on everybody in the International League." He said, "I don't care how long it takes you. We'll pay all your expenses and I'll give you $3,000. I just need a report on every player in the International League."

I did that. I went to Rochester and Lee MacPhail asked me if, while I was doing that, I would give him a report on the Rochester players and I said, "Yes, I'd be glad to." Well, the three best players in the league that year were Boog Powell at Rochester, Donn Clendenon at Columbus, and Tommy Tresh at Richmond.

I did that and Hoot Evers said he'd give me more money if I'd do it again the next year. I had an insurance agency here in town and I was working at that full-time. I used to do it just between seasons. And Lee MacPhail says, "Bill, if you're going to get back into baseball, we'd like you to work for Baltimore on a full-time basis." And he says, "Speaking to various groups selling tickets — no free agency scouting, but being our minor league infield instructor and managing our rookie league [team] and at the end of the rookie league season doing National League scouting."

I ended up taking that offer from the Orioles and I went to their minor league camp when it was time for baseball in Thomasville, Georgia. That's when [Earl] Weaver was managing in Elmira, I think, and [Joe] Altobelli was someplace, Cal Ripken was someplace, Billy DeMars, Jimmy Frey — all of these people were in the minor league system. I told Lee that I would take that job with the understanding that when there was a coaching job available in Baltimore that I would be considered for it.

I had gone to see Mark Belanger play his last high school game in Pittsfield, Massachusetts. From there, I flew to Tampa, Florida, to see Tony LaRussa play his last game and I was supposed to go to College Station in Texas to see Davey Johnson, but while I'm there I get a call from Harry Dalton saying, "You don't have to go to College Station. We've already signed Davey Johnson."

The Orioles felt they were the top three shortstops in the country — this was before the draft when you could sign anybody — Belanger, LaRussa, and Davey Johnson and we signed two of the three. Well, Belanger played for me [at Bluefield] and Davey Johnson played out in Stockton, California, that first year.

After the first year, they made one coaching change in Baltimore but it wasn't me and they offered me my choice of managing a couple of other clubs in the organization. I think they sent Weaver to Rochester and they wanted to know if I wanted the Elmira job. I said, "No. I'll go back one more year to Bluefield, but if there's nothing after that year I'll have to take another look at the situation."

We won the pennant both years down there [at Bluefield] and after the second year they [the Orioles] changed managers. [Billy] Hitchcock was fired and [Hank] Bauer became the manager and at that time I became the third base coach and I happened to be there for 13½ years. During that period of time, we probably had the best baseball team in the country, either American League or National League. It was when Frank and Brooks and Boog and Blair were there and we had Palmer and Cuellar and McNally.

You left the Orioles to manage the Rangers and you still have the best record of anyone who ever held that job, yet you left at the end of your second season. Why?

I really wasn't fired. I took over in '77. They were two games under .500 when I took over, and I think we were 60 and 33 for the remainder of the

'77 year and, as a matter of fact, went into first place at one time. Kansas City won 20 out of their last 22 games and beat us.

Then the following year was my first year in spring training with them and we were going to open up with the Yankees at home that year and there was a lot of interest in our club because of our success the year before. On national television in spring training — I think it was with [Joe] Garagiola — I told everybody that we had the best team in baseball and that we ought to win it.

Right after that workout was over, we had a meeting with our coaching staff and our owner and our general manager and so forth and I said, "Now I've told the world that we have the best team in baseball, but I want to tell you that there's *no* way we can win this pennant with the infield we have." [Bert] Campaneris, you know, was at the end. He was like Rizzuto when I went to the Yankees. And Bump Wills was a rookie second baseman that was gun-shy on the runner coming down from first base and [Mike] Hargrove was a very good offensive player but certainly not too good defensively and Toby Harrah was out of position at third base. He had been a shortstop.

So I said, "If we're going to win the pennant, we've gotta do something. And the other thing we need is relief pitching." I had more starting pitching than anybody in baseball, you know, with the likes of Ferguson Jenkins and [Jon] Matlack and [Bert] Blyleven and [Doyle] Alexander and Doc Medich and Dock Ellis, but some of 'em were five-inning pitchers and I didn't have much other than Reggie Cleveland, who was like a starter. You know, if he relieved today he needed two or three days' rest before he could pitch again. He did a good job for me. I got him from Zimmer. We went into Boston early on and Zimmer said, "I gotta get rid of Reggie Cleveland," and I said, "I want him." And I had Roger Moret, who did a fine job for me, but he wasn't doing well and we found him in a catatonic state early on in the season in our clubhouse.

Anyway, we're playing decent. Midseason, [owner] Brad Corbett called me up after a game with Detroit and he said, "I'm gonna have two contracts on your desk tomorrow. You sign whichever one you want." One was for five years and one was for three and I picked up the telephone on my desk and called Baltimore to talk to my wife, who was not going to live in Texas, and she says, "I don't want you to sign either one. I know how much you want to win it and I can put up with it for another year. If you want to sign a one-year, it's all right."

So I talked to Brad the next day and I told him. As the season was coming to a close, he thought, if I'm gonna have to make this move a year from now, why don't I make it now. So that's how it all came about.

I came here to Towson State as the baseball coach the next year and everybody that knew me thought that I was just biding my time to take another job somewhere else. I had people asking me my interest and I said, no, I was done. Nobody believed it for about five years. I kind of missed it the first couple of years, but then I didn't anymore.

Our athletic director died very suddenly in 1984 — developed leukemia and he was gone within six months — and they went through a search where they offered the job and the candidate turned the job down. In the second search, they asked me to be the interim because in the first search the interim was a candidate and they didn't offer him the job. I told 'em that I would do that with the understanding that I would *not* be the athletic director, so I wasn't even a candidate.

As it turned out, they did the same thing and offered the job and it was turned down. That's when they asked me if I would be the athletic director and I said, "I thought we had a deal. There's about 12 things that would have to be changed around here." And our president said, "Well, put them down on paper and let me look at them." I did and they took care of those 12 things, so I ended up with this job.

For the first two years I tried to do both jobs and I didn't do too well with either one. I told some of my cohorts — Steve Hamilton down at Morehead State and Bobby Richardson and Alan Worthington down at Liberty; right now there's one up at LeMoyne, Dick Rockwell — "You may do it for a year but you're not gonna try and do it forever," and they all agreed with me after a year. I think Rockwell is still doing both jobs.

Going back to your baseball career, is there one game that stands out?

I think probably the thing that stands out more than anything is [Don] Larsen's perfect game in the World Series in '56. That was the most excited I'd ever seen Stengel — you know, the last couple innings of that game. He was up on the steps of the dugout yelling almost on every pitch. The electricity in the air was special.

Probably my biggest disappointment as a player was not getting into the World Series in '56. We played seven games and I'm on the bench for all seven.

The other thing that was special to me was the '66 World Series when I was coaching with the Orioles and we beat the Dodgers four straight. The funny thing, Bob Hunter — you know, the same last name as me — was one of the writers out in Los Angeles and the headlines in the paper as we opened the Series read, "Hunter Picks Dodgers in 4." Needless to say, that was over my locker in Los Angeles. (Laughs) It didn't say what Hunter.

The most disappointing thing was losing to the Mets in '69. We had a very good ballclub. I think the Dodgers felt that way about us in '66, you know, with [Sandy] Koufax and [Don] Drysdale and [Claude] Osteen and so forth. They couldn't believe it, especially three shutouts.

Who was the best player you saw?

Oh, golly. I oft times wonder what [Mickey] Mantle would have been had he been healthy. He used to wrap his legs from the ankles up to the groin. He'd come in in *pain* after every ball game, just sit there kind of in a coma after a ball game yet would go out there and run as fast as anybody on the field, hit the ball as far as anybody ever hit it. I don't know that he had the mental makeup to be that exceptional. [Willie] Mays was a wonderful player, [Henry] Aaron was a wonderful player. I didn't get to see them as much because I was in the American League. Frank Robinson did a great job for us.

Mantle was phenomenal, there's no question about that. Left-handed or right-handed. I remember — it might have been '56 on Opening Day in Washington — where he hit two over the center field fence. He was something. I'm not saying Mickey was a great outfielder, but he would run down balls that other people would never touch and, of course, played in that big center field out there in Yankee Stadium.

I oft times wondered while I was involved with it if he had been healthy what *might* have been. I think that he certainly made the most of what was there with all his pain. It was real — his pain was real. A lot of people aren't aware of that, but if you saw him in the clubhouse you had to feel pity for him.

If you ask me who was the best third baseman, why, Brooks Robinson was. You hear people talk about Pie Traynor, but Brooks was just *amazing.* I recall late in every year when we would bring up players from the minor leagues. The first night they sat on the bench they'd say, "That's the best play I ever saw!" You know, I saw that every day. He was just *amazing.* But, of course, he didn't run very well but was a good base runner and was a real clutch player and that's what Frank was, too. I saw Frank hit two low and away sliders that are *unhittable* off Dean Chance. Most people would go on back and sit on the bench after those pitches.

To pick one would be very difficult. Ted Williams, of course, was a hitter personified. Joe DiMaggio was done just before I came into the big leagues, but everybody says he was a hell of a ballplayer and I'm quite sure he was. But to pick out *a* player would be very difficult for me. There were a lot of good ones.

Who was the best pitcher?

I don't know who the best pitcher was, but I know, when I was with the Yankees, I always liked to see [Whitey] Ford get the ball. When I was coaching with the Orioles, I always liked to see [Jim] Palmer get the ball. Palmer really didn't become a pitcher until he hurt his arm. He was a thrower, but he learned how to pitch. Jimmy was one of those rare guys, pitching-wise, that I think knew the game well enough to be manager. [Paul] Blair used to get really peeved at him; he'd turn around and move him one step.

Weaver always got peeved at Paul because he played too shallow. He said,

"You know, if the ball goes over your head, it's extra bases. If the ball drops in front of you, it's a single. We have the best infield in baseball; we'll get a double play on the next pitch." And Blair says, "Skipper, there won't be anything fall in the ballpark behind me." And there wasn't much, I'll tell you that.

Who was the toughest pitcher on you?

Frank Lary. Frank Lary was a pitcher that I could *never* distinguish his slider. It always looked like a fastball to me, until it got there and then it wasn't there. If anybody felt helpless — I don't know if I ever got a hit off Frank Lary, but if and when I did it was a real accomplishment because I felt so inferior at the plate when he was pitching. Early Wynn threw a slider, but it wasn't like Frank Lary's. Frank's kind of exploded on you. Early's was kind of a flat thing.

In fact, Early was the only pitcher in the big leagues that I hit two home runs off of in one game. That's when I was on Kansas City and I hit eight. That was my best day at the plate. We beat Cleveland, four to three. I hit a home run the first time up to put us ahead, one to nothing. The next time I came up, I hit a home run with a man on to tie the ball game, three to three, and I came up in the ninth inning with the bases loaded. Under other circumstances, I would've lost my hat but if he hit me, the ball game's over. I looked down at Harry Craft coaching at third and the squeeze is on and third base coaches, they don't know what's going on anyway. (Laughs) I stepped out of the batter's box and hit my spikes with the bat; you see that on television and so forth, but that was really the acknowledgment of receiving the squeeze.

I got back in and it was kind of like stop-action. I bunted the ball down the third base line — it was fair by about six feet — and Early doesn't move after the ball, the third baseman doesn't move after the ball, Hector Lopez, the runner on third, has not broken for the plate. Then Hector kind of set things in motion. He started home, and Jim Hegan, seeing the third baseman and pitcher were not going after the ball, went out to get it and while he's going out, Lopez passes him on the way in. And I stood in the batter's box. There was only one man out and they gave me a hit on it. My lifetime batting average was probably a correct .218 rather than .219 because they gave me a hit. It ended up that I drove in all four runs in a four to three victory over Early Wynn. Three-for-three and two of 'em home runs.

Did you save souvenirs along the way?

Yeah. I have quite a few. I have one on my shelves here in my office: a plaque that Larsen sent to all the teammates as a Christmas card. It portrays him delivering the last pitch of the ball game in the perfect game. In the background it has the right field scoreboard, it has Billy Martin down in his position, and everything; the scoreboard shows the count and no hits and so forth. It says, "Presented to Billy Hunter" and signed "Don Larsen." It's one that I treasure.

How much fan mail do you receive?

Bev, my wife, just mentioned last night, "Do you realize that you're getting about three or four pieces of fan mail a day?" That's just since those '53 and '54 Topps reprints. I told Cy Berger at Topps, I said, "I don't know whether it was worth the $500 that you gave everybody to take care of all this extra fan mail."

It's kind of nice. My mailman's probably not too happy about it 'cause I'm one of those guys that goes home every night and does it and puts the return envelope into the mailbox to go out. If you let it gather up, it becomes too much a chore and you say, "Why am I doing this?" We usually eat around 5:30 and I leave the office between 4:30 and 5:00 and the first thing I do when I go in is get down and take care of that before I have dinner that night and then it's taken care of for that day.

Bev says to me, "Why does it take you so long?" and I said, "Well, I read everything." Now I don't respond to questions a lot of 'em ask — you know, "Who's the best pitcher you ever faced?, What was your greatest thrill?" I don't respond to those because I just don't have time to do that, but I do sign everything that's sent my way and a lot of people will send a letter, "If I send you something, will you sign it and return it?" They treasure whatever it is. It may be a team picture or something like that where they have several people on it and they don't want to lose it. I usually respond yes.

Now I'm getting, "Thank you for signing the previous stuff I sent you. I picked these two cards up at a recent show. Would you be so kind as to sign them, too?" And I just do it. I guess if it were 20 or 30 a day I might not be doing it, but being what it is it's not that big a deal.

For the stars it could be a headache and I don't know what Brooks Robinson gets and Jim Palmer gets and a lot of dealers are getting them for sales and some of the people don't feel that they have an obligation to help somebody else make a living. Some people abuse it.

Would you go back and be a ballplayer again?

Oh, I'd love to! (Laughs) Today I'd have to have an agent and an accountant and all of those things. I think it was a lot simpler in my day. I enjoy the memories.

GORDON WILLIAM (BILLY) HUNTER
Born June 4, 1928, Punxsutawney, Pennsylvania
Ht. 6'   Wt. 180   Batted and Threw Right

Year	Team	G	AB	R	H	2B	3B	HR	RBI	SB	BA	SA
1953	StLA	154	567	50	124	18	1	1	37	3	.219	.259
1954		125	411	28	100	9	5	2	27	5	.243	.304
1955	NYA	98	255	14	58	7	1	3	20	9	.227	.298
1956		39	75	8	21	3	4	0	11	0	.280	.427

Year	Team	G	AB	R	H	2B	3B	HR	RBI	SB	BA	SA
1957	KCA	116	319	39	61	10	4	8	29	1	.191	.323
1958	KCA	22	58	6	9	1	1	2	11	1	.155	.222
	CleA	76	190	21	37	10	2	0	9	4	.195	.264
Yankee years		**137**	**330**	**22**	**79**	**10**	**5**	**3**	**31**	**9**	**.239**	**.327**
Career		630	1875	166	410	58	18	16	144	23	.219	.294

Courtesy New York Yankees

DERON JOHNSON
Tough with Men On

Yankees 1960–1961

Deron Johnson signed a minor league contract upon graduation from high school in 1956. This was at the peak of the Bonus Baby era, when players who signed for more than $4,000 had to be kept on the major league roster for two years.

Deron was probably a more sought-after football prospect. Several colleges were after him, but the major league baseball teams knew about him, too. Five eventually showed serious interest: the Yankees, Braves, Red Sox, Indians, and Pirates.

The Yankees had signed two young men to bonus contracts: Frank Leja in 1954 and Tommy Carroll in 1955. Neither panned out. Manager Casey Stengel just wouldn't use them, so the team played on with two idle roster spots. In mid–1956 the Yankee front office was not keen on the idea of handing out a large amount of cash to another young man who would occupy a roster spot and not contribute to the team.

Rather than take a lump sum and stagnate on a major league bench, Deron and his dad figured he would be better off in the minor leagues where he could play every day, but with a better salary than a minor leaguer would normally have. The result: Deron signed a Class D contract for $1,000 a month. This was essentially the major league minimum ($6,000 a year) at the time, but the Nebraska State League played only 63 games, or just a little more than two months. Deron and his father figured if he had a good season, he'd get a raise. They figured correctly; he had a very good season and he got the raise.

Playing for Kearney, the 17 year old blasted 24 home runs to lead the league by nine over runner-up and future major league All-Star Jimmie Hall. Johnson also led the NSL with 78 RBIs and in slugging (.687 to Hall's .686), and he batted .329, a seventh in the league. He also walked 63 times in 63 games.

The next year, 1957, he moved all the way up to Binghamton of the Class A Eastern League. Again he led in home runs with 26. Then he made the jump to Triple A Richmond (International League), where he spent the next three years and homered a total of 79 times.

Overall, he put up outstanding power and run production numbers every year in the Yankee chain, but there was no room at the top. Deron was an outfielder then and New York had men like Mickey Mantle, Hank Bauer, Roger Maris, Yogi Berra, Norm Siebern, Enos Slaughter, Elston Howard, and Johnny Blanchard playing out there. The decision was made to try to make a third baseman out of him, but Andy Carey, Gil McDougald, Clete Boyer, and Hector Lopez were already in pinstripes. First base was another possibility, but the Yankees had Bill Skowron, Siebern, and the ever-promising Marv Throneberry.

The result was Johnson played a grand total of 19 games for the Yankees. A couple of trades eventually led him to the National League, where he found a home for a decade.

Before he established himself in the major leagues, though, he was a minor league terror. In the five minor league seasons in which he was still the property of the Yankees, he belted 128 home runs and drove in 465 runs. Alto-

gether, he totaled 162 homers in the minors; added to the 245 he hit in the big league equals a lot of lost baseballs.

Early in 1973, his tenth NL season, he was sold to Oakland and returned to the American League. That season he became the first man in major league history to hit 20 home runs while playing in both leagues.

You were a big, strong boy. You tore up the minor leagues at every stop for five years.

Deron Johnson: I was lucky.

Lucky? What were the pitchers doing, hitting your bat? You weren't lucky.

(Laughs) God gave me strength. That helps.

With all your minor league numbers, it took you a while to establish yourself in the majors. The Yankees had no room at the top.

Yeah, they won the World Series every year. A great bunch of guys. I got to go to spring training with 'em every year and I got to meet 'em all and they were really good to me — Mickey and Yogi and them guys. In fact, I still see 'em.

You were only in New York a short time and they traded you to Kansas City. What did you think of that?

I got traded for Bud Daley. It was my first trade and it was kind of a shock, but I was kind of happy 'cause I knew I was gonna get to play.

Then I had to go in the army. Actually, that turned out to be my break. Kansas City sold me to Cincinnati and I got married. I got a shot to go in the National League. I liked the National League.

In 1964, you guys almost won the pennant.

That was my first year. That was a hell of a pennant race. There was five teams right there: us, the Cardinals, the Phillies, the Braves, and the Giants. There was so many damned teams there, if you won one day you'd go from fourth to first. It was really fun. Once we were tied for first. Every day you go you know it means something.

They just played ball different then. They were a little bit meaner. You were playing for next year every year. There weren't any long-term contracts. And you were playing for the team. Everybody wanted to win and if you won you were gonna get a raise. You didn't play for numbers; you wanted 'em, but they didn't mean that much.

Your '65 year was fantastic.

I had a good year. I was on a good ballclub. We had some good hitters. We had Pete Rose and Vada Pinson. I had Frank Robinson hitting in front of me. I had a hell of a year, really.

Later in your career, with the Phillies, you tied the major league record with four home runs in four at bats.

That was something. Everybody brings it up and it's something ain't too many people done. It was just one of them things. Every time I hit the ball it went in the air. It was against Montreal, just before the All-Star break. [July 10 and 11, 1971]

Other than that, is there a game that stands out in your memory?

There's so many of 'em, you know — you knock in a run and win a game. But, no, just knocking in the winning run was my thrill. I got paid for knocking runs in. I prided myself in being tough with men on base. I can remember a lot of big hits. You've got a lot of memories in this game. In fact, that's all you've got.

You're still in the game as a coach.

With California. I love it. I've seen the game change. You've just gotta change with it. You can't talk about the old days. Every once in a while, they'll [the young players] come around and talk to me and they'll wanna know things and I'll tell 'em and they'll sit there and say, "Nah" — they won't believe it.

Pitching's changed. They don't pitch inside no more. If they do, the umpire runs out there and tells 'em they can't. The batter has a fit. I laugh. And they'll dive into the ball. If you're gonna dive in, you're gonna get hit anyway. I respected a pitcher that pitched inside. I wanted him to know that I wasn't afraid and I knew that he wasn't. It was more competitive.

The plate is there. The pitcher thinks he owns it and you think you own it and that's what it's all about.

(Laughs) That's right. Pitch inside, they'll get out of the way. Hell, they've got the head protected now.

Who was the best player you saw?

I seen a lot of 'em. Mickey, Frank Robinson, Henry Aaron, Mays, Clemente — I mean, I played against all them Hall of Famers. They could all hit with power and they could all run. They were all total ballplayers in my opinion. And they played hard. I had the privilege of playing with Mickey and Frank Robinson and Aaron and they had that little extra. They're Hall of Famers.

Who was the best pitcher?

Oh, I faced a lot of good ones. Probably Gibson. Koufax, Drysdale, Seaver, Marichal, Bunning — these guys were not fun going to work against. They were something — you knew you was gonna have a tough day at the office. You had to figure 'em out. They had patterns. I think we studied the pitchers more in them days than they do now. You know, like when a certain guy would get you out one way he wouldn't change. He'd make *you* change. Nowadays they say, "That guy really throws hard." Christ, all these guys threw hard. We didn't have no radar guns.

The gun seems to be overused.

We use it to see if he's starting to lose it. That's the only way we use it, but as long as I've been in the game I can tell when a guy's losing it. You can see him start getting shorter. Scouts and them guys, they can see it. When the scouts are watching kids, half the time they're [the guns] lying because they got it set at a different mileage. It's gonna read 95 and the kid's only throwing 85 'cause they got the gun set up ten miles an hour so the other scout can't read it. They've got a lot of tricks.

Who was the toughest pitcher on you?

Probably Gibson and Seaver. Seaver threw hard and he had great control. He was a pitcher and a real competitor.

Would you go back and do it all again?

A hundred times over.

Do you have any regrets from your career?

No. It's a great life. I've raised three kids and I've got a wonderful family and the only thing I owe it to is baseball. This is all I've ever done — I've never got a paycheck nowhere else. I didn't go to college, so if I didn't play ball I don't know what I'd do. It's a great life. You meet a lot of great people. I've got some great friends and I've got some great memories, so whatever happens you can never take it away.

I've got lung cancer right now, and I've got guys calling me from out of the blue. It's unbelievable.

How are you coming with it?

Oh, it's gonna be all right, but you never know when you gotta go. I've gotta go make that team up there and they got some pretty good ballplayers. That's gonna be tough.

I suspect some of the good ballplayers aren't up there.

(Laughs) There's some good ones down there, too. I gotta figure which team I'm gonna try for.

I hope you don't have to try out too soon.

No. I'd like to wait a couple, three years.

What do you think of the salaries today?

Christ, the number one draft picks now, they get a lot of money! A kid don't earn what he gets. I think there's players out there worth four million dollars, but not as many as will get it. It's just like a standard rate: if you do this, you get this. It's kinda weird right now.

I like what we did. If we had good years, we got a good raise. And then you went back and tried to do better the next year so you'd get another raise. If they brought that back, I think we'd see different baseball. Instead of having one good year, I think they'd try to have about five or six in a row. You had to get two good years when I played. They figured if you got to the third year, you could play. TV's paying the freight now. Everybody ought to get up and kiss that thing.

Four months after this interview, Deron Johnson was called up to a higher
league. I imagine he's playing first base there and probably batting fifth or
sixth so he can drive in the important runs.

DERON ROGER JOHNSON
Born July 17, 1938, San Diego, California
Died April 23, 1991, Poway, California
Ht. 6'2"   Wt 200   Batted and Threw Right

Year	Team	G	AB	R	H	2B	3B	HR	RBI	SB	BA	SA
1960	**NYA**	**6**	**4**	**0**	**2**	**1**	**0**	**0**	**0**	**0**	**.500**	**.750**
1961	**NYA**	**13**	**19**	**1**	**2**	**0**	**0**	**0**	**2**	**0**	**.105**	**.105**
	KCA	83	283	37	61	11	3	8	42	0	.216	.360
1962		17	19	1	2	1	0	0	0	0	.105	.158
1964	CinN	140	477	63	130	24	4	21	79	4	.273	.472
1965		159	616	92	177	30	7	32	*130	0	.287	.515
1966		142	505	75	130	25	3	24	81	1	.257	.461
1967		108	361	39	81	18	1	13	53	0	.224	.388
1968	AtlN	127	342	29	71	11	1	8	33	0	.208	.316
1969	PhiN	138	475	51	121	19	4	17	80	4	.255	.419
1970		159	574	66	147	28	3	27	93	0	.256	.456
1971		158	582	74	154	29	0	34	95	0	.265	.490
1972		96	230	19	49	4	1	9	31	0	.213	.357
1973	PhiN	12	36	3	6	2	0	1	5	0	.167	.306
	OakA	131	464	61	114	14	2	19	81	0	.246	.407
1974	OakA	50	174	16	34	1	2	7	23	1	.195	.345
	MilA	49	152	14	23	3	0	6	18	1	.151	.289
	BosA	11	25	0	3	0	0	0	2	0	.120	.120
1975	ChiA	148	555	66	129	25	1	18	72	0	.232	.378
	BosA	3	10	2	6	0	0	1	3	0	.600	.900
1976		15	38	3	5	1	1	0	0	0	.132	.211
Yankee years		**19**	**23**	**1**	**4**	**1**	**0**	**0**	**2**	**0**	**.174**	**.217**
Career		1765	5941	706	1447	247	33	245	923	11	.244	.420

*Led League

League Championship Series

1973	OakA	4	10	0	1	0	0	0	0	0	.100	.100

World Series

1973	OakA	6	10	0	3	1	0	0	0	0	.300	.400

DON JOHNSON
The Youngest Yankee

Yankees 1947, 1950

The 1947 Yankees were a veteran team. The average age was 30; only the Chicago White Sox in the American League had an older squad.

The entire New York outfield was over 30: Tommy Henrich (34), Joe DiMaggio (32), Johnny Lindell (30), and Charlie Keller (30). George McQuinn at first base was 38. Rounding out the infield, Snuffy Stirnweiss (2B) and Billy Johnson (3B) were 28 and Phil Rizzuto (SS) was 29. Number one catcher Aaron Robinson was 32 and backup Ralph Houk was 27. The pitching staff had 39-year-olds Spud Chandler and Bobo Newsom and 32-year-old Allie Reynolds. Butch Wensloff was 31, Bill Bevens 30. Three others were 29.

There was some youth, however, but very little of it. Of those who spent the entire season with the club, there were three under the age of 25: backup infielder and future doctor and American League president Bobby Brown was 22; reserve catcher/outfielder Yogi Berra turned 22 a month into the season; and pitcher Don Johnson was 20.

Don Johnson spent the whole season with the team. Although manager Bucky Harris used him only sparingly, he contributed four wins to the cause. The only younger player in the league to see more action was Art Houtteman of Detroit.

Don never quite lived up to that early promise, but he eventually put in seven big league seasons, mostly with such wretched teams as the Browns, Senators, and Orioles. His best year came in 1954 with the third-place White Sox, when he went 8–7, with a 3.14 ERA. He continued to pitch professionally through 1960 and then left the game to return to his home town of Portland, Oregon.

You played with and against some awfully good ballplayers.

Don Johnson: Oh, I played with some *good* players. Ted Williams, all those guys. Bobby Doerr — he lives up the road from me here a little ways, up in the Rogue River Valley. He's a great guy. Hall of Famer. Old number one.

The best I ever seen was Williams, and DiMaggio was the best all-around ballplayer that ever lived. I faced Ted over a hundred times in my career and he never hit a home run off me, but he had a lot of line drives, I'll tell you that. (Laughs) You couldn't fool him. I could throw pretty hard, so I just threw the ball down the pipe and if he hits it, he hits it. What are you gonna do?

Old Luke Appling, you remember him? He passed away. He'd foul about 25 pitches off before he'd hit me, but he was a good ballplayer. There were some good ones around, there really was. The guys today are bigger and stronger, but I don't know...

I follow Ken Griffey, Jr. I think he's gonna be a *superstar.* He's something else, that kid. I wish I had his future instead of my past. (Laughs)

I can't believe where the years went by. I can remember when I was 20 years old and figured this was gonna last forever. But it doesn't, you know that?

I had a little trouble with liquor here and there, but who didn't in them days. God, I tell you, I couldn't believe it. (Laughs) When I joined the Yankees — I got out of the Army — I didn't play but one year in the minor leagues and that was with Kansas City in '44. That was the American Association and then I went in the service. I was barely 17. When I got out I joined the Yankees. In them days, there was only eight teams in the American, eight teams in the National. It was hard to make it. You were just lucky to make it.

I spent all of '47 in New York. Yogi Berra was my roommate — first roommate I ever had. (Laughs) He was something else. He was 21. We had a hell of a ballclub that year. We had DiMaggio and Henrich and Vic Raschi — who passed away — Allie Reynolds — hell of a pitcher.

[Eddie] Lopat came in '48. He didn't even break a sweat, that guy. He couldn't break a pane of glass, but he was sure uncanny out there. (Laughs)

A lot of the old-time players I played with, we didn't make any money. Now, it's not like nowadays. You know, if you made 35 grand back in '50, you really made something. The minimum when I broke in was $5,000 a year. Nowadays they've got their briefcases and their agents and all this crap. I never heard of anything like that. (Laughs) It's a different world, not a better one. I really enjoyed playing back in the '50s and the guys I played with — DiMaggio, Berra, and all those guys.

Remember George Stirnweiss? He was a nice guy. Good friend of mine. He *hated* to fly and remember when he died on the train when the train backed into the bay? The train went off the pier or something and he died on a train and he was so scared to fly.

You and he were involved in a big trade. (Stirnweiss, Johnson, Duane Pillette, Jim Delsing, and $50,000 went to the Browns for Joe Ostrowski, Tom Ferrick, Leo Thomas, and Sid Schacht on June 15, 1950.)

Eight players. At least I can say I played for the Browns.

There's not many of you guys left who can say that.

(Laughs) It brings back a lot of memories. Old Sportsman Park. We had a pretty good ballclub. Zack Taylor was the manager. In 1950, we did knock Cleveland and Detroit out of it. We went into Cleveland and Detroit the last two weeks of the season. We beat Cleveland four straight. We beat Lemon, Feller, Wynn, and Garcia — remember that Big Four? Beat 'em four straight, knocked 'em out of the pennant.

We went to Detroit. We beat Hal Newhouser and a couple others. We won three out of four from Detroit and we knocked both of those out and the Yankees slipped in. I remember that. They made fun of our club, but we were the spoilers then. (Laughs) That was a lot of fun. There's a lot of good memories there.

You went from St. Louis to Washington and became the number one starter there in 1951.

We kinda had a bad ballclub there. We had Mickey Vernon, remember him? American League batting champion. We had Bob Porterfield. I think he's passed away. God, a lot of my friends are gone. I can't believe it.

Remember Bill Bevens? He's from about 50 miles up the road from me. Hubbard, Oregon. He passed away. He had a stroke before.

How far do you live from Pee Wee Reese?

He's over in Louisville, about 70 miles from here.

That's an awful pretty state you're from there. I know I used to go into Louisville once in a while. I'd get those hominy grits. (Laughs) I didn't know what they were, but, geez, they were good. How's Pee Wee doing?

I hear he's fine but he doesn't respond to fan mail anymore.

How about DiMaggio?

DiMaggio doesn't answer letters.

Doesn't answer letters. That figures. You know what I used to do when I was a rookie? I was 20 years old. Hell, I could throw hard and had a hell of a fastball; I had everything going. Joe liked me, see. We'd go on the road and he couldn't walk on the streets. They'd mob him, you know that. He'd call me up to his room. He'd sit and stare out the window for two, three hours at a time. Wouldn't say nothing to me, just liked to have me there. Then we'd go to them western movies, have to sneak down the back alley. Isn't that something?

Can I ask you something? I got in the mail today two picture postcards. I don't remember those; I don't remember posing for those things. Do you know where they come from?

There are photographers who have been taking pictures of ballplayers for years, some for decades, and they sell these photos in different sizes. That's probably where they're from.

That's a real big business nowadays, that and these baseball cards and everything.

Joe lives down in St. Petersburg now, doesn't he? He and Dom have got a condominium down there now, is that right? I heard that on a radio show, either in Orlando or St. Pete. "The Big Dago" we called him. (Laughs)

You were only on two good teams, the '47 Yankees and the '54 White Sox. When you were on a good team, you were a good pitcher. In '54, you had three complete games and all three were shutouts.

The first part of the year I beat the Red Sox, one to nothing, and pitched against a guy named Tom Brewer, remember him? They had a good ballclub, Boston. That was in Chicago and Jack Brickhouse, he was the announcer. I can't remember who the other two were. It's been so darn long.

We had some good ballplayers on that Chicago club. We had Nellie Fox, he's gone now; we had Billy Pierce; we had Johnny Groth in center field and we had Jim Rivera and the catcher, Sherm Lollar — he's gone, too. All those friends of mine are gone. I can't believe it. We were all having a good time, making eight, ten grand a year, you know. (Laughs) And lucky to get it. I was in 46 games that year. I had a good year that year.

You led the Sox in games and saves and were fifth and fourth, respectively, in the American League.

That's not bad, is it?

Then I had to go to Baltimore. I wanted to stay in Chicago, but Paul Richards was mad at Chicago so he took me to Baltimore. I didn't want to relieve over in Baltimore, but what are you gonna do?

Then I went down to Toronto [International League]. Jack Kent Cooke was the owner. He owned the Redskins. I had some good years there, I tell you. (Laughs) I made more money there.

The San Francisco Giants got you from Toronto in 1959. I was at Seals Stadium the day you arrived. You just stepped off the plane and they put you in the game. I thought they should have given you a day to adjust after the long flight.

Against the Chicago Cubs. All I wanted was for them to start me every four or five days, but [manager] Bill Rigney and I didn't get along too good.

I walked in the clubhouse and I wanted to shake hands with [Willie] Mays. I said, "I'm Don Johnson. You just bought me for a couple ballplayers and some cash." And he wouldn't shake my hand. I said, "Okay, Mr. Mays, let me tell you something. You couldn't carry Joe DiMaggio's jock strap!" That's what I told him, right to his face. I shouldn't have said it, I suppose, but that's what I said.

He does a lot of card shows and doesn't interact well with the fans. Most people feel he's rude to them, not like fellows such as Ernie Banks and Brooks Robinson.

Wonderful man, that Ernie Banks.

You went back to Toronto in 1959. How long did you play after that?

I retired in '60 and went back home. I had played winter ball in Cuba ten years. I played with the Alimendares Blues down there. Havana, Cuba. I played with Mike Goliat. Whiz Kids in '50. Robin Roberts, Richie Ashburn, Curt Simmons — brings back a lot of good old names, you know that? We had quite a few good name players down there — Mike Goliat and a few others. Is he still around?

He's still with us. He lives in Seven Hills, Ohio.

Seven Hills, Ohio. Wonderful little town. Beautiful country around there. He's about my age.

Is there one game that stands out?

There's three games I pitched against Bob Feller and I lost all of 'em, one to nothing, one to nothing, and two to one. I was with Washington. I remember it was so hot in Washington one night and it was nothing to nothing going into the top of the ninth and a guy named Bobby Avila — remember him? — he bunted his way on and went to second and one of the best friends I ever had in baseball, Ray Boone, the shortstop, knocked him in. He's one of my favorite people.

There was a game when I was with Chicago and we were playing the Yankees. I came in in relief in the sixth inning against New York and they had Mantle and they had all them horses out there. We went to the 14th inning. From the sixth to the 14th inning we couldn't get a run, we couldn't do nothing. Mantle came up in the last of the 14th inning and hit a ball about 480 feet off me. (Laughs) I threw him a good curveball and he golfed it right off his shoetops into the upper deck in left field, batting left-handed. When he rounded third base, he said, "Don't worry, Don. I'll buy you a couple drinks down at Toots Shors' after the game." (Laughs) He was a hell of a hitter, wasn't he?

One thing about me, I never gave up many home runs. In the old days, you know, you get two strikes on the batter and you'd brush him back a little bit 'cause you have to let him know you're out there. Nowadays if you do that, they come out there with the bat at you! I can't believe what's happened to baseball.

Who was the best pitcher you saw?

The two best pitchers I've ever seen in my life — I know there's a lot of 'em around — are Bob Feller as my right-hander and a guy named Hal Newhouser. He made the Hall of Fame. He was classy, he'd pitch inside, his curveball was sharp, he kept it down. Of course, he got beat a few times but he won over 200, you know. Then my next choice would have to be Bob Lemon. He was a good pitcher. Of course, I didn't see much of the National League. Warren Spahn was great, we all know that. And Lew Burdette and Johnny Sain and Vic Raschi.

Just look at that Yankee pitching staff we had in '47: Reynolds, Raschi, Joe Page — remember him? He passed away; he lived in Springdale, Pennsylvania. We had a darn good ballclub. The '47 Yankee team was outstanding! I would say in the top ten all-time teams.

Did you save souvenirs?

I had so many of 'em. I had jerseys, a lot of hats, a few bats. I still have an autograph book. I had some pictures of me and Joe DiMaggio with his arm around me. I lost those someplace; I don't know what happened to 'em. Boy, I'd like to have those back! They'd be worth some money.

It's amazing what things from your time are worth today.

Yeah, isn't that the truth. We didn't think about it at all.

How much fan mail do you receive?

I get about ten letters a week, something like that. I'm glad to sign 'em. Really I am. It's nice to be remembered.

Any regrets from your career?

I say if I'd probably laid off the sauce a little more I could maybe have been a lot better. There were a lot of guys in my boat. I would say that cut me maybe two or three years off my big league career and maybe 20 wins, or something like that. Who knows?

But that's okay. I'm fine now! I do the best I can. I get a little pension and social security and I'm doing the best I can. I'm retired. I wasn't trained for nothing else except baseball. It was my whole life.

I'm glad you remembered me. There's probably a lot more ballplayers a lot better than I was that would be worthy of this. It makes me feel good.

DONALD ROY JOHNSON
Born November 12, 1926, Portland, Oregon
Ht. 6'2"   Wt. 200   Batted and Threw Right

Year	Team	G	IP	W	L	Pct	BB	SO	H	SHO	SV	ERA
1947	**NYA**	**15**	**54.1**	**4**	**3**	**.571**	**23**	**16**	**57**	**0**	**0**	**3.64**
1950	**NYA**	**4**	**18**	**1**	**0**	**1.000**	**12**	**9**	**35**	**0**	**0**	**10.00**
	StLA	25	96	5	6	.455	55	31	126	1	1	6.09
1951	StLA	6	15	0	1	.000	18	8	27	0	0	12.60
	WasA	21	143.2	7	11	.389	58	52	138	1	0	3.95
1952		29	69	0	5	.000	33	37	80	0	2	4.43
1954	ChiA	46	144	8	7	.533	43	68	129	3	7	3.13
1955	BalA	31	68	2	4	.333	35	27	89	0	1	5.32
1958	SFN	17	23	0	1	.000	8	14	31	0	1	6.26
Yankee years		**23**	**72.1**	**5**	**3**	**.625**	**35**	**25**	**92**	**0**	**0**	**5.23**
Career		198	631	27	38	.415	285	262	712	5	12	4.78

Courtesy Ray Kelly

RAY KELLY
The Babe's Mascot

Yankees 1921–1931

You could call it a dream come true, but what kid would ever dream such a dream: to be chosen by baseball's greatest player to sit in the dugout with him? And not just one time, but all the time, year after year! He was even allowed to accompany the team on the road!

That's exactly what Ray Kelly got to do. For a decade, he was Babe Ruth's personal mascot. Can you imagine?

How did you meet Babe Ruth?

Ray Kelly: When I was three years old, in 1921, my dad would take me down to an area called Riverside Drive in New York City and he and I would play ball together. As a result, people, thinking I had a little more talent than I did have, would form a crowd and watch my dad and I play ball.

The Babe was coming back from a game one day up at the Polo Grounds and he used to drive down Riverside Drive. He saw this crowd and thought perhaps there was an accident or something and maybe he could be helpful, so he stopped his car and came over to this crowd of people and he saw what was going on — this little child playing ball with his father.

After watching us for ten minutes or so, he walked over to my dad and introduced himself and asked my dad if he wouldn't mind bringing me up to the Polo Grounds the next day. He wanted to see me and talk to us. That's how it started. We went up the next day, and he had left word at the players' entrance to let us in. We went in and watched the game with him from the dugout.

When did you start actually staying for all the games with him?

He asked my dad that day, down near the end of the game, "Would you mind if I had your son, Little Ray," he always called me Little Ray, "as my personal mascot? " Of course, my father was delighted.

In a few days, he had uniforms made for me. He had about three for me — one that said "Babe" and one that said "The Yanks" and another that said "New York", as I remember. And then as I matured and grew older, why he had to get new uniforms made for me. I was always in uniform.

How often did you make road trips with him?

When I was younger I didn't do much traveling, but as I matured and got a little older I went often, particularly during the summertime when I was on vacation from school. Those were the years when I started doing more traveling.

Is there any particular performance by the Babe that you remember?

No particular performance. Seeing him hit so many home runs was just fantastic! Those first two years — '21 and '22 — the Yankees were playing in the Polo Grounds still because the Yankee Stadium hadn't been built. In 1923

Previous page: Ray Kelly and Babe Ruth, Opening Day, 1923, before the first game ever played at Yankee Stadium.

the stadium was built and I really got interested more than I was a couple of years earlier. I was a little older, you see.

Nineteen twenty-three was a phenomenal year for him. I can't remember how many home runs he hit, but it was an awful lot that year. I do remember specifically that he batted .393 that year and he was voted the Most Valuable Player.

How long were you with him?

Until I started high school. I think I left him in 1931; I started high school in '32.

You were there for the "Called Shot" in the 1932 World Series.

I had just started high school and the Yankees were playing the Chicago Cubs in the World Series. He got in touch with my dad and asked my dad if he wouldn't mind bringing me up to the Yankee Stadium for the start of the World Series. They played the first two games up in the Yankee Stadium and they won those first two games. After the second game, he asked my dad, "Can I take Little Ray out to Chicago? I have a feeling we're gonna take these guys in four straight."

My father resisted at first, saying, "C'mon, he just started high school. Let him get an education." But Babe insisted and finally my father gave in.

So I went out to Chicago with them and in the third game — it was sometime in the middle innings, I think the fifth or sixth inning — that's when this business with the "Called Shot" developed. Charlie Root was the pitcher for the Cubs and he threw the first pitch and Babe missed that one, so it was one strike. That's when he put up one finger and I always assumed what he was saying was, "Okay, that's one strike."

The next pitch was a ball and the third pitch was a ball and then came a called strike and that's when the Babe put up two fingers, indicating, "Okay, that's two strikes."

That's four pitches: two balls and two strikes. The Cubs were all yelling at him and before the next pitch, the Babe stuck up his hand — elevated his arm with his palm up, pointing over Root's head out to the center field bleachers. The next pitch came in and he creamed it! He hit the longest home run that was ever hit in that stadium up to that point.

A lot of people don't realize, and I've read practically every book about the Babe, and I don't recall reading the fact that Lou Gehrig came up after him and hit one out, too. Back to back.

Was that the last time you were with him?

Yeah, physically. I saw him the next day. They took the fourth game. They swept the Cubs four straight. We came back to New York together and separated and we never got together again. I was in school, but we still kept in touch. Then in '35 he got traded to the Braves and then we really lost touch.

The Babe Ruth Conference [at Hofstra University] really had an effect on me. I've often heard of people talking about flashbacks and things like that, but from this conference I've been getting flashbacks of things I haven't even thought about in years and years.

Did any of the other Yankee players make an impression on you?

Oh, sure. An awful lot of 'em did. I got quite friendly with Whitey Witt. He played center field for the Yankees. I used to chat with him in the dugout and I have a number of pictures taken with him, more than with anybody else for some reason. I have pictures with Bob Meusel and Joe Dugan, who was Ruth's roommate on the road.

Witt later, I think it was '25, was traded from the Yanks to the Brooklyn Dodgers and the Dodgers came back to the stadium one time for an exhibition game with the Yankees and he insisted on having a picture taken with me in my Yankees uniform and him in his Dodger uniform. I was very fond of him. He was one of the pallbearers at the Babe's funeral.

"Little Ray" Kelly grew up to be an accountant, not a baseball player. Today he is retired from a partnership in a New York accounting firm. Few people ever knew Babe Ruth as well.

CLIFF MAPES
Three Retired Numbers

Yankees 1948–1951

Many ballplayers have had their numbers retired, but how many have had three numbers retired? Only one: Cliff Mapes. And one of those was retired while he was still playing.

When Mapes joined the Yankees in 1948, he was given number 3. That number had been worn earlier by another Yankee outfielder named Ruth. In a ceremony honoring the Babe later that same year, number 3 was retired right off Mapes's back and he was given number 7.

In 1951 Cliff was traded to the St. Louis Browns and number 7 was given to yet another Yankee outfielder, a kid named Mantle. That number, in time, was also retired.

After the '51 season Mapes was traded again, this time to the Detroit Tigers where he was given number 6. He left Detroit after that season and number 6 remained unused until June when it was assigned to a bonus baby outfielder named Kaline. Now, of course, it's retired, too.

Maybe Mapes wasn't Ruth, Mantle, or Kaline, but he did the numbers he wore justice, especially in 1949. Joe DiMaggio's foot limited his playing time and Cliff played more games in the outfield that season than any Yankee outfielder. Here are the New York outfielders that season and the number of games and at bats of each:

Outfielder	G	AB
Cliff Mapes	*108*	*300*
Gene Woodling	*98*	*283*
Hank Bauer	*95*	*296*
Joe DiMaggio	*76*	*272*
Johnny Lindell	*65*	*198*
Charlie Keller	*31*	*89*

The figures are for appearances as outfielders only and
do not include games and at bats as pinch hitters.

Before we get on with Cliff Mapes and baseball, let's first touch on him and horses. He has always loved them and owns a paint filly that is more of a pet than anything. One of his favorite memories is "meeting" the great horse Secretariat. He spoke of his earliest memories of horses.

"When I was about three years old, we went back to Nebraska to visit and I disappeared. I was only three, I didn't know what I was doing. I seen these horses down there in the field—and my mom was goin' crazy, they couldn't find me around the house or anything—and they found me out in that pasture with them horses, just walkin' around under 'em and over 'em and all and they wasn't botherin' me at all. They was just so gentle. I always did love horses, as long as I can remember."

Okay, on to baseball.

How old were you when you decided you wanted to be a ballplayer?

Cliff Mapes: Oh, I knew that from the time I was eight years old. I was born in Nebraska on a farm and my dad always said when he was younger —

he didn't get a chance to play 'cause he was the oldest one of ten kids and he was wanted on the farm to help out and his dad wouldn't let him try out 'cause he had to go away to get looked at — so he says to himself, "If I ever have a boy, I'm gonna move to California where he can play year 'round." And he did. I was about a year old, and they moved to California. I was raised in Long Beach, California.

He'd come off work and he had a hard job — he was a hod carrier, eight hours of *real* heavy work — and he'd come out there 'til dark and throw balls to me or play pepper or whatever and he made me a good ballplayer.

He came [to the World Series] when we played Brooklyn in 1949 and he really enjoyed that. The only thing he didn't like about New York was he couldn't get coffee black. He always liked his black and it was already mixed with sugar and cream. He hated that. (Laughs) He was a good man.

You signed in 1940 and joined Flint in the Michigan State League. Were you Yankee property then?

No, that was Cleveland. I signed with Cleveland when I was about 16 years old, maybe 17.

How did the Yankees get you?

In '46 after I got out of the service, I was supposed to go to Wilkes-Barre [Eastern League] and they decided to hide me out in the Pacific Coast League 'cause I was subject to the draft. I went to Seattle and Bill Skiff, the manager, knew the situation I was in and he mentioned to the Yankees that I was available in the draft. The Yankees drafted me that fall and I was with the Yankees from then on.

You were a catcher when you signed.

Yeah, I caught the first two years. I was a temporary first baseman. I can play just about anywhere, but I liked catchin' the best. Then they switched me to the outfield. It was a good move. I lasted longer probably.

You were in the service in 1944 and '45. Did you play ball there?

We did when we was goin' through boot camp. I played with the San Diego Navy. As soon as I got through boot camp, though, I went aboard a Merchant Marine ship as a gunner and I spent the next two years goin' from here to the Philippines and back carryin' cargo — foodstuffs and all that.

When the Yankees got you, you became a different ballplayer.

I was developin' all the time. There was two years out for the service and I was a little rusty there, but in '47 I went to spring training with the Yankees. Right at the last minute, just before the season started, they optioned me to Kansas City 'cause they was yellin' for outfielders. That was a farm club of the Yankees at that time — American Association. I had a good year — the best year I ever had — at Kansas City and then I stayed up with the Yankees 'til the last part of '51.

In 1948 with the Yankees, half of your appearances were as a pinch hitter.

Most of the time, yeah. I didn't play a whole lot, but if anybody got hurt in the outfield I played.

That was a tough outfield to break into.

It sure was. Charlie Keller and [Tommy] Henrich and [Joe] DiMaggio. And they lasted longer than I did. (Laughs)

In 1949 when DiMaggio's foot was bothering him, you saw a lot of action.

I played more that year than I ever did.

Do you remember the first game of the July 4, 1949, doubleheader against the Red Sox in Yankee Stadium?

[In that game, New York was leading, 3–2, with one out in the top of the ninth inning. Vic Raschi was pitching, but Boston had loaded the bases. Johnny Pesky, who singled, was on third; Ted Williams, who also singled, was on second; and Vern Stephens, who walked, was on first. Al Zarilla was up and Bobby Doerr was on deck. Zarilla, in an 0 for 14 slump, lined what appeared to be a single to right, where Mapes was playing.]

The bases were loaded, see, and the ball was hit to me on a line — it hit about 10 to 12 feet ahead of me, just perfect to get a quick throw off and get a lot on it. I was throwing to Yogi [Berra] to catch Williams comin' from second and ol' Yogi caught the ball and just stood there on home plate and Pesky slid in by him and the umpire [Art Passarella] called him safe. (Laughs) Ol' Yogi jumped right in his face, says, "That was a force out! Pesky was on third!" And I started lookin' around and the bases was still loaded. I couldn't figure it out right away that it was Pesky comin' in from third. Evidently he hesitated just a fraction to make sure I didn't catch the ball. Zarilla really hit it hard and everything was perfect for me. He just hesitated because he had to.

[Thus Doerr came up with the bases still loaded, but now there were two outs. He hit a long, high drive to right, but Mapes caught it two steps from the fence and the Yankees won, 3–2. When the season ended, New York won the pennant by one game over Boston.]

Several Boston players said that was the most frustrating game of the season for them.

(Laughs) We always came up with something to beat them. We were lucky against them.

In the World Series that year, your hit in the fourth game off Don Newcombe sort of broke the whole Series open.

[The first three games of the Series had all been decided by one run and the Yankees led the Dodgers, two games to one. Entering the fourth inning of Game 4, neither team had scored.]

Yeah, it did that in that fourth game. He [Newcombe] opened up the first game and Henrich hit a home run in the last half of the ninth and beat him [1–0]. I couldn't touch him that first game, but they brought him back too soon and he didn't have enough rest after goin' nine innings that first

Cliff Mapes *(courtesy New York Yankees)*

game. I got a double to left center and knocked in two runs and then Jerry Coleman knocked me in from second, so I actually knocked in two and scored one. I was responsible for three runs. We lost one game there [in the Series].

You lost the second game. Preacher Roe shut you out, 1–0.

That's the only game I didn't play in. Preacher Roe was a left-hander and he [Stengel] put Hank Bauer in.

In 1950, you again were close to being a regular outfielder. Four of you had

400 or more plate appearances, but no one was going to replace the three guys who were usually out there. Were you looking to go to another team?

No, not really. I thought maybe Charlie Keller or one of 'em would leave. Well, he did go, but on account of his back. I thought there'd be a place for me there sometime in the near future, but [Casey] Stengel didn't want to wait that long, I guess.

What did you think of your trade to the Browns in 1951?

Oh, that was a trade! That broke my heart, goin' from the top to the bottom and I got nothin' out of it, too. If I'd have been traded to the other league — the National League — or sent down, I'd have got a full [World Series] share, because I was there that long, you know. That's the ruling. I can understand it, too, 'cause that nullifies any chance of a baseball player traded from a pennant contender to lean toward lettin' 'em get a run or two "accidentally", you know.

The Browns gave four players and a minor leaguer for you. They really wanted you.

Yeah. I won a couple of games against the Yankees that year when I was traded to the Browns.

The year after you were with the absolutely horrible Browns, you went to the worst team the Tigers ever had.

Yeah. I went from bad to worse. (Laughs) That was a fun team, though; they was all over the hump — pretty near all. [Hal] Newhouser and [Bob] Swift and a bunch of those guys. We had has-beens mostly and we couldn't beat no one hardly.

After that season, you were traded back to the Browns.

Yeah, but they farmed me out to Toronto in the old International League. I played up there about a half a season. I tore my arm up in the spring of '52. I could throw pretty good once in a great while and I'd have that one good throw and it was gone for a week or ten days — just too much pain. About two-thirds through the '54 season I retired. I was in Tulsa, actually. Couldn't do much good. Outside of my arm I could have done it, you know; everything else was all right.

Phil Rizzuto, your shortstop with the Yankees, finally got into the Hall of Fame.

By gosh, he should've been in there! And Allie Reynolds — I think he deserves it. Him and I were buddies.

I'll give Stengel one thing: he used him and [Ed] Lopat *really* good. If Lopat would start a game and get in a little bit of trouble in later innings — throwin' that junk up there, you know — he'd bring ol' Allie in and he would just mow 'em down. That change of speed. And the reverse on the other side — Lopat would relieve him sometimes, throw that junk at 'em and they couldn't hit it.

Is there one game that stands out?

I guess that game against Newcombe, that fourth game of the World Series. That made me feel real good. And then that throw. We always seemed to be up with Boston in the last series we played 'em and they couldn't do nothin'. We got ol' Ted Williams out pretty easy.

Ol' Williams, he played that short left field wall [in Fenway Park] pretty darn good. He studied that and he worked at it and got to where he could hold guys to singles off the wall. That was the shortest field I believe I ever performed in. And I was battin' the other way. (Laughs) I hit it a few times, you know — a line drive to left field.

Batting left-handed, unless you pulled it sharply there, it was a long poke to right field.

Yeah. You had the bullpen to go into.

Speaking of Williams, who was the best hitter you saw?

He was *definitely* the best hitter. Joe DiMaggio was the best overall player. He wasn't the long ball hitter, but he made contact. He hit quite a few home runs, too, but not like [Mickey] Mantle did. Mantle, oh, he was the hardest-hittin' ballplayer I've ever seen! He was strong! And he could bunt — he could drag bunt. All he had to do was hit it fair and it was a base hit. He'd even get behind in the count — two and two or somethin' like that — and he'd drag bunt and get to first base.

Who was the best pitcher?

Reynolds was one of the best I ever saw, and one I really thought was a bear-down man was Vic Raschi. He was out there to win and he didn't want *no* foolin' around about it. He wanted to get at the opposition and get 'em outta there. I roomed with him for about a year and a half.

How was he after a loss?

Oh, you couldn't talk to him. He'd go out and have a few beers and cool off. I wouldn't see him 'til about midnight. He never drank beer until after he had pitched again.

Do you get much fan mail?

It dribbles in. It kinda picks up pretty close to the start of the season and all during the season and then it kinda drops off in the winter time. I enjoy it. I get letters back from some of 'em, about how they appreciate my response and all that.

Any regrets from your career?

Well, not really. The only regret I really have is tearing my arm up. I just never was the same after that. I wasn't a hundred percent and it affected me all the way around, I think. It didn't seem to bother my swing, though.

Would you go back and do all this over again?

You betcha! Twice. (Laughs) I loved the game.

CLIFFORD FRANKLIN MAPES
Born March 13, 1922, Sutherland, Nebraska
Died December 4, 1996, Pryor, Oklahoma
Ht. 6'3"   Wt. 205   Batted Left and Threw Right

Year	Team	G	AB	R	H	2B	3B	HR	RBI	SB	BA	SA
1948	NYA	53	88	19	22	11	1	1	12	1	.250	.432
1949		111	304	56	75	13	3	7	38	6	.247	.378
1950		108	356	60	88	14	6	12	61	1	.247	.421
1951	NYA	45	51	6	11	3	1	2	8	0	.216	.431
	StLA	56	201	32	55	7	2	7	30	0	.274	.433
1952	DetA	86	193	26	38	7	0	9	23	0	.197	.373
Yankee years		317	799	141	196	41	11	22	119	8	.245	.407
Career		459	1193	199	289	55	13	38	172	8	.242	.406
World Series												
1949	NYA	4	10	3	1	1	0	0	2	0	.100	.200
1950		1	4	0	0	0	0	0	0	0	.000	.000
2 years		5	14	3	1	1	0	0	2	0	.071	.143

Courtesy New York Yankees

BOB MARTYN
Never in Pinstripes

Bob Martyn almost was not a professional baseball player. The scouts were aware of him, but they were not beating a path to his door or trying to lure him with big bucks. Or even little bucks. He finished college in 1952 and no offers came, so he went to work.

A few weeks later, however, he was offered a chance to play and he made the most of it. Moving steadily up through the Yankees chain for five years, he produced a .311 minor league average, but this was the Yankees. There were plenty of talented outfielders in their system: Bob Cerv, Bill Renna, Art Schult, Woodie Held, Dick Tettelbach, Lou Skizas, Norm Siebern, Zeke Bella, to name a few. And on the big club were Mickey Mantle, Hank Bauer, Irv Noren, Enos Slaughter, Gene Woodling, and Elston Howard. The competition was tough.

In 1957 Billy Martin fell into disfavor with the Yankee management, and a deal was struck with the Kansas City Athletics. This was probably a Martin for Harry Simpson trade, but accompanying Martin to K.C. were Martyn, Held, and Ralph Terry. Going with Simpson to New York were Jim Pisoni, Milt Graff, and Ryne Duren. Simpson and Duren gave the Yankees solid help, but this trade actually benefited the team more down the road. Held eventually was sent to Cleveland for Roger Maris, who was later traded to New York, and Terry learned how to pitch at the major league level with the A's. He was then swapped back to the Yanks, where he starred for several years.

Bob Martyn benefited from the trade, too. He had two solid seasons with the Athletics before another deal in early 1959 carried him back to New York. The Yankees still had Mantle, Bauer, and company, so Bob's major league career ended. He played through 1960 in the minors.

You have a degree in sociology.

Bob Martyn: Sociology and mathematics. I had a dual major.

Did you use them?

Primarily I used the sociology one. I had initially intended — that was before I went into pro ball — to use the math in statistics in the sociology field and do statistical research in that regard. But as it turned out, ultimately when I finished up with baseball and started looking around I ended up using the sociology side of it, but not the statistics part much because I went into personnel administration — human resource management they call it now. I spent the last 30-odd years doing that.

Has it been a satisfactory career?

Oh, very much so. I went to work for a company that became the largest employer in the state of Oregon — a very highly regarded electronics company called Tektronix. They've run on to rough times the last ten years, but it really was an extraordinarily good place to work.

Then a few years ago they had an early retirement program, and they were starting to size down some so I took it and so did three of the fellows

Previous page: Bob Martyn in spring training with the New York Yankees.

that I'd worked with for 23 years. We went across the street and put a consulting business together. We're still doing the same thing.

How were you signed to your first professional baseball contract?

I signed in early July in 1952. I'd been out of school about a month. I had actually graduated and nobody came around and seemed much interested in signing me. I'd had more interest after my junior year than my senior year, so I went to work for the State of Washington. Then the first of July I had a call from the Yankee scout in the Portland area, Syl Johnson, wanting to know if I was interested in playing pro ball. He and I had become acquainted during my days at Linfield [College]. He called me and said to meet him the next night in Seattle, which I did, and I decided I'd give pro ball a try.

You broke in with a bang. They sent you over to Boise [Pioneer League] to finish out the season and you really had super numbers [63 games, 10-11 .341].

It was a good start. I think one of the things that I enjoyed more — or made the baseball career so enjoyable — was I didn't have any high expectations going in as compared with, for example, the younger fellows, particularly right out of high school, who, because they had been signed on big bonuses and so on, had extraordinary expectations in terms of where they were gonna be and how quickly. That was right near the start of the bonus babies. I was just there enjoying playing and the chance to do it and having fun. Good things kept happening to me and that was fine.

The next year, 1953, Uncle Sam got hold of you. Was that his idea or yours?

That was his. I had intended to spend the winter at Washington State University working on my master's degree. In fact, just before the end of the season at Boise, I got my draft notice and so I ended up the second of October that year reporting at Fort Lewis, Washington, for a two-year stint with Uncle Sam.

You made it back for a portion of the 1954 season.

What happened, in '53 I played ball for the camp team where I was in the service — San Luis Obispo, California. The next year I was at Camp Kilmer, New Jersey, and was playing ball there with the camp team. That was the end of the Korean affair and it was winding down and they came up with an early-out for the draftees — letting a number of 'em out three months early — so I contacted the ballclub and said there was a chance I could do that. I had saved up all my leave.

So I took leave immediately and thought I could bridge with my leave up to the last three months I had left. I ended up down in Norfolk [Piedmont League] and played about three or four weeks there. Then one day I got a phone call from one of the fellows in our headquarters office at the camp indicating that my request for an early-out had been turned down.

In 1955, you went to Birmingham, [Southern Association] and had an excellent season [12-87-.318].

That was my first full season. I played for Phil Page. I was lucky to have very good managers — at least I enjoyed playing for them — all the way through my career.

In 1956 at Denver, you had another fine year [12-75-.314, 183 hits], then at the major league trade deadline in 1957, the Yankees and Athletics had one of their big trades. What was your reaction to that?

Well, nothing but good because it gave me a chance. Back in those times, of course, the Yankee organization was so large and there really weren't any spots on the Yankee roster. I went to spring training with 'em three years and never went north with 'em, so that trade was the opportunity to get into the big leagues. That was one of the highlights of my career for that opportunity to come along.

With the Yankees' depth, there were an awful lot of players like you who were not going to get the opportunity. You were a good ballplayer, but you weren't Mickey Mantle.

That's right. I kept thinking, "Gee, I ought to be able to beat Hank Bauer out of a job," but he kept doing a good job so there wasn't a spot in the lineup for anybody.

When you joined Kansas City, you were, I guess, best described as the fourth outfielder there for two years.

One of my best friends there, Woodie Held — 'til he got traded to Cleveland — and I traded off in the outfield. In fact, there was almost a four-man rotation at times, although [Bill] Tuttle and [Bob] Cerv played almost all of the time. Yeah, I think that'd be most accurate. I had periods of time when I was starting regularly. That third position in the outfield was never nailed completely down by anyone, I guess.

As I remember, you were very fast, but that was not an era in which bases were being stolen.

There was not much base stealing going on at that time, that's right, so that aspect of it wasn't at all utilized.

With the philosophy of today, it would appear that you would be given more playing time for that reason alone.

Probably a good possibility.

An impossible question, but that won't stop me from asking it: How would you have done had you been allowed to run?

Oh, I think I'd have done probably a little above average in terms of base stealing. One of the things that would have happened, of course, is learning much better to get good jumps and to make things happen. That's what the base stealing game has done is to make other things happen on the field in terms of that threat and, of course, impacting the pitcher's attention. Once that ball starts getting thrown around, well, some other things happen. It would have been more enjoyable.

Bob Martyn with the Kansas City Athletics *(courtesy National Pastime)*.

Just after the 1959 season you went back to the Yankees. What did you think of that?

It was a disappointment, of course. I thought I'd had a good spring training, although at the same time I recognized that that was the nature of the game. One of the things that may have been a factor — I never asked anybody — was that I was a little bit older than some of the younger fellows coming up.

So on one hand it was disappointing, on the other hand I wasn't too terribly surprised. It was the nature of the game in those days. Of course, there was no protection for players in some respects, as far as no union, so you were an individual negotiator. I took it in stride. If I made it back, fine; if not, I'd been able to do something very few people ever had an opportunity to do.

Where did the Yankees send you?

They sent me to Richmond [International League], which is where I was when I got traded a couple of years before. I finished out that season with Richmond, then the next year in the spring, in fact all through the winter, I kept in close contact with 'em and told 'em if I was going to continue to have to play minor league ball that I'd sure like for 'em to make a deal and get me out here on the West Coast in the Pacific Coast League.

A lot of conversation went on. I held out at the start of that season, in spring training, not for money but for the fact that I was hoping they'd still work out something. Before I signed a contract I traveled down to where spring training was and hung around for a few days and finally signed when they somewhat convinced me that they had tried as best they could and couldn't find someplace to get me.

I started out the season there at Richmond. Almost daily, it would seem, but on a regular basis, I was still hounding 'em about trying to get me to the Coast League, particularly before my family moved there with me because we had a couple of kids in school by then and they'd be coming out in early June. The day that my family was on an airplane flying to Richmond, they notified me that I'd been traded to Seattle. (Laughs) So they got there and I met 'em at the airport and we spent one day there for me to find somebody else to rent the house I'd rented and to sell the car back that I'd bought from the auto dealer. We turned around and flew back here to Portland and spent a couple of days in McMinnville where we lived and then went up and joined the team in Seattle a couple of days later.

Was there not talk at one time of you being traded to the Cincinnati Reds?

I was aware that there may have been a little bit of it. Of course, there was not very much interleague trading going on back then. There was a minimal amount of it. I was just slightly aware that there had been some talk along those lines.

The team that I'd loved to have played with was the Cubs. They played all their games in the daytime and I suspect I was probably 30 or 40 percentage points better in the daytime than at night. The more in the daytime, the better I liked it.

Is there one game that stands out?

Probably one of the better ones was the All-Star game in 1956 in the American Association. I hit two home runs in that game and Denver was the host team and we beat the All-Stars. I ended up with two home runs, one of 'em off a left-hander that *always* gave me trouble, a fellow named [Gene] Host, and got the MVP for that game. It was the biggest crowd of the year in the stadium, and my folks were there, so it was hard to have a much better outcome than that one.

One of the better hitting days I had in the majors was a game we lost. I hit a home run and a triple off of Bob Turley. When I hit the triple and was on third base, our pitcher, Jack Urban — we played together at Denver — was batting. The base coach put on the squeeze bunt signal. Jack seemed to acknowledge it and so, as the pitch was heading to the plate, I was heading to the plate, too. I'll never forget. Jack backed out of the way and there was Elston Howard with the biggest grin on his face standing there waiting for me. (Laughs) Jack had not seen the signal, and it just happened that the return signal was something that he kind of did habitually anyhow.

Who was the best player you saw?

Three that always stuck in my mind were Luis Aparicio and Nellie Fox, an extraordinary combination, and Ted Williams, who was still playing then. Watching him and playing against him was a tremendous thrill and an opportunity.

Of course , there were some good players then. Mantle was playing then; that whole Yankee team was extraordinarily strong. Some of the typical ones you see around that were getting the notoriety then, they were the ones to watch, also. I enjoyed them, certainly. I guess that was part of it — the admiration and the awe that I had in the whole situation anyhow, as far as being there and having a chance to play with those guys essentially as peers.

I imagine just being on the same field with Ted Williams was something else.

Oh, yeah, it was. It was always amazing that when he took batting practice — the batting cage was surrounded by players of the other team. It amazed me 'cause I was right there with 'em, too. He was fabulous to watch.

Who was the best pitcher you came up against?

Interesting thing. For me, the most difficult pitcher I came up against was [Luis] Arroyo, playing for Havana in the International League. He was a left-hander — that was part of it, too — but for me he was the most difficult pitcher that I ever faced, in terms of facing over a period of time. Some of the better pitchers in those days were a little tough on me, but off and on I think I had my licks on 'em, but I never did solve him. (Laughs)

That was 1959, I believe, and, of course, the next year they [Havana] got kicked out of the league. It happened on Cinqo de Mayo or that kind of celebration. Maybe it was '61. That was an interesting town to go to.

I bet the Havana road trips were looked forward to by the players.

Particularly when [Fulgencio] Batista was in power. Havana was a wide-open, fun, interesting place, regardless of what you did or where you went. When Castro came in, he shut the thing down, supposedly — at least drove it underground — all of the pleasurable things that some people followed around: the gambling, the casinos, and the girls and the shows and everything. The atmosphere, particularly in 1960, was very, very tense. You basically didn't leave the hotel. You spent your time either at the ballpark or between the hotel and the restaurant, which was about a half a block away.

Once you got in the ballpark, it seemed more relaxed 'cause then you concentrated on the game. Of course, Castro was an excellent baseball fan and so things seemed very calm and down to what you were there for at the baseball stadium.

I remember I even got to meet Fidel Castro at the end of the '59 season. We finished up the playoffs there and they beat us in the seventh game in Havana and Castro came up to the clubhouse to meet all the players. I stood there and shook hands with him in my birthday suit just coming out of the shower. (Laughs) My claim to fame is Fidel Castro.

What's your opinion of Harry Craft as a manager?

I enjoyed Harry as a person. Managers for me were not particularly an issue because I tended to be able to get along pretty much with them and adjust to whatever kind of style an individual had. Harry was pretty easygoing. Of course, I was essentially a rookie the year that he came aboard. I didn't see anything wrong with Lou Boudreau, for that matter, so the change was nothing that I had too great a perspective on. I enjoyed playing for Harry.

As I said, there were not many others playing too exciting a brand of baseball in terms of a lot of running and a lot of strategy and so on. It was pretty much a cut-and-dried approach to things, so I didn't have any feelings necessarily strong one way or another about Harry. As I say, I liked him as an individual and enjoyed playing with him and knowing him. He was not the best manager I ever played for.

In respect, I guess, to putting everything together, it was Ralph Houk at Denver. That was his first year of managing. He was fiery and fought hard for his ballplayers and gave you a lot of additional encouragement. He pushed you a little harder, but he did it in a very constructive, pleasant way. He'd let you know when things weren't going right, too, but made you feel good about it.

Did you save souvenirs from your career?

Not all that much, as I think unfortunately now, not that mine were in great demand. (Laughs)

It is interesting that it turned out the baseball cards started getting popular in recent years. I have eight grandchildren and I didn't even have any cards left to give them so I'd go out and buy cards to give them. One grandson, who is the most avid in terms of he'd like to play a little ball and collect things and so on, I think cornered the market on my cards in the Portland area. (Laughs) I think if I was looking that aggressively now, I'd be bidding against him for any cards I wanted to accumulate. He showed me a book and I don't know how many he had in there.

What's your opinion of card shows?

My particular attitude has to do with the current players who seem reluctant to give many autographs to kids at the ballpark. They want to charge for them, and I guess that's where it then translates into the card shows and so on. I always thought that that was one of the, I guess you could say, obligations or one of the things that you repaid the fans with. The fans were the ones that supported the game and made it possible for you to be there in the first place and giving autographs was one of the things that went with the territory. I guess it's my own attitude that that was one of the things you did for the fans. I'm willing to give anyone an autograph anytime they want it. (Laughs)

You played professionally for eight years. Any regrets?

I played in eight different seasons, through '60. I didn't play at all during the '53 season.

Regrets? None at all. If I had it to do over again I sure would, even anticipating it might have been a couple of years compared to a whole career of it. As I said, for me I was just almost in wonderment that each year I progressed like I did and enjoyed it to its fullest. I have no regrets at all. The whole thing is a very fond memory.

ROBERT GORDON MARTYN
Born August 13, 1930, Weiser, Idaho
Ht. 6'   Wt. 176   Batted Left and Threw Right

Year	Team	G	AB	R	H	2B	3B	HR	RBI	SB	BA	SA
1957	KCA	58	131	10	35	9	4	1	12	1	.267	.366
1958		95	226	25	59	10	7	2	23	1	.261	.394
1959		1	1	0	0	0	0	0	0	0	.000	.000
3 years		154	358	35	94	19	11	3	35	2	.263	.383

LINDY MCDANIEL
A Nice Return on the Investment
Yankees 1968–1973

Lindy McDaniel was a product of the Bonus Rule of the mid–1950s that required any player who received more than $4,000 to sign a contract to remain on the signing club's roster for two years. It was a bad rule and effectively destroyed the careers of most of the young men signed under it, as they rusted on the major league bench rather than being allowed to play and develop in the minor leagues.

The rule had its successes, however. Hall of Famers Al Kaline, Harmon Killebrew, and Sandy Koufax were all bonus babies and there were a few other long-term major league performers who overcame the Bonus Rule. Clete Boyer, Mike McCormick, and McDaniel are three who enjoyed prolonged major league success.

Returns on these young men were slow to come in most cases. It was years before Koufax and Killebrew came around, but Kaline and McDaniel responded quickly and by the time their bonus time was over both were established major leaguers.

McDaniel received $50,000, an extremely large amount for the time, to sign with the Cardinals in 1955. Two years later, his brother Von also received $50,000 from St. Louis and two years after that, with the Bonus Rule gone, another brother, Kerry, received a like amount plus $30,000 for their father. The two younger brothers, pitchers like Lindy, never made an impact due to injuries, but Lindy's career more than atoned.

A successful starter at the beginning of his career, Lindy McDaniel eventually became a relief pitcher and at the time of his retirement he ranked second all-time in both games and relief wins (119). He led the National League in saves three times and was named Fireman of the Year in 1960 and 1963. He made a strong run at the same honor in 1970, when he won 9 and saved 29 with a 2.01 ERA for the Yankees.

He joined New York on July 12, 1968, in one of the most one-sided trades of all time. New York sent former 20-game winner Bill Monbouquette to San Francisco for McDaniel. Monbouquette posted an 0–1 with one save for the remainder of the 1968 season, his last in the majors. The Yankees received one of the premier relievers in the American League, as McDaniel recorded 38 wins and 58 saves for the Yankees in his five seasons with the club.

Along the course of his career, McDaniel was a teammate of many of the legends of the game, including Stan Musial, Ernie Banks, Willie Mays, Mickey Mantle, and George Brett. In 21 years, that $50,000 bonus was repaid many times over.

Lindy McDaniel: Fred Hawn was the Cardinals' scout that scouted me. When I signed, I signed in St. Louis and Joe Mathes was the head of the scouting system and Mr. Meyer was vice-president of the club and Bing Devine was the general manager at the time. Harry Walker was the manager of the big league ballclub.

The Philadelphia Phillies had offered me a contract, but I didn't try to shop around, I guess mainly because the Cardinals had always been my team when I grew up as a kid. I had a kind of a goal since I was 16 to sign with the

St. Louis Cardinals and to sign for $50,000, and that was kind of a coming-together of that goal. I signed in August and I didn't join the club until September the first, when they expanded the roster, so that I wouldn't knock anyone off.

We had some older players like Murry Dickson and Walker Cooper [who returned to the Cardinals in 1956] and some of the older players kind of took me under their wing, in a way, to help me in adjustments and things like that, so I didn't feel that much pressure at all. In fact, when I started games, I think Walker Cooper did a lot of the catching and he was just like a father to me.

I only played for [Harry] Walker that one month, and Fred Hutchinson took over the next year. Walker was very helpful when I tried out in St. Louis. Everything went really well in the workout and throwing batting practice. I did have a lot of poise and I had a lot of experience to be an amateur, so I had a very mature arm for age 19.

I threw batting practice two days in a row, and they could hardly get a solid hit. When we negotiated, that all played for me and Walker was extremely in my corner, as far as wanting the Cardinals to sign me. He's the one that had to talk to Mr. [August] Busch to convince him, because initially he [Busch] turned it down totally. When he found out what I wanted, then he turned it down. Bing Devine was the one that was talking to him and then Harry Walker got on the phone with him. He was in his railroad car somewhere in the country — I don't know where — and they had to contact him by phone. When Walker got through talking with him, then he said yes. I don't know exactly what he said.

Hutchinson was a good man to play for and he was protective, I think, of the younger players and he was like a father image to the players, to the younger players especially. He brought them along slowly and was concerned about not putting too much pressure upon them too quick.

I was kind of worked in gradually. I was used as a long relief pitcher and a spot starter at times. I won my first four games and then I lost six in a row, and then I won my last three.

My first game was in Chicago the first day I joined the club. I came in in relief and pitched two innings. Walker Cooper [playing for the Cubs in 1955] hit a home run off of me. I think I gave up one run in two innings. I think he hit the home run in the bottom of the eighth. Home plate looked like it was a *long* way off. I guess it was just the excitement of being in the big leagues and all this and you're out there the first time and it looked like it's about a hundred feet away.

I had a lot of raw ability and I could throw hard, but you've got all that adjustment. Walker Cooper said that all he wanted to do, because I did have a very live fastball, was just to bat and get out of there and not get hurt. I gave him too good a pitch to hit.

Lindy (left) and Von McDaniel with the Cardinals, 1957 *(courtesy Lindy McDaniel)*.

In '58 I went down [to the minor leagues] one month. I was having a terrible adjustment because my normal way of pitching was about three-quarters overhand and a lot of side motion, a lot of twist in my body, and a long stride, and a natural sinker. In '58 I started losing my natural stuff on the ball so that the sinking fastball was not sinking as well and hitters were waiting on it a lot more. I had to bring it up in the strike zone and I was getting hurt bad with it.

What I did, I had to adjust totally to a new way of pitching — straight overhand, with a short stride, a different way of getting the power that I wanted. So I made a total adjustment at the big league level, which is very hard to do. But I was forced to do that.

In '59, when I made the adjustment to straight overhand pitching — that was in May when I went to the bullpen. The next three months I actually picked up enough wins and saves that assured me of the Fireman award if they had had it at that time.

Then in '60 was when I came up with the forkball in addition to the speed I had, so that's when I had it all together. At that time, when I made the adjustment straight overhand, I was very natural in a way that I was in a pattern and I didn't have to think about it very much. In another way, it wasn't natural because it was not the way that I was trained to pitch from a kid on up. Then in '61 I started having mechanical problems because what seemed to be natural all at once was falling out of place — then I had a terrible adjustment.

I had to make a real severe adjustment in '69 when they lowered the mound and that was rather devastating to my particular delivery until I adjusted. Then I found out I didn't need the high kick, I didn't need a lot of these other things that were extra motion that really didn't contribute to my control or speed. Once I made that adjustment with the Yankees it was real good.

After being with the Cardinals for eight years, you were traded to the Cubs in 1963. How did you feel about the trade?

At that time, I was mentally adjusted because I had come off of two mediocre years with the Cardinals. Basically I would have liked to stay with the Cardinals, but the only way I could was to make some severe changes in my delivery that they felt like I would have to make to be successful. It was basically going back down to three-quarters overhand pitching and other things I didn't think would work because I'd been through that. I knew I'd lost the natural sink on my fastball and I had to make it with control and speed. I didn't think that would work but I didn't have the answers of what would work and I couldn't put the pieces together with the Cardinals. I started getting a lot of pressure from the Cardinals and from the manager [Johnny Keane], and I think the pressure really built up to the point that I was willing to be traded. To me, it was the lesser of two evils at that point.

I found out after I was traded to the Chicago Cubs that one reason I was traded was that Fred Martin, their pitching coach, believed that he could convert me into pitching the way he used to pitch. That was three-quarters overhand and curl my leg and throw the sinking fastball. Their idea was, they got me in order to convert me, which I didn't realize that was the case, and in my own heart I didn't think that would work.

They worked on me from the first day of spring training and I said, "Oh, no. I'm in trouble." I had a lot of pressure on me there, so that's when I hurt my arm. I was really trying to overextend it without having my timing and my coordination correct.

I asked them, "Give me three weeks and if I don't satisfy you in three weeks the way I'm throwing, then I'll do whatever you tell me to do. I'll go ahead and throw your way." So what happened, after three weeks of whirlpool and everything, I started coming out of it. I went into a beautiful delivery and coordination that I can't really explain, but my old stuff was back and my old forkball was back and my control was back and my delivery was back. When they put me in the games, I was successful.

The Cubs traded you to the Giants in 1966.

I never wanted anything handed to me, but I wanted the opportunity and I did not get the opportunity with the San Francisco Giants. Things occurred there where I was not given a good situation at all. Then I was traded to the Yankees in which it was a total reverse of that, where they really stood behind me. They gave me a *real* good shot to do what I could do, so I was able to succeed.

'Course, I'm looking at relief pitching. A relief pitcher is only as successful — he cannot be any more successful than the people that manage him feel like he is because a relief pitcher is dependent totally almost on the manager's opinion of him in *how* he is used. There has to be that support, otherwise this can be very devastating. Ralph Houk in New York had confidence in me, felt I could really do the job.

The Bonus Rule gave you an early chance to play in the major leagues. In retrospect, what do you think of it?

I think it helped me. I don't know that I would have gotten the same opportunity without it. To say whether or not it was good overall, I can't.

I believe in the free enterprise system. Some people today feel if a ballplayer makes a million dollars or two or three million dollars how terrible it is. Here's teachers not making very much compared to ballplayers, but I don't think that's the fault of the ballplayers. I think it's part of the system and it's also part of the value system that we have in this country where people are willing to pay the ticket prices and watch the TV and all this. Without that, it wouldn't work.

LYNDALL DALE MCDANIEL
Born December 13, 1935, Hollis, Oklahoma
Ht. 6'3"   Wt. 195   Batted and Threw Right

Year	Team	G	IP	W	L	Pct	BB	SO	H	SHO	SV	ERA
1955	StLN	4	19	0	0	.000	7	7	22	0	0	4.74
1956		39	116.1	7	6	.538	42	59	121	0	0	3.40
1957		30	191	15	9	.625	53	75	196	1	0	3.49
1958		26	108.2	5	7	.417	31	47	139	1	0	5.80
1959		62	132	14	12	.538	41	86	144	0	*15	3.82
1960		65	116.1	12	4	*.750	24	105	83	0	*26	2.09
1961		55	94.1	10	6	.625	31	65	117	0	9	4.87
1962		55	107	3	10	.231	29	79	96	0	14	4.12
1963	ChiN	57	88	13	7	.650	27	75	82	0	*22	2.86
1964		63	95	1	7	.125	23	71	104	0	15	3.88
1965		71	128.2	5	6	.455	47	92	115	0	2	2.56
1966	SFN	64	121.2	10	5	.667	35	93	103	0	6	.266
1967		41	72.2	2	6	.250	24	48	69	0	3	3.72
1968	SFN	12	19.1	0	0	.000	5	9	30	0	0	7.45
	NYA	24	51.1	4	1	.800	12	43	30	0	10	1.75
1969	NYA	51	83.2	5	6	.455	23	60	84	0	5	3.55
1970		62	112	9	5	.643	23	81	88	0	29	2.01
1971		44	72	5	10	.333	24	39	82	0	4	5.01
1972		37	68	3	1	.750	25	47	54	0	0	2.25
1973		47	160.1	12	6	.667	49	93	148	0	10	2.86
1974	KCA	38	107	3	1	.750	24	42	109	0	1	3.45
1975		40	78	5	1	.833	24	40	81	0	0	2.89
Yankee years		**265**	**545.1**	**38**	**29**	**.567**	**135**	**363**	**486**	**0**	**58**	**2.89**
Career		987	2139.1	141	119	.542	623	1361	2099	2	172	3.45

*Led League

IRV NOREN
Teammate of Mikan and Mantle

Yankees 1952–1956

How often does a rookie come along who leads his team in nearly everything? We're talking about doubles, triples, home runs, RBIs, batting average, slugging average—all the glory stats.

The Washington Senators had such a rookie in 1950, a 25-year-old center fielder who also led American League outfielders in assists and was second in total chances per game. He was Irv Noren and his performance was really no surprise; he had been MVP of his minor league the two previous seasons. In 1950, he hit 14 home runs in cavernous Griffith Stadium, drove in 98 runs and batted .295, despite missing 16 games.

In most years, Noren's performance would have earned him Rookie of the Year honors, but the rookie crop in the AL in 1950 was outstanding. Whitey Ford of the Yankees and Chico Carrasquel of the White Sox also had stellar first years and in most other seasons would also have won, but Walt Dropo of the Red Sox had one of the top rookie years of all time and took the award.

Playing in the anonymity of the nation's capital didn't help Noren's cause with the writers or the fans, but the rest of the league was fully aware of his ability. In 1951 he again put up solid numbers—and despite missing nearly a month because of a broken jaw he led the league's outfielders in putouts and total chances per game.

Taking special note were the New York Yankees. In 1951, Joe DiMaggio was winding down rapidly, but the Yankees felt they had their outfield covered. Mickey Mantle and Jackie Jensen spent a great deal of that season in New York, and the plan for 1952 was for Mantle to take over in center field and Jensen to fit in with the rotating left and right fielders, Gene Woodling and Hank Bauer.

But Mantle, especially, struggled in 1951 and it was uncertain if he would be ready in '52. At the beginning of that season, though, he looked as if he would be able to do the job, but then Jensen couldn't get untracked. So about two weeks into the season the Yankees sent Jensen and three others to Washington for Noren and Tommy Upton, whom everyone knew would not make the Yankee roster. It was then, in essence, four men for Noren. It turned out to be a trade which benefited both teams. Jensen and Spec Shea gave Washington two good seasons each and Noren worked right into the New York outfield with Mantle, Woodling, and Bauer.

Noren's best season as a Yankee was 1954, when he led the majors in batting for most of the year and was selected for the All-Star game. He ended up batting .319, third best in the league.

Noren retired as an active player after the 1960 season, then managed in the minors and coached in the majors for many years.

You signed originally with the Dodgers.

Irv Noren: Yeah. I got out of the army one day in '46, March 15, and met Tom Downey, a Dodgers scout, that afternoon and that night I went down to the hotel in L. A. and signed. I went in the army at 18, and got out three years later. I played at Fort Ord and helped run the team, but the scout that signed me saw me around Pasadena at school.

From Santa Barbara I went to Fort Worth in '47 and '48. Forty-seven I had a decent year, but that was an awful tough league down there and then in '48 I went back there again and had a good year — MVP. Then I thought I was goin' to the Dodgers but they had so many players. [At this time, Brooklyn had more than 500 players under contract.] I sorta threatened to quit because they were gonna send me to Montreal, which was their other Triple A club, and I just told 'em I wouldn't go because I thought I should get a shot with the Dodgers in '49.

We were at Vero Beach and my wife and young daughter were with me. I told Branch Rickey I was goin' back to my dad's bakery and get in the baking business. In them days you had to sorta fake your way in there and tell a few fibs cause there was no union. I told 'em I was goin' back; I probably wouldn't, but I told 'em that.

Rickey said, "Wait a minute. Wait 'til tomorrow morning. Don't leave tonight." So I waited and went in and saw him again. He says, "How 'bout Hollywood in the Pacific Coast League?" Growin' up out here and followin' the Pacific Coast League, I said, "Okay, I'll go." So I came out here in the Coast League in '49.

Fred Haney was the manager and we won it all and I was the MVP of the league. Bucky Harris, who was managing San Diego that year, he knew that he was gonna go back to Washington and manage the Washington Senators. Branch Rickey the year before had lost some money in the football team they were gonna try to start — the Brooklyn Dodgers — so to get it back — hell, he had 500 players in the Dodger organization in them days — he just sold me to Washington for $70,000 and a player, and he sold Chico Carrsaquel to the White Sox and Sam Jethroe to the Boston Braves. That's what I understand was how he got his money back. [Noren's and Carrasquel's rookie years were mentioned above; Jethroe was National League Rookie of the Year in 1950.]

In the meantime, Bucky Harris told Clark Griffith if there's any chance to get me out of the Dodger chain to do it. I think the White Sox and the Red Sox wanted me, too, but I ended up with Washington.

Your rookie year was great.

I'd have hit over .300 if I hadn't had my appendix out near the end of the season. I was hittin' over .300 and Clark Griffith said, "I want you to go back and play center field. We don't have anybody." I'd been out a while and I was a little weak, but in them days you said sure, so I went back in and in the last month or so I dipped under .300. I had 98 RBIs and I'd have gotten over 100 easy if I don't get hurt. But that year I wasn't gonna get the Rookie of the Year anyway. Walt Dropo got it; he drove in about a hundred and eighty, (Laughs)

Playing in Washington didn't help.

I was hittin' over .300 and leadin' the league in doubles, I think, at the All-Star break, but when you got DiMaggio and Williams and the other DiMaggio and guys like that, they're not gonna take many other outfielders, especially one from the Senators.

Were you fast?

No, I wasn't very fast. The only thing that saved me, especially in the outfield — center field — was my reflexes. I just had good reflexes; I was gone at the crack of the bat, like they would say. Like Jackie Robinson — he was fast but he was faster because after two steps he was goin' as fast as he was goin' after ten steps. He accelerated real fast and I think that's what enabled me, with the little speed I did have, to play center field. And on the bases, it's probably the same way.

The Yankees traded for you in 1952.

They gave Jackie Jensen, Spec Shea, Archie Wilson, and Jerry Snyder, I think — a couple little guys that didn't go — for me and Tommy Upton, an infielder. I felt good, of course, goin' to the Yankees, but at the same time I was enjoying myself and Mr. Griffith was takin' good care of me. He made it like a family deal. He was very active as far as family. He told me when he called me in Saturday, he says, "I've traded you upstairs. The Yankees want you to play center field tomorrow in Yankee Stadium against the White Sox in a doubleheader." He called me in before I went to the ballpark that day and his secretary said, "Mr. Griffith wants to see you. Don't get dressed. Come into the office." And that's when he told me.

The Yankees had another center fielder coming along then, a boy named Mantle.

(Laughs) Yeah, and Jenson had gone about 1 for 50, I guess. Couldn't get started. 'Course, with the Yankees you gotta produce. There's no waiting around with them. That's when they got me cause I always hit fairly good against 'em and beat 'em a few ball games when I was at Washington.

It just takes a while to get used to the Yankees. You walk in the clubhouse and you see all those guys you've played against and the Yankees are the Yankees. They just had that air about 'em. You walk in the clubhouse and you're lookin' around and you say, "I'm really here!" and it takes a little while to get situated, I think. (Laughs)

You and Bauer and Woodling pretty much rotated.

After a while we had four outfielders — Mantle, Bauer, Woodling, and myself. 'Course, Mantle after a while stayed there, but other than that, we did rotate. Stengel liked that; he liked to move guys around and hit you first or hit you eighth or whatever. He was always tryin' to do something different.

[In 1954] I guess everything came about and I had a good spring, but I don't think I got goin' until May —'til I played regular, you know. Stengel was funny. If you won a ball game or got a pinch hit single, you had a good chance of playin' the next day. (Laughs) I think I won a ball game one night in the tenth inning with a home run and I just kept goin'. At mid-season I was leadin' both leagues. I don't know what it was, .365 or something like that. But then my son was born in August. (Laughs) I tell him that's why I dropped. His cryin' kept me up at night. (Laughs)

It's pretty tough, number one, to end up hittin' .360 or .350 anyway, and in them days I think the pitchin' was tougher. They tell me pitchin' is better now than it was then but I just don't believe it. When you go into Detroit and have Dizzy Trout and Virgil Trucks and Hal Newhouser and Freddie Hutchinson; then you go to Cleveland and face Feller, Lemon, Wynn, and Garcia; then you go to the Yankees and face Reynolds, Raschi, Lopat, and Ford; then you go to Boston and face Parnell — you can just keep goin'. And you can tell me that you got guys like that now? And they were mean. They'd tell you they were gonna knock you down if you dug in on 'em. There was none of this where the guy holds his hand up now and digs in with is back foot, I mean, holy cow! There's no way you could do that! You'd be knocked down four times.

Today it's a different game. The umpires today are different. They just sit over there and look for trouble. They just agitate you, try to get you goin'. In the old days, they'd say, "Hell, you wanna knock a guy down? Knock him down. I don't care." (Laughs) If you wanna argue with him, you'd argue, then they'd say, "Okay, you've had enough now. Let's go." If you kept on you'd get thrown out, but at least you could say something, get it off your chest.

About three days before the [1954] All-Star game, I was facing, I think it was Mickey McDermott and he threw me a pitch on the outside and I tried to hold up and I strained the top of my hand. It was really hurtin' and I went to the [All-Star] game anyway, and 'course, I wasn't gonna play left field. Stengel asked me if I could pinch hit and I went to get a bat and I just couldn't hold it, so he put me in left field in the last inning to get me in the game. I wanted to hit because he wanted me to go and hit with the bases loaded and one out and the score tied off [Carl] Erskine, but I just couldn't swing. I had played with Erskine at Fort Worth and I had confidence. With the way I was goin', it would be a nice spot to hit in. It was a big thrill just to be in it, but you always like to be able to play.

You played in three World Series with the Yankees.

I didn't have a very good '55 when we got beat. Bein' there is a big thrill; of course, everybody, as a kid, always dreams about bein' in the World Series. I also coached in two with Oakland — third base coach at Oakland when we beat Cincinnati in '72 and the Mets in '73.

The A's let you go during the '74 season. Why?

Dick Williams quit after the '73 Series with the Mets, when Charlie Finley made him replace the second baseman. Mike Andrews made an error and

Charlie came in and wanted to get him off the team and have the commissioner put a replacement player and have Dick tell the commissioner Mike Andrews is hurting. Dick didn't do it. He just said, "Screw you. I'm through."

We had another year on our contract — the coaches — so we stayed there and Alvin Dark took over. I played with Alvin with the Cardinals and the Cubs in '59. I went to him that year and I said, "Alvin, if you want your own third base coach, I understand." You know, all managers like to have their own third base coach and Dick Williams hired me and he says, "No, I want you here. You know the league, you can help me."

So, about the middle of the season — All-Star break or just past it — he called me in and said that I'd missed a sign on purpose 'cause I wanted to get his job. I told him a few words I don't wanna repeat. I told him, "That's the worst thing I ever heard. Why would I do that with these guys I've played with two years, got me two World Series, and we're six games in front now?" And he said, "I want you to move over to first base and I'll put Jerry Adair at third." And he called Jerry Adair in and Jerry said, "I can't coach third. Irv's been here for three years and we've won it every year." So then Alvin says, "Go on back there and coach third." I said, "Alvin, I've gotta have confidence in myself and confidence in you when I'm out there coachin' third, 'cause I look at you every pitch of the game."

Charlie calls me and wants me to quit. I said, "I'm not gonna quit. You fire me." He said, "I can't afford to fire you." And I said, "I can't afford to quit." So I went back out there and about a couple weeks later, maybe after the All-Star game, Alvin called me in and said that Finley gave him the okay to let me go. I had a few words and left.

Finley was all right. He was no dummy, he just bugged the hell out of his managers and called 'em all night long and drove 'em crazy. Dick Williams, he put up with it as long as he could. He was a very good manager.

He deserves to be in the Hall of Fame off his managerial career, but his matter-of-factness may prevent it.

Yeah, you're right. He just told it like it was — you knew where you stood. He couldn't manage today with these players.

Is there one game that stands out?

I think my most memorable game was my first time in the big leagues. You know, as a kid you're always wantin' to get to the big leagues and my dad was always pushin' me to get there and finally opening day in Washington. President Truman threw out the first ball and just bein' in the major league ballpark with all the hullabaloo, then you come out and go out there on the field and you're just thinkin', "Ever since I can remember — ten years old — this is what I was dreamin' about! It's finally come true!"

I got a base hit the first time off of Bobby Shantz in the bottom of the first. I drove in a run. Eddie Yost was leadin' off, then Gil Coan. I don't know

Irv Noren *(courtesy National Pastime)*

who I drove in. Then I scored in the inning and I crossed home and Truman yelled at me and I went over and shook his hand. It was pretty exciting.

I'm sure I was as excited as all get-out playin' in my first World Series and a couple of times I won ball games in the tenth inning with home runs and different things like that. But I think, as far as just remembering things, that stands out.

And, of course, bein' traded to the Yankees and goin' out the next day and playin' center field — it was a doubleheader and I got a couple hits first game. There's a lot of thrills in the game as you go along.

I grew up in Jamestown, New York, and my folks moved out to Pasadena when I was 12 years old. My dad kept saying that I kept sayin' I was with the Yankees when I was younger — I don't remember that — but that was his goal in life — for me bein' able to play baseball in the big leagues. In the minor leagues wherever I went, he followed me. He'd bake all night and go up to Santa Barbara and watch the game. I told him I got sold and he was there opening day in Washington. That was big thrill for me *and* him.

My mother's still alive. She's in her 90s. My dad died at 60 when I was with the Dodgers. My mother says my dad was really proud of me and I think that's as important as anything.

Who was the best player you saw?

DiMaggio. You can argue. I roomed with Musial when I was with the Cardinals. He's a super, super guy, nicest guy in the world. And he was a great player. He could go get 'em in the outfield, great arm, good base runner, hit .300, knew the strike zone, hit home runs, nice guy — the whole bit.

Who was the toughest pitcher on you?

The toughest on me was Mike Garcia. I didn't like knuckleballers and they had a few then, but for an all-around guy I had trouble with Mike. The last couple of years I hit him pretty good, but it got so bad, when Mike Garcia was pitchin', my wife would say, "You better have a headache today." (Laughs) I could hit Early Wynn and Lemon and Virgil Trucks and all those guys that were good pitchers and Mike Garcia wasn't any better than they were. But that happens in the game; certain guys can get certain guys out. Herb Score was tough, 'course he was left-handed. I faced Koufax later on in the National League and he was awful tough.

You were associated with professional baseball for 30 years. Did you save souvenirs?

Yeah. Balls signed by Cy Young and Ty Cobb and World Series bats and programs. Things like that.

Do you receive much fan mail today?

I get around two or three a day. I sign 'em and send 'em right back. The guys today want money to sign. My dad told me years ago that greed is a terrible thing.

You also played professional basketball.

It wasn't very long. (Laughs) We had a pro team out here called the L. A. Red Devils in 1946. Jackie Robinson, George Crowe, Art Stoffen, who just passed away — he was a center at Stanford with [Hank] Lusetti — and Ziggy Marcell, who played with the Globetrotters for a number of years, and Eddie Oram, an All-American at USC. We had a guy by the name of Bob Cotton out of Texas Wesleyan who was about 6'10" or somethin' like that. We played all the teams from the East — played the Chicago Gears, the Sheboygan Redskins, the Harlem Renaissance — and we played at the Shrine Auditorium and the Olympic Auditorium. The teams would come out here and we'd pack the places.

When the Gears came out with [George] Mikan and those guys, we played 'em two days and I had a couple of good games and scored 25–30 points. Our team broke up — the guy that was runnin' it just couldn't keep it goin' — so the Gears called and wanted to know if I'd come back and play for them. Art Stoffen and I did — we went back and played with 'em, with Mikan and all those guys. We played at the Amphitheatre in Chicago. I finished the year with 'em and then Branch Rickey heard about it and he said, "Son, if you wanna play basketball, play basketball. If you wanna play baseball, play baseball."

So my mind was made up right away. (Laughs) I loved baseball and basketball in them days wasn't like it is today and it wasn't like baseball then. I never played pro basketball anymore, but it was fun. In school, I was better in basketball than I was in baseball. I was player of the year in Southern California at Pasadena High and that first year at Pasadena Junior College I was state player of the year. I had scholarships to SC and UCLA and Kentucky and all over the place. Sam Berry was the coach at SC in them days and my dad had the bakery in Pasadena. He said he [Berry] went up there to talk to my dad so often he got to like the Swedish rye bread my dad made there. (Laughs) He was tryin' to talk him into gettin' me to go to USC.

Any regrets from your athletic career?

No, not really. The only regret that I would've had was if my dad hadn't seen me play. My mother said that's all he wanted — to see me play in the major leagues. That was his dream. Otherwise, I think I did everything I felt like I wanted to do.

BK: Would you do it again?

IN: Oh, yeah. Yeah, I'd do it again.

IRVING ARNOLD NOREN
Born November 29, 1924, Jamestown, New York
Ht. 6'   Wt. 190   Batted and Threw Left

Year	Team	G	AB	R	H	2B	3B	HR	RBI	SB	BA	SA
1950	WasA	138	542	80	160	27	10	14	98	5	.295	.459
1951		129	509	82	142	33	5	8	86	10	.279	.411
1952	WasA	12	49	4	12	3	1	0	2	1	.245	.347
	NYA	93	272	36	64	13	2	5	21	4	.235	.353
1953		109	345	55	92	12	6	6	46	3	.267	.388
1954		125	426	70	136	21	6	12	66	4	.319	.481
1955		132	371	48	94	19	1	8	59	5	.253	.375
1956		29	37	4	8	1	0	0	6	0	.216	.243
1957	KCA	81	160	8	34	8	0	2	16	0	.213	.300

Year	Team	G	AB	R	H	2B	3B	HR	RBI	SB	BA	SA
	StLN	17	30	3	11	4	1	1	10	0	.367	.667
1958		117	178	24	47	9	1	4	22	0	.264	.393
1959	StLN	8	8	0	1	1	0	0	0	0	.125	.250
	ChiN	65	156	27	50	6	2	4	19	2	.321	.462
1960	ChiN	12	11	0	1	0	0	0	1	0	.091	.091
	LAN	26	25	1	5	0	0	1	1	0	.200	.200
Yankee years		**488**	**1451**	**213**	**304**	**66**	**15**	**31**	**198**	**16**	**.272**	**.402**
11 years		1093	3113	443	857	157	35	65	453	34	.275	.410
					World Series							
1952	**NYA**	**4**	**10**	**0**	**3**	**0**	**0**	**0**	**1**	**0**	**.300**	**.300**
1953		**2**	**1**	**0**	**0**	**0**	**0**	**0**	**0**	**0**	**.000**	**.000**
1955		**5**	**16**	**0**	**1**	**0**	**0**	**0**	**1**	**0**	**.063**	**.063**
3 years		**11**	**27**	**0**	**4**	**0**	**0**	**0**	**2**	**0**	**.148**	**.148**

DUANE PILLETTE
Streak Stopper

Yankees 1949–1950

A pitcher who spends his career on a good team—a contender—can look back on that career and point to a couple of important games he pitched here and there, maybe a pennant-clincher or a post-season effort or something like that. However, a pitcher who spends his career at the other end of the standings doesn't have the opportunities to pitch many memorable games because there just aren't many that are worth remembering.

Duane Pillette spent eight years in the majors—five full years plus parts of three others. The five full seasons were spent with the St. Louis Browns and the Baltimore Orioles. During those five seasons, Pillette's teams finished seventh three times and eighth twice, amassing a .366 winning percentage and averaging 44 games out of first each year. Important games were few and far between.

But noteworthy games did occur.

On June 15, 1953, the New York Yankees, en route to yet another world title, had reeled off 18 wins in a row. They were within one of the club and American League record, set six years earlier. The Browns, Duane's team, had equaled their club's all-time losing streak record—14 straight, originally set in 1911.

St. Louis was in New York for a four-game series and Pillette was the first game starter for the visitors. He stopped both streaks, winning 3 to 1 with relief help from Satchel Paige.

Later in 1953—September 27, the last day of the season and the Browns' last game ever—Duane pitched against the Chicago White Sox. The Browns had been losers for decades; for them to go out a winner would be against the laws of nature. It was only fitting that the biggest loser in all of baseball should go out that way—and they did. Duane dropped a 2–1 decision. It was typical of the frustration of the Browns' pitchers: a good performance for nothing.

The team was supposed to have new life in Baltimore in 1954. Some writers, as the new season neared, even predicted the Orioles would be in the hunt, and they were—right up until Opening Day. Don Larsen lost to the Detroit Tigers, 3–0, as Steve Gromek tossed the shutout.

The next day, however—April 14, 1954—the new Baltimore Orioles won the first game in their history. Pillette went the distance, downing the Tigers, 3–2. The giddy heights of .500 ball were not to last. The team wound up its first year in Baltimore at 54-100, the same record it left St. Louis with the year before.

This was a team with good pitching, though. In addition to Pillette and Larsen, the starters were Bob Turley, Joe Coleman, and Lou Kretlow. The team ERA was half a run lower than it had been the previous year, but the offense balanced this out: The team scored half a run fewer per game.

Pillette pitched in 25 games that season, all starts, and had a 10-14 record, with only one no-decision. The team's winning percentage was .351, his was .417. For the five years, Duane consistently won at a better rate than his team. He led the Orioles in ERA; his 3.12 was a third of a run better than any of his teammates' and was twelfth best in the A.L.

Previous page: Duane Pillette with the Baltimore Orioles.

He came by his pitching ability honestly. His father, Herman, won 19 games as a Tiger rookie in 1922 (the year Duane was born) and a total of 298 games in the majors and minors in one of the longest professional careers on record.

Elbow problems ended Duane's major league career before the Orioles climbed to respectability, so he was denied the chance to ever pitch healthy for even a decent team, much less a good one. You have to wonder what might have happened had he stayed sound.

When I was a kid, you were one of my favorite players. I got to see you pitch when you were with the San Francisco Seals at the start of the 1957 season, but then you went to the Seattle Rainiers.

Duane Pillette: The Seals at that time had a very strong working agreement with the Boston Red Sox. They wanted to send down young pitchers and the Seals had a number of older pitchers. The year before that I had had a sore arm, although at that particular time I happened to be leading the ballclub in ERA, and I don't know if I was making any more than the next person who had just come back from the majors.

In any case, they were very nice. They gave me my choice: Do you want to be traded or do you want to go out on your own and maybe get a couple dollars to sign 'cause you're obviously playing quite well, etc.? So I said, "I'll take my chances." I called Lefty [O'Doul at Seattle] and he said, "Sure." I got a few dollars to sign and I went with a ballclub that I really appreciated being with. I wasn't happy about leaving [the Seals] because I was living at home [in San Jose].

On Camera Day at Seals Stadium, you posed for a picture for me and some kid came up and asked, "Who's that guy?" I was amazed that everyone didn't know you.

(Laughs) Let's face it, the greatest fans in the world really only know the stars — the name ballplayers. Even though I started out with the Yankees, I ended up with the Browns and Baltimore and we were in last place for years and the last place ballclubs just don't get the notoriety.

June 15, 1953. The Browns had equaled their all-time losing streak and the Yankees were within one of their all-time winning streak. You stopped both streaks in Yankee Stadium.

We were getting frantic. Obviously, when you're playing with the Browns we had more losing streaks than winning streaks, but I think the thing that really bothered us was when we came in to New York City and the scribes were saying, "Gee, if we win one more we're gonna break our record and now we've got the Browns in here for a four-game series and now we haven't won 18, we've won 22." I suppose that's the feeling that every good ballclub like the Yankees would feel, but for the scribes to write about it made us pretty angry. I truly never appreciated the New York scribes. I didn't care for 'em, to be honest; they took advantage of a lot of good ballplayers and they seemed to want to write the worst about people, rather than the best.

As far as the ball game is concerned, I remember it totally. It's one of the real highlights of my life. I was interested in stopping our losing streak because 14 had tied our losing streak [record] at that particular time, but when you go out to pitch a ball game you're not really interested in the streaks — you're interested in winning that ball game. But I think somehow or other you get a little more incentive in those situations.

I was a little miffed at our manager [Marty Marion]. I got taken out in the eighth inning with a man on second base, I believe, with two outs and they put Satchel [Paige] in. Not that Satchel wasn't a great reliever, but I *really* wanted to stay in for a full nine innings, especially since we were ahead at that time, 3 to 1. But managers do what they have to.

My strengths were usually in the later innings. I was usually stronger as the game went along. If I had a weakness it was getting through the first two or three innings. I seemed to feel my way through a lot of ball games unconsciously and I would get hurt with a lot of runs early. Probably what really hurt my ERA was the fact that they would score early and I'd get out of the ball game in a hurry, but I pitched a lot of complete ball games considering that we didn't win that many, and I also went extra innings in ball games, as much as 12 innings in St. Louis one time on a day where you could hardly stand the sun *or* the humidity. That's one of the reasons why I really hated to leave.

You pitched a couple of other milestone games. You lost the last Browns' games and you won the first game the Orioles won.

(Laughs) That's right.

The [Browns'] last ball game was against the White Sox. I think the score was 2 to 1. You get used to losing the one-run ball games. They always say the mark of a good pitcher is when he wins the close ones. I think the one thing that people don't realize is the fact that, depending on what kind of a ballclub you are, you have to be able to turn the double play, you have to be able to do the things that the top-notch teams do more often. That's why they're a better ballclub than you are.

Consequently, a one-run difference — we give up those one runs a lot more quickly than somebody else does — can mean the ball game. One ball-club will have a man on third and first and one out and a ground ball is hit and they get the double play and the run doesn't score. Our ballclub has the same play and we're not quite good enough; we don't get the double play so the run scores. That's the difference.

I just had a lot of bad luck against the White Sox, too. For whatever reason, things would happen. I seemed to pitch well against them, but I just didn't seem to beat them.

The first game for the Orioles happened to be when we were on the road

Duane Pillette *(courtesy National Pastime)*

and I believe Don Larsen pitched the first game in Detroit and pitched well but we lost. I pitched the second ball game. The reason I really remember it is that it was *really* cold there. In fact, the ground was frozen and I slid into second base — I don't remember whether I was on first and went into second or whether I actually got a base hit and tried to make it into second base — but I got a strawberry that lasted all season. It went down through about seven layers of skin. (Laughs) We don't wear sliding pants when we're pitchers, so I remember that one.

Ned Garver, one of your teammates in St. Louis, said that the Browns always seemed to be able to give up that one run at the wrong time.

It always seemed to happen. I don't know whether it was because we just didn't have the players that could make the plays or sometimes it gets to be a habit. You always kind of waited for the other shoe to drop, so to speak. Especially in the real close ball game — what's gonna happen now? You're a little tentative. Sometimes you'll pitch a little differently because, quite honestly, maybe you don't feel that they [your teammates] can do it.

In my case, I was a sinker ball pitcher so they hit a lot of ground balls and I always wanted to have the double play. I'll be very frank with you, when we got Billy Hunter [to play shortstop], especially with the Orioles where we had a nice infield where you could hit the ground ball without it flying through like it did over at Sportsman's Park [in St. Louis], then I was very confident and I think I threw a lot of good sinker pitches and made them hit the ground ball all the time. At times I would change my mind when we were in Sportsman's Park to different hitters. If they were low-ball hitters I would pitch them up and that wasn't my strength. I think sometimes I lost ball games because I went away from my strength worrying about, "Well, gosh, we're not gonna get the damned double play anyhow."

Sometimes it was just a *fraction*. Double plays are usually all a very close play at first base anyhow, unless the ball is hit very, very hard one-hop right to somebody. But when the ball is hit to one side or the other, it's only a fraction of a second whether the man turns properly at second base or whether the shortstop gets the ball to him at the right level where he can make the turn. The matter of talent is minor, but it's enough to make a difference. I noticed it more, as I said, because I was a sinker ball pitcher, because I made 'em hit the ball on the ground.

It really hurt my ego in 1955, after having a decent season in '54 with Baltimore; I really felt like we were gonna have a better ballclub because Paul Richards was gonna be the manager and he's gonna get more talent out here, etc., and then I hurt my arm in '55. It just crushed me.

I felt it [1954] was my best year; not necessarily did I win any more games maybe than I did in another season, but I felt like I pitched much better totally. My wins were against better ballclubs. I'm not sure, but I think I beat Cleveland quite often and Cleveland that year had set a record for wins. I always seemed to pitch pretty well at Boston, too. I'd win my ball games at Boston. Boston, Cleveland, and the Yankees — I always seemed to pitch fairly well against them.

The Orioles were last in the major leagues in runs scored in 1954, so it was hard to win, but the defense really had improved over '53.

That's the reason you pitched with a little more confidence. When your ballclub's playing a little better you're more confident and you can do a better job.

You were nearly 24 years old when you signed a professional contract. Had you been in the service?

Yes. I signed with the Yankees. They gave me a bonus but I had a Newark contract. In the International League. The one thing that I felt good about was that most all of the rookies that were signed in the Yankee organization, because they wanted them to play, went to a lower classification. I not only played with Newark, I was probably one of their better pitchers, if not their best.

There again, I lost some tough ball games when I really didn't think that I should have. But that happens to everybody. I enjoyed the first year and I enjoyed playing with the Yankees' organization. I really did.

You never pitched below Triple A. If there hadn't been a logjam at the top, you'd have been a Yankee much sooner.

They had an awful lot of talent, there's no doubt about it. They used their young rookies [to trade] to get the ballplayers to replace the spots where they were hurting and, of course, we all knew that. If you look back through the league in the mid–'50s, you'd probably find one or two ex–Yankee ballplayers on each ballclub.

That's what they used you for in 1950. They were a little light in the bullpen and figured Tom Ferrick and Joe Ostrowski could help them.

[Joe] Page was having a bad year and they needed relief pitching. An article in the paper said George Weiss [Yankee general manager] had made a lousy deal, but they won the pennant again and they won the World Series. You couldn't fault what they did. They had the personnel that they could play with. They might have given up a little more than what they should have at that particular time, but they did what they wanted to accomplish. And they did for five years in a row, so you can't knock what they were doing.

What did you think of the trade?

Going from first place to last place is like going down in the elevator from the 50th floor to the first in a hurry. (Laughs)

I was perturbed only from this standpoint. Previous to the trade, Casey [Stengel] liked me very much. He had shipped me to Kansas City and said, "I don't care whether you pitch or not. Just stay in shape; we'll bring you right back after the trading deadline [June 15]."

Well, Bob Porterfield got hurt and Weiss looked back to Kansas City and Newark to see who could replace him and he said, "What the hell is Pillette doing down there?" So he brought me back. Had I stayed in Kansas City 'til after the trading deadlines, I probably would have stayed with the Yankees. I pitched well for them.

You had only been in Kansas City about two or three weeks.

Less than that. I think it was about ten days.

The thing that was really the crusher was that we went to St. Louis and midnight came — 'course everybody's sitting down in the lobby waiting for the trading deadline — and we've got a doubleheader with the Browns the next day.

I went up in the elevator with Casey and we got out of the elevator about five or ten minutes after 12 and 12 o'clock was when we were supposed to be in our rooms, but everybody waited to see who was gonna be traded. Nothing came through the wires that we had made a trade, so I went into my room, got undressed, and went to bed. I got a phone call about 2:30. My wife had called me. She was in Kansas City still and she told me I'd been traded. (Laughs)

I really hit the fan. Casey brought me up. He liked me. I pitched well against him when I was in the [Pacific] Coast League and Jim Turner was the [pitching] coach and he had been my manager at Portland. They were the people who were responsible for my getting a real good shot with the Yankees — they recommended me highly and they liked me. They really thought I was gonna be a good ballplayer *for* the Yankees.

But when Casey didn't tell me [about the trade] I thought that he knew and didn't tell me, so I called him right away on the phone and I said, "That was rotten. That was a lousy thing to do." He swore up and down he didn't know. And I believe him 'cause Casey was not that kind of guy. He was always 100 percent with his players.

I admired the guy. I thought he was psychic. He did things at times with the Yankees, with pinch hitting at certain times and doing things that were actually against all the rules of baseball — as we say, "playing the percentages" — and they turned out. I said to him, "I know you're psychic, Casey." He said, "Hell, I've managed for 30 years and I never was on a good ballclub. How could I be psychic?" (Laughs)

Everyone struggled in St. Louis. You played before crowds of 500 people and it had to be a pretty sobering experience, then you moved to Baltimore. What were the players' feelings about the move?

I think everybody was *100 percent* happy, not only because you like to have the fans in the stands rooting for you — that gives you a lot of incentive and makes you feel like you're wanted. But I don't want to slight the St. Louis fans. The people who came out there when the Browns were in last place as long as they were have got to be hard-nosed fans. When you come out to watch the Browns, you've gotta *love* baseball and love the guys that you see. I get more calls for autographs right now from people who were kids in St. Louis and saw me play than I do from other people. Those people were *really* fans.

Moving to Baltimore was great. They had a brand new stadium. The

infield was nice, plush grass and I had the greatest time of my life in Baltimore. Fifty-four was probably the finest year I ever really enjoyed as far as
playing in a town.

I had severed one-half of my triceps muscle on a bone spur that had been
chipped off. We get little bone chips in our elbows from spurs and I had a little saw-tooth spur right at the edge of where the triceps muscle has two little
connections and I severed one-half of the muscle off of my elbow.

Dr. Bennett, one of the finest orthopedic surgeons for athletes at that
time, said I'd never be able to throw a baseball across the street again. He told
Baltimore that and that's when they shipped me out. I told them I could pitch
and they said, "We're gonna send you back to the Coast League with Lefty
O'Doul. He's got a last-place ballclub, but if you can pitch once a week we'll
pay you." At that time, they didn't have to pay you. They could just let you
go and that was it.

I was fortunate enough to work with a very fine orthopedic surgeon here
and we didn't operate, but he re-attached that little connection by taping it.
I kept it on for about six weeks and then I did minor exercises and then the
following year I went to the Cleveland spring training camp. They were the
one team to invite me. I had pitched that well against them in the past that
they were willing to take a chance with me.

Al Lopez, the manager at that time, had said, "You've made my team.
We're very proud of you." That was great. They had 20-game winners up the
kazoo, they had [Art] Houtteman and [Bob] Feller and guys like that in the
relief corps. I felt real good about having made the ballclub and two days later
[Hank] Greenberg, the G.M., said, "I don't want to take a chance with a sore-
armed pitcher."

Lopez felt so bad he said, "I'm gonna get you a job. You can still pitch."
He called everybody and finally the Phillies said, "Put him on a plane and
send him down here and if he looks good we'll sign him." So I signed Opening Day [1956] with the Phillies, but I didn't play much. It was another second division ballclub. They wanted me to be a relief pitcher and when you're
down in the standings like that you throw every day in the bullpen and my
arm didn't take that. I could pitch as long as I threw every fourth day, but I
couldn't come back and throw in the bullpen every day. It kept the arm ten-
der.

But Baltimore was great. I wish to God I had been healthy and had the
opportunity to continue playing in Baltimore. I would have really enjoyed it.

*You were still sound enough in the Coast League to be one of the top pitch-
ers out there and that was a good level of ball, much better than the high minors
today.*

Everybody at that time was trying to call it the third major league. It
really wasn't, but it was a lot sounder than the International League or the

American Association. There were some teams there that were better than the Browns. (Laughs)

You threw four shutouts in your major league career. Is there one that really stands out?

I didn't know and really didn't care about how many shutouts I had and I don't remember too much about the shutouts. Sometimes I think I pitched much better allowing one and two runs.

There was a ball game in Detroit that I pitched where I had a perfect ball game for 7, 7⅓ innings — something of that nature. At the time, the last perfect ball game that had been pitched in the major leagues was against my father in the same ballpark. Charlie Robertson of the White Sox pitched a perfect ballgame against my father in Detroit in 1922, the year I was born. Since that time there had not been another perfect ball game.

I got that many innings and then you start to realize it. I think it was Harvey Kuenn, but I'm not quite sure, who hit a ground ball to shortstop but it was in the hole between third and short. The shortstop made a good play on the ball and threw the ball over to first base and it was just a slap-slap play — you could have called the guy either safe or out. Truly, I think the umpire made a great call in calling him safe, but as soon as he called him safe he turned around and slapped his thigh and said, "Oh, shit!", 'cause he realized what he had done. That kind of was a letdown. We finally ended up winning the ball game but I don't remember what the score was. That could have been the greatest thrill I would've had, especially with the last one being against my father. I would've remembered that one. Bu the other shutouts, no. You always want to shut the other team out, but I didn't pitch that many.

We had a guy for the Browns who came up — God knows where he came from, San Antonio or somewhere. Bobo Holloman. Bobo had 20 line drives and 27 outs and pitched a no-hitter in St. Louis. Sure, it's a no-hitter and you're proud of it, etc., but, my God, there were line drives all over the park and everything happened to be hit right at somebody.

[It was Holloman's first major league start and it was the first, and only, time this century that a pitcher tossed a no-hitter in his first start. He found fame fleeting, however, and was back in the minors, never to return, before the season was over.]

Anytime you have a perfect ball game, you not only have to pitch well, but your control has to be a little bit better than average because you usually walk somebody during a ball game. Not only that, but you have to be fortunate where somebody doesn't make an error. Those things happen quite readily. I think in order to pitch a perfect ball game, you *do* have to be lucky.

I may have pitched better in other games than the would-be perfect game, but I think I remember that because I *didn't* get the perfect ball game because of the play.

Speaking of your father, he pitched forever—29 years.

Yes, he did. He was my idol. They put pretty good stuff in those farm boys at that time. He has the record for the most games pitched in the Coast League [704] and he broke it, I believe, in 1940 or '41 and he pitched through 1945. He was a relief pitcher at that time. It was 629 or thereabouts when he broke it. In 1934, they gave him the name "Old Folks" and he was a starting pitcher at that time and continued to be a starting pitcher for another several years.

[Herman Pillette also holds the record for most years pitched in one minor league — 23 in the PCL (1920–21, 1925–45). His brother, Ted, was also a minor league pitcher.]

Who was the best pitcher you saw?

There's a lot of reasons why one person will think one's a better pitcher than another. I liked people who went out and took charge of things and I also liked a type of pitcher who would be a stopper.

I think as far as being a stopper was concerned—he was *not* the best pitcher that I'd ever seen, but as far as having to win a ball game—I thought Vic Raschi was probably one of the better ones. As far as being a tough pitcher who would intimidate the hitter—Early Wynn, and I never saw the guy hit anybody, okay—but he let you know, "Don't dig in on me!" He was a tough Indian, he really was. I think the Cleveland staff amazed me more than anything else, rather than just thinking about one pitcher.

I liked Whitey Ford an awful lot, but Whitey was the kind of guy that had a very large ego for not a very big man and if you crushed his ego a little bit, whatever, then you could get the best of him. I thought Mel Parnell was a hell of a pitcher. He was not a very big man and he pitched in a tough ballpark with Boston and won 20-some ball games a couple of times. That's a tough ballpark for a left-hander.

There were a lot of good pitchers and I never really thought of one. I couldn't compare myself with those people 'cause I felt like I wasn't on their level, but what about the best hitter you ever pitched against? In my theory, I thought [Ted] Williams was probably the greatest hitter I *ever* pitched against, although there were a lot of *real* good hitters. One guy that I only pitched against a few times, 'cause we only played them in spring training, was [Stan] Musial, but he was an entirely different type of hitter than Ted. Ted was this kind of hitter: He said, "I don't give a damn if you put 12 guys on the field. If I hit the ball good, you're not gonna catch it anyhow." And he proved it.

When he hit .400, he could have been removed that last day but what'd he do? He went out and got six hits in the doubleheader. But he was that kind of guy. Had he not been called over to Korea, God knows how great he would have been. He missed a lot of good years right out of the center of his career when he was hitting the ball real, real good.

Who was the best all-around player you saw?

I didn't play with Joe [DiMaggio] that much — he quit in '51 and I saw him at the tail end of his career. When I first went up in 1949 I thought he was the greatest ballplayer I ever saw. He made everything look so easy. He had a great arm. Even though he didn't look like he could run, he ran real well.

He played the hitters so well. I remember one time I was pitching against Cleveland and Larry Doby was a *good* low-ball hitter. I threw him a sinker and he hit the hell out of the ball to center field. I turned around and thought, "Oh, my God," and Joe just ran and ran and ran and stopped and turned around and hit his glove with his hand and caught the ball. I played with a lot of guys who were good outfielders but they made plays look a lot tougher than they really were, or maybe that was their style of catching, but Joe just made it look so easy.

Basically, base running, throwing, hitting, fielding — he was probably one of the greatest ballplayers that I saw, but I only saw him that short period of time when he was really playing good ball. He admitted that the slider was his downfall. He said, "I can't hit that goddamned thing! I think it's a fastball and I can't pick the sucker up. I'm just not gonna play anymore."

And Joe didn't have the best ballpark to hit in. The left-center field fence was nine miles and center field — you couldn't hit the ball out of center field. Even [Mickey] Mantle couldn't hit the ball out of center field and he hit the longest balls I ever saw.

I think Mick could have been one of the greatest all-around ballplayers, but he had some problems. He had bad legs. He was so muscular he used to pull muscles in his legs. He'd tape himself before the ball games so he wouldn't pull muscles. He couldn't steal bases because I think he had osteomyelitis — if he broke a leg he might lose it or something of that nature. I think he could have been and should have been one of the greatest all-around, but he just had problems and couldn't go all out. He sure was a hell of a ballplayer.

He tore me up pretty good. I liked to pitch him away even though he could not hit that ball hard up and in. If you could hum that ball a little up and in, you could strike him out a *lot*. The guys that could throw that ball hard up and in could strike him out. Well, I tried, but I couldn't. And it was dangerous — if I missed a little bit it was adios. I found that out in a hurry. When he broke in, he probably hit his second home run off me. Maybe it was his first.

I pitched him low and away, and he used to hit those line drives or little one-hop line drives back to the box and just kill me. I was always knocking 'em down or trying to knock 'em down or get the hell out of the way or something.

One of your ex-teammates, J. W. Porter, said that Mantle in 1956 was the best ballplayer in the history of the game.

I think that what happens is that each ballplayer sees something that he really admires and maybe it's just that one year or maybe it's just that one series. That's why I say Joe; I saw him do things in 1949 I've never seen any ballplayer do. Line drive hit over second base and he comes in and catches it off his shoetops and the next ball's hit 455 or 460 feet to center field and he turns around and waits for the ball. You wonder, "What the hell is this guy?!"

And you watch him run — he was no Willie Mays as far as running was concerned, but he was a lot faster than he looked. He was a loper but he covered ground and he played the game so instinctively well that anybody that says there was a better ballplayer, I'd have to see him.

While we're talking about hitters, you hit a home run.

(Laughs) Yeah. One. We were in Philadelphia and I think the pitcher was Marion Fricano — no big name, no more than I was. We were both playing for bad ballclubs. He threw me a fastball right down the middle with two strikes on me and I just swung. I hit the ball as good as I'd ever hit it and it went into the upper deck.

The nice thing about it: My father never really had much opportunity to see me play because he was playing. This was a *Game of the Week* on a Saturday — God knows why the Browns and the Athletics got on the *Game of the Week* — and he happened to see that ballgame when I hit the home run. (Laughs) That made me feel good. I hit one home run in my whole life. I didn't even hit any in the minor leagues.

Did you save souvenirs?

No. My wife would sometimes make me bring home the newspaper when I pitched a ball game [on the road] and she tried to save a few things. Some of the clippings got lost; we were in a flood in '48, when I was with Portland, and a lot of things she had saved from college — I met her in college — and semipro ball got so wet she couldn't save them.

What we have are a few things here and there. She said, "Let's put it together in a scrapbook and maybe the grandkids will know who you were." So we started doing that, but we haven't finished it yet. Before I leave this earth I suppose I'll get it done.

Where did you go to college?

University of Santa Clara, one of the best colleges in the world. In fact, when I came back I spent 14 years on the Board of Fellows for them. I didn't complete college. The service came along and I got married when I was in the service and when I started pro ball my second child was born in spring training, so I had two children and a wife to take care of, so I never got a chance to go back.

Do you ever see any of your old teammates?

Don Larsen had his 35th anniversary for his perfect ball game and he had it down in Gilroy [California]. There must have been 300 people there anyhow and probably in the neighborhood of a hundred ballplayers. It was in the Elks Club and I walked in and Charlie Silvera, who was my catcher in Portland and with the Yankees — we're pretty good buddies — was standing next to this gentleman and he said, "Hey, Dee! Do you recognize this guy?"

And it was Jim Turner, the pitching coach — 88 years old. I'll be willing to bet you the guy looks as good as I did and I wasn't 70 yet. It was wonderful to see him. Jim was my manager for two years and also pitching coach when I was with the Yankees. I really admired Jim. I thought he was a great, great guy and a great pitching coach.

Hank Bauer was there and Tommy Henrich was there and Moose Skowron was there. We must have had ten or twelve ex–Yankees from the area. Bill Renna was there. It was great to see those guys.

Do you receive fan mail?

I average 12 or so a month. About every other day. They send a card or whatever. Some even ask for pictures — hell, I ran out of pictures years ago. I sign. Why not? I'm thankful that they want my autograph, that they remember me.

Any regrets from your career?

I don't think so. I suffered a number of injuries that set me back. Everybody wishes that they hadn't gotten hurt.

My first year I pulled a groin muscle in the playoffs at Montreal when I was at Newark. They were taking five or six of us up — Raschi was on our ballclub, and Yogi [Berra] and Jerry Coleman and Frank Coleman, an outfielder. They were taking us up for the last few weeks of the season and I pulled this groin muscle and they taped it. I pitched the last game and I injured it so badly that I couldn't go up. I think that's a regret, along with the other injuries.

Would you do it again?

Sure.

DUANE XAVIER (DEE) PILLETTE
Born July 24, 1922, Detroit, Michigan
Ht. 6'3"   Wt. 195   Batted and Threw Right

Year	Team	G	IP	W	L	Pct	BB	SO	H	SHO	SV	ERA
1949	**NYA**	12	37.1	2	4	.333	19	9	43	0	0	4.34
1950	**NYA**	4	7	0	0	.000	3	4	9	0	0	1.29
	StLA	14	73.2	3	5	.375	44	18	104	0	2	7.09
1951	StLA	35	191	6	*14	.300	115	65	205	1	0	4.99
1952		30	205.1	10	13	.435	55	62	222	1	0	3.59
1953		31	166.2	7	13	.350	62	58	181	1	0	4.48
1954	BalA	25	179	10	14	.417	67	66	158	1	0	3.12
1955		7	20.2	0	3	.000	14	13	31	0	0	6.53

Year	Team	G	IP	W	L	Pct	BB	SO	H	SHO	SV	ERA
1956	PhiN	20	23.1	0	0	.000	12	10	32	0	0	6.56
Yankee years		**16**	**44.1**	**2**	**4**	**.333**	**22**	**13**	**52**	**0**	**0**	**3.86**
Career		188	904	38	66	.365	397	305	985	4	2	4.40

*Led League

Courtesy National Pastime

BILL RENNA
Baseball Over Football

Yankees 1953

Bill Renna started his professional baseball career a little later than most. He had been in the military and completed college before turning to baseball in 1949. Even then, he had to consider other offers. He had been drafted by teams in two professional football leagues and was considered a top prospect, but baseball was his first love and he elected to try his hand there.

Joining Twin Falls of the Pioneer League well into the season, he started off with a bang. In only 330 at bats, he hit 21 home runs to lead the league, drove in 96 runs, batted .385, and slugged .667, also a league-leading figure.

He continued to show power in the minors. In 1951, with the 3-I League's Quincy team, he led the circuit in homers, this time with 26, and in '52 with Kansas City, he belted 28, second in the American Association to teammate Bill Skowron's 31. But the Yankee outfield of that era was a tough one to crack. (That is the most oft-repeated phrase in this book and we're not always talking about the same era.) In 1953, Renna spent the entire season in New York, but with an outfield quartet of Mickey Mantle, Gene Woodling, Hank Bauer, and Irv Noren, he found little playing time and had only 104 at bats as an outfielder.

Still, he did well, batting .314 in his limited action. There was reason to hope for more playing time in 1954, but he was traded. The Philadelphia Athletics of this day were not unlike the St. Louis Browns — no money and little talent, with a minor league system bereft of prospects. Anyone who showed anything was usually traded away for unproven players of potential who then manned the various positions around Shibe Park until they, too, showed enough to be traded away in return for more prospects. Such was the case with Renna. He and five other excellent prospects were sent to the A's for two proven players, Harry Byrd and Eddie Robinson.

And it enabled the A's to field a lineup that would have been difficult to do otherwise. Renna, Jim Finigan, and Vic Power were everyday players; Don Bollweg and Jim Robertson shared playing time at their respective positions; and John Gray joined the rotation at mid-season. Finigan led the club in hitting and Renna was second in team RBIs, but this, Philadelphia's last season in the American League, was a disaster as they won only 51 games and finished 60 games behind Cleveland. The next year, the A's were in Kansas City.

Renna again became Yankee property in 1956, when, interestingly, he was traded back to the Bronx Bombers for Eddie Robinson.

Did you sign originally with the Yankees?

Bill Renna: I did, yeah, when I graduated from Santa Clara University in 1949.

You were an excellent college football player. Were you drafted?

Yes, I was drafted by the L.A. Rams and the L.A. Dons. That's when they had the All-American Conference. The Dons wanted to use me as a linebacker and blocking back in the single wing and the Rams wanted to use me as a center/linebacker.

Why did you choose baseball?

I always wanted to play baseball since I was a young kid, and I figured I'd fare better financially and physically and play longer in baseball.

You were a tremendous power hitter in the minor leagues.

Yeah, I had my days.

Your first season was one of the better seasons ever.

Well, I got started well and just continued hot. I was kind of a streak hitter. When things were going well, they went *real* well and then there were times when I wasn't that good.

When you first came up, the Yankees had a pretty tough lineup. Did you think you had a chance there?

I knew there was one place open in the outfield, that was understood, and I was hoping it would be me. I figured I had a pretty good chance in lieu of what happened the year before at Kansas City. I had a fair year [in Kansas City]; I played right field and then center field when the center fielder got hurt early in the season. I was the most experienced outfielder. They had Bill Skowron in left and Bob Cerv playing in right. We had a pretty powerful ball-club there.

[The 1952 Kansas City Blues had a very strong lineup, led by minor league Player of the Year Bill Skowron (31-134-.341), Renna (28-90-.295 in 110 games), Cerv (12-48-.297 in 60 games), Vic Power (16-109-.331, 46 doubles, 17 triples), Don Bollweg (23-81-.325), and Kal Segrist (25-92-.308). The pitching was led by veteran Ed Erautt (21-5). In spite of all these, the Blues finished the regular season in second place, 12 games behind the Milwaukee Brewers, to date the last American Association team to win 100 games, but K.C. bounced back to win the playoffs, 4 games to 3.]

After batting over .300 as a part-time Yankee in 1953, you were traded to the Athletics after the season. What did you think of that?

At the time I was kind of surprised because it was mentioned to me after the season that I'd be all right for the next year because the Yankees were going to make some trades. I thought that meant I'd be all right as far as the Yankees were concerned, but I was one of the two off the major league roster who were traded. And there were a number of others in the minor leagues who went with us to the A's for Harry Byrd and Eddie Robinson. It was a big trade. I thought it would be an opportunity for me and it was. I was able to play regularly, but unfortunately I didn't have the year I wanted to have.

It [a trade] does have an effect. You grow up in an organization that had winners and had the winning attitude, then you go to a poorer team. My roommate with the Yankees, Don Bollweg, and I were traded and remained roommates with the A's. It was very unfortunate for us. It was a good opportunity, but it just didn't work out.

They moved the franchise to Kansas City in '55 and I was there in '55 and part of '56 and then they traded me back to the Yankees, who in turn

Bill Renna *(courtesy New York Yankees)*

sent me to Richmond in the International League. That was in June. I finished the year out there and told the Yankees if I was going to play minor league ball I wanted to play on the [West] Coast. They said they'd try to get me back in the major leagues.

I had a fair year there at Richmond. I got screwed over in the draft. They shifted me to their Denver roster in the American Association. They moved so-called suspects from Richmond over to Denver. At that time, if one man was drafted off a minor league club it would freeze the roster. They could only lose one. It was a maneuver that was done and part of the game. It hurt some of the players, but that's the way it went.

At Richmond I hit .314 or .317 from the time I got there in June until the end of the year and I hit, I think, 20 home runs and had 75 runs batted in or something like that. Then they wanted me to report to Richmond again the next year and I said no. I said I'd quit if I can't play in San Francisco.

The Yankees traded me to the Boston Red Sox and they sent me to the Seals. I think Eli Grba and Gordy Windhorn and $10,000 went to the Yankees and I went to the Red Sox. I went right to spring training with the San Francisco Seals and spent the year there. The Red Sox took me up in '58. I was with them all that year and part of '59 and they sold me to the San Diego Padres in the Coast League and I retired after that year.

Who was the best player you saw?

I was fortunate enough to go to spring training with Joe DiMaggio in 1950. Joe was probably the best, but I played with Ted Williams, I played with Mickey Mantle. I spent some time with Enos Slaughter, but he didn't compare with the rest of these guys. Yogi Berra, [Jim] Piersall, [Jackie] Jensen — I was very fortunate to play with some great ballplayers, but I think Joe DiMaggio was far and away the best. The only thing is that I didn't see Joe when he was in his prime. Yes, Joe, without a doubt, but Ted Williams was up there, too.

What about pitchers?

Billy Pierce was the toughest guy for me to hit. He was a left-hander and I was a right-hander, but that's the way it is. Fortunately I saw Bob Feller at the tail end of his career. Mike Garcia was tough. Cleveland had the good pitching — Garcia, Feller, Herb Score, but I think I only faced him once before he got hurt, Bob Lemon. [Bob] Turley was pretty tough. I didn't face many right-handers when I was with the Yankees, mostly left-handers because that's the way [Casey] Stengel played it.

Whitey Ford was very crafty. Eddie Lopat was probably the craftiest of them all. He was very difficult to hit because he had a lot of motion, a lot of change of speeds, and very good control. I played for him when I was at Richmond — he was the manager — and I couldn't even hit him in batting practice! He was uncanny. And a great guy, too.

Is there a game that stands out?

The game I probably remember the most is the day our son was born. I was with the Yankees in '53 and my wife was in Lennoxville Hospital in New York giving birth to Barry. She called me just before we went out on the field. Ted Gray was pitching for Detroit and I was starting that day because he was a left-hander. The first time up I hit a home run. That was probably the biggest thrill to that point in my life. I was very, very happy but when I got to the bench everybody gave me the silent treatment. Then the following year,

I hit another home run on his birthday. Then the year after I was on the bench so I didn't have a chance.

I had some hot streaks when I was with the Kansas City Blues. I think I hit seven or eight home runs in a span of five or six or seven days. And when I was with the Seals, too, I used to get hot.

There have been a lot of changes in baseball since you began playing professionally nearly 50 years ago. What do you think are the major changes?

Number one, the money is unbelievable. It kind of blows your mind to think of guys making a couple million dollars a year. But that's due to television. Without TV, the owners couldn't do it. The owners complain about the large salaries, but I think it's due to their own greediness. They've allowed themselves to get in the position they're in.

And I think the pension plan has been enhanced considerably; I think it's great for the players. Fortunately, I was able to participate because they dropped it from a five-year man to a four-year man. I missed five years by 71 days. I've been drawing a small pension since I was 50 years old. You can take it at 45 if you want.

The current players have a tremendous pension plan available to them, but the guys in the beginning who did a lot of the leg work and who contributed financially to the plan aren't really getting their just dues. Naturally I'm prejudiced, but I think they should be enhanced, too. Early Wynn and his group have tried to get a few things mandated so that some money can be put in for the older guys.

In my day I was just a chattel. I wanted to play and that's the way it was. Now there's so many options — a two-year man, a three-year man, arbitration, and all. I don't know the technicalities but it gives them more flexibility and the players are in a better position.

What was your top salary?

I earned $15,000 at the time I quit. My first year out I heard on the radio the average major league ballplayer makes $15,000 and the average major league ballplayer plays four years. I think what they were doing was talking about the pension plan, but it sounded like the guy was talking about me. I guess you can say I was average.

I wish I could have started a little sooner. I was 27 before I got to the major leagues. I had gone in the service, but I always felt if I'd have had a few more years to work at it I might have been a better player. I had to work hard. I wasn't a natural, I guess. I had to hustle like hell and there were always two or three people after your job.

I think the Yankees held me back. They wanted me to go down to Puerto Rico and play in the winter there, but I'd been down there in '53 and if they didn't know what I could do by then, for crying out loud, another winter wasn't going to show them. I just didn't want to do that.

About a year or two after I quit, they had the expansion teams. Maybe I could have hooked on, but I was ready to quit. I was married and had three kids and I had my obligations.

What did you do when you left baseball?

I had a business degree. I went to work in sales and I've been in construction and sales ever since. I've been in various parts of construction — general contracting, subcontracting. I've been very comfortable in what I've been doing. I've enjoyed it.

Did you save souvenirs from your career?

Not very many. I've got a bag out in the garage. It's got a glove in it and an old pair of shoes. I've got some bats, some World Series bats, and a World Series tray and some trophies I won.

Do you get much fan mail today?

Yeah, I get maybe one or two a week, maybe a little more. The baseball card situation has created a lot of this. What bothers me is sometimes they'll send maybe 12 index cards and want me to sign all of them. I sign one or two cards and send a note asking them not to send all those cards. They're commercial guys. I don't mind signing somebody's card — it's fine — but I sure don't want to have somebody making money off my signature.

I really have mixed emotions on card shows and charging for autographs. I can't see myself doing that. Seeing some of these guys — Bob Feller and guys like that who you have a lot of respect for — sit down and sign for money, I just don't know how it looks. I know they're paid for it and then the fans are charged, but I just don't like it.

I've had offers [to do shows]. They really don't want a Bill Renna, anyhow; they want a [Jose] Canseco or somebody like that who's a big star. That guy's got the wrong outlook. He's obligated to do certain things; it's not a one-way street. Like not showing up to meet the president. He's got to take care of his ballclub, to show he's a human being.

If you had it to do again, would you?

Yes, sir! Even knowing I ended up like I did, I'd do it tomorrow. I was fortunate; I had a World Series ring my first year. Most guys never get one. I made decent money. When I was through, I was through. I never looked back.

What advice would you give a kid who wants to play baseball?

If he really wants to play, he's got to bear down, he's got to hustle, he's got to learn as much about the game as he can and pay attention. The most important thing is practice. Learn as much as he can about hitting, learn to play his position. But, mainly, practice. And hustle.

What about education?

Oh, yeah! It helps considerably, especially if you're fortunate enough to go to a place that has good coaching. I was fortunate because Paddy Cottrell was my coach. He was well-versed in professional baseball and he taught us the basics. When I went into professional baseball they were trying to teach us things I was taught in college.

It also gives you something you can put in your pocket and when you need that education and can use it, it's there. And the clubs know you have that education, you're not just some stumblebum that will hang on. It's an ace in the hole. I have a business management degree. It makes you so much more flexible.

Go to college, get your degree, play your baseball. Learn and hustle.

WILLIAM BENEDITTO (BIG BILL) RENNA
Born October 14, 1924, Hanford, CA
Ht. 6'3"   Wt. 218   Batted and Threw Right

Year	Team	G	AB	R	H	2B	3B	HR	RBI	SB	BA	SA
1953	**NYA**	**61**	**121**	**19**	**38**	**6**	**3**	**2**	**13**	**0**	**.314**	**.463**
1954	PhiA	123	422	52	98	15	4	13	53	1	.232	.379
1955	KCA	100	249	33	53	7	3	7	28	0	.213	.349
1956		33	48	12	13	3	0	2	5	1	.271	.458
1958	BosA	39	56	5	15	5	0	4	18	0	.268	.571
1959		14	22	2	2	0	0	0	2	0	.091	.091
Yankee years		**61**	**121**	**19**	**38**	**6**	**3**	**2**	**13**	**0**	**.314**	**.463**
11 years		370	918	123	219	36	10	28	119	2	.239	.391

STEVE SOUCHOCK
A Career of Bad Breaks

Yankees 1946, 1948

The breaks did not go well for Steve Souchock. First, when he first made the Yankees' 40-man roster, World War II, where he was a decorated war hero, took him for three years. When he returned in 1946 after those three lost seasons, he was kept on the Yankees' roster because of the rule in effect then to protect the jobs of returning servicemen. He wasn't ready to play in the major leagues at that point, so he sat for most of the season, hence a fourth lost year.

Later, after a trade to the White Sox, he was caught in a power struggle between people in the front office and once again saw limited playing time. Then things went pretty well in Detroit, and he was a key man off the bench for the Tigers for three years. Finally, he had earned a regular job; he was scheduled to be the Bengals' regular right fielder in 1954. But the bad breaks kept coming. In the winter before the '54 season, he crashed into a wall while playing in Havana and fractured his wrist. The Tigers made do with a kid named Al Kaline instead of Steve that year and that essentially ended his career.

Even with the breaks against him, Steve Souchock had an eight-year career in the major leagues and says baseball was good to him.

You began your professional career in 1939. Did you originally sign with the Yankees?

Steve Souchock: No. I signed with a local team, Greensburg [Penn State League]. They sold me to New York. I was there [Greensburg] five, six weeks and then I was with the Yankees right along, and then I went back with them a little later on.

The Yankees bought me that first year I was in baseball. I went to Easton, Maryland [Eastern States League], from June on in '39 and then I was with Akron [Mid-Atlantic League] the following year. I had a good year there [25-105-.310].

You were the Eastern League MVP in 1942 at Binghamton, leading the league in runs, hits, doubles, triples, RBIs, and batting average.

Right. I had a good year. Right after the season I went to the service. I was in three years with old General George Patton.

When you came out in 1946 you spent the season with the Yankees. Were you on the protected list?

Yeah. I suppose at the time it was a good rule that they try to do something for the GIs that came home, but in my case, and I'm sure many other cases, it hurt me because I had missed three years of baseball already and I wasn't ready to play for the Yankees. We kept 30 players in those days and I wanted to go back to the minor leagues to see if I could still play. Because of the rules, they had to have waivers on me and when they put me on waivers somebody claimed me, so I sat around and missed almost a full season. I got a little chance to play, but I needed to go someplace where I could play every day, so in a sense you might say I lost four years.

In 1947 you went to Kansas City (American Association) and had a big year (17-99-.294).

I didn't get to playin' down there — to play real good ball — until late June. You know, I missed all those years. When you miss that length of time and are not doin' any playin', it's very difficult to start over again and get back in your old form.

When I had that good year [in 1942], I was put on the 40-man roster. I was just a kid — I was goin' up to the big leagues at 23. It looked like a good future at that time, but when you miss all that time you've gotta, in a sense, start all over again.

You were traded to the White Sox for the 1949 season and it looked like a good opportunity for you but it didn't work out. What happened?

Again, I didn't get much chance to play there. I was kinda caught in the middle between Frank Lane and Jack Onslow. Jack Onslow was hired before Frank Lane and those two didn't get along. After Frank Lane came, he got me from the Yankees and Onslow made the statement out in Anaheim, California, at a Chamber of Commerce breakfast that the players he had had at Memphis had got up to the big leagues and he had to take care of 'em. That put me back out in left field and I didn't get much playin'. I don't remember how much I played there; I played some outfield, a little bit of first base.

They sent you to Sacramento in the Pacific Coast League the next year and you had another real good season (30-99-.291) and the Tigers drafted you.

The story I've been told is they were fightin' for a pennant in 1950 and they tried to make a deal for me with Sacramento, but Jo Jo White, the general manager, wanted too much for me, so Billy Evans [Tigers' general manager] says why should we pay that much for him, we'll take him in the draft. So that's what happened. [White wanted cash and a couple of players.]

From what they told me in Detroit, they needed somebody to fill in and pinch hit. I think they lost the pennant by just a few ball games in 1950. They needed a player to come in once in a while and deliver as a pinch hitter, a spot player. They drafted me and I stayed there for several years.

Jo Jo White was an old Tiger and he wouldn't do his old team a favor.

He was the general manager and naturally when you're making a deal you're trying to get the best you can for yourself. I had a great year out there and he thought I was worth more than Detroit was willing to pay, so he lost me [in the draft] and got much less than he would have otherwise. That's a gambling situation that you've got to take once in a while.

For three years you were the number one man off the bench for the Tigers.

Yeah. I did a fairly good job there. Utility player — I played most all the positions and did some pinch hitting.

You broke your wrist in 1954 and that cost you almost the entire season.

That cost me my career.

You closed it out the next year with a pinch hit single.

I really couldn't play anymore. I lost my power. I broke my right wrist. I came in to pinch hit against Herb Score and I got a line drive single to center field. I might be the only player that hit a thousand and went to the minor leagues. (Laughs)

How did you break the wrist?

I ran into a wall in Havana, Cuba, trying to catch a fly ball. I was playin' in the Winter League. I really wasn't that anxious to go because I had a pretty good year with Detroit and they kept buggin' me down in Havana. The guy was in the States chasin' me all over and he made the deal so good that I had to go.

After that at-bat, where did you go?

I went to manage Little Rock, Arkansas, in the Southern League for the Detroit Tigers. I managed there for a year and a half. I went down there, I think, in late June and I finished that year and the next year.

Then Lee MacPhail with the Yankees got in touch with me. Lee MacPhail is a very fine and honest man and he used to bring some older guys that come up through the Yankee organization back and put 'em to work. He asked me to manage and I went to Binghamton [Eastern League] and stayed there two years and then I went to Richmond in the International League for two years as manager. Then I went troubleshootin' for the Yankees for a lot of years.

I was with 'em 'til 1975, when the [Major League Scouting] Bureau came into existence. Then I was with the Bureau and had to retire because my wife had been real sick. After she passed away, the Tigers put me on.

You spent more than 50 years in baseball. What's the biggest change?

Players in the old days had more fun playin'. With the long term contracts, I'm not sure everybody's puttin' out. There's some that always try hard, some really good ballplayers.

I think players in the old days were a little more generous and helped the younger guys more so than they do today. There was a lot of compassion. Just to give you a little idea, when the pension started in 1946, each player had to put in $250. People like myself, and there was many of us, that had just come home from service, didn't have any money. Two hundred fifty dollars was a lot of money. There was five of us on that [Yankee] ballclub, just like there was on every ballclub — the extra five players who made it 30 — and there was three players on the Yankees that came up to me — and I'm sure some of 'em went to the others — and said, "Listen, if you don't have the money, we'll put it in for you. If you ever get it, pay us back; if you don't, don't worry about it." I'll never forget that.

When I was with the Yankees, the first four clubs finish in the money and everybody gets a little bit, includin' the clubhouse boys and the groundskeepers and the bat boys. I can remember not too many years ago,

Steve Souchock *(courtesy Detroit Tigers)*

and I'm not gonna mention the club, one club didn't give their bat boy a quarter. It was very embarrassing. Even though we didn't win the pennant the couple years I was there [with the Yankees], they didn't leave anybody out. Nowadays I've heard some stories, whether they're true or false, they don't cut a lot of people in.

There's so much money bein' made in baseball today by the players — which I'm not faultin' them at all — but I don't think they share as much as they did in the old days. What would it cost each player to give a couple thousand [from his World Series share]? What difference would it make if he got a hundred thousand or ninety-eight thousand? (Laughs) That's one of the changes.

There's a lot of good players around, but in the old days there was more good ballplayers on one club than there are today. Today they might have four or five real good ballplayers. In the old days, they had maybe eight or nine good players on the ballclub and some good ballplayers couldn't make the ballclub because there was that many good players. It's expansion. And they're gonna do it again.

That's why you see a lot of big scores. You'd go to Cleveland and they had Early Wynn and Bob Lemon and [Mike] Garcia; they had a great staff and they had a great bullpen. You'd play against Detroit and you got [Hal] Newhouser and [Virgil] Trucks and it would be a battle. And the Yankees and the Red Sox. Games used to be 2 to 1 and 3 to 2 and 1 to nothin'. You don't see that much anymore because that's the lack of pitchin'.

Who was the best pitcher you saw?

Satchel Paige was old. I'm not gonna say he was the best pitcher — there was a lot of good ones — but I remember in Detroit, Johnny Groth and Pat Mullin and myself was to pinch hit in the ninth inning against St. Louis and Satchel Paige was old in those days. He threw ten pitches and he struck three of us out and not one of us even hit a foul ball! (Laughs)

You gotta put Bob Feller in that category and Hal Newhouser and Allie Reynolds, and Vic Raschi was a good pitcher, and Bob Lemon. There was many, many of 'em in those days. Each club had at least three or four real *good* pitchers. It used to be a duel. Newhouser used to pitch against Feller and you had to scrape to get a run. But it was real interesting.

Is there one game that stands out?

Freddie Hutchinson is dead now and he was a great, great person, probably had as much respect as any ballplayer in baseball as a manager. He knew how to handle people and he was very competitive when he was a player. When he had taken over the Detroit job as the manager he had to coach third base for a week or so during the home stand. I hit a home run in the ninth inning against the Yankees, who were fightin' for a pennant; we weren't goin' anywhere. I hit the home run to win a ball game and that was his first night of managin' and he greeted me at third base and he run all the way to home plate with me. (Laughs)

That's why I got such a great kick out of it. I was tickled to death to hit the home run, but I was more tickled for Freddie Hutchinson. I had that much respect for him along with everybody else. He had a temper but he didn't hurt anybody. He was that competitive. He was one great, great person.

Who was the best player?

I can only speak of the American League. I'd have to say Joe DiMaggio was the most complete player I had seen. I didn't see that much of Willie Mays or Stan Musial. I would call Joe DiMaggio the complete player because he could do everything a little bit better than everybody else. He had a great arm, he was a great outfielder, he was a good hitter with power, he was a good base runner — he was a complete player.

Maybe Ted Williams might have been a better hitter, but overall I would say Joe DiMaggio, all-around, was the best player. And on top of that, he had a great attitude.

Do you receive much fan mail today?

I get some, not a lot. After all, I'm over 70 years old and I played many, many years ago, but I still do get mail. I would say two, three times a week. Autographs — pictures to sign.

There's some things I don't believe in; the players are signing autographs and chargin' for 'em. I never was a good ballplayer, but I'm never gonna charge anybody for anything like that. After all, these are the kids — it's their game. They're the future fans, they're the future ballplayers. In a sense, I can't fault the ballplayers because somebody's makin' a profit out of it and the ballplayers probably want their share, but for me I think it's wrong. I'm not sayin' it's wrong for them — to each his own — but I'm against it. You know, it's the people's game. They're the ones that really pay the salaries for the players.

Would you go back and be a ballplayer again?

I would have to say yes on that because that's all I know. I've spent my lifetime in baseball and it's been a very exciting life. It's had its ups and downs — you go 0 for 4 and you're on the bench.

It's very educational and you meet some really wonderful people in baseball and they stick together pretty close, particularly as you get a little older. You get to thinkin' about all the fun you had and all the good guys.

One thing that bothers me, and I've been fortunate — the good Lord's been good to me, number one I came home from the war and number two I've been healthy and been able to stay in the game — but you've got good ballplayers with money problems. Kenny Keltner was a great ballplayer for many, many years and he was getting that little pension. His wife was in a nursing home. He said if it wasn't for that Social Security he'd have probably had to go on relief.

They give us a pretty good raise [on the pension] but how many guys are left that are in my category — you know, that are 65, 75 years old — where they could have done that several years ago and made it easier on those guys that started this pension. That, I think, is a sour note to most of the old-timers.

Like I say, for me, I never made a lot of money and I was able to pay my bills, but I think about all the guys that played baseball that were good ballplayers in the old days and played in the big leagues for eight or ten or twelve years who are getting very little on the pension. I really don't know the rules anymore, but with this new contract that the players got, they did up that to a certain degree. How much, I don't know.

But this is what I'm talkin' about. If the players would have done that years ago — to give these people a chance once they get a little older to have a little better livin'. I don't think it's fair because the old-timers paid to get into it, started it. Early Wynn worked his tail off so the old-timers could get a little more money. He's been workin' for years. It's happened but it happened a little bit too late. There's an old saying, "Smell the roses while you're alive." A lot of 'em are gone.

Do you have any regrets from your career?

I don't think about it any more, but I did when I was younger. I thought I should have been a better ballplayer. For a big guy, I didn't have good speed but I run pretty good. I didn't have any outstanding tools — I had some power — but I had about average ability.

I think the wartime hurt me. I'm not complainin' about that at all. I had to go to war like everybody else and I came home, that's number one. After I came home from the war, I really never got a chance to play that much. I did a pretty good job as a utility player, but every year I played in the minors I had pretty good years. When I got to the big leagues I platooned. I suppose the record speaks for itself — it says I couldn't hit right-handers well. I never got that much of a chance to hit right-handers, so we'll never know. But I thought I should have been a better ballplayer. I'm not blamin' anybody for that. You can only blame yourself. I enjoyed the game and I've met a lot of wonderful, wonderful people.

When the Bureau started, a bunch of us were at Jacksonville and every day the telephone would ring and somebody would say, "I just got let go." Bill Fischer was really a hell of a guy and funny and I had a lot of laughs with that guy. I had taken him to dinner one night and he says, "Steve, you know you're really happy. You must have a job." And I says, "Fischer, I have a job but I don't know whether I'll have one when I get home. The only reason I wanted to take you to dinner — you and I had a lot of laughs together and if it wasn't for baseball I'd never have the opportunity to have those laughs with you because you may get fired, I may get fired, we *both* may get fired, but this is my way to say thank you for all the laughs. If it wasn't for baseball, I'd have never known you."

I took Jack Tighe to a ball game one day. Jack Tighe's an older guy and his wife died shortly after my wife died. He was like a little kid. He got a chance to be around some ballplayers. There was a couple scouts there. Cy Williams was workin' for the Tigers a long time and he and Jack had been together a long time and he was at the ball game. He was like a little kid. This is what happens when old guys get together. There's a lot to talk about; you don't see 'em too often. It's exciting.

STEPHEN (BUD) SOUCHOCK
Born March 3, 1919, Yatesboro, Pennsylvania
Ht. 6'2½"   Wt. 203   Batted and Threw Right

Year	Team	G	AB	R	H	2B	3B	HR	RBI	SB	BA	SA
1946	**NYA**	**47**	**86**	**15**	**26**	**3**	**3**	**2**	**10**	**0**	**.302**	**.477**
1948		**44**	**118**	**11**	**24**	**3**	**1**	**3**	**11**	**3**	**.203**	**.322**
1949	ChiA	84	252	29	59	13	5	7	37	5	.234	.409
1951	DetA	91	188	33	46	10	3	11	28	0	.245	.505
1952		92	265	40	66	16	4	13	45	1	.249	.487
1953		89	278	29	84	13	3	11	46	5	.302	.489
1954		25	39	6	7	0	1	3	8	1	.179	.462
1955		1	1	0	1	0	0	0	1	0	1.000	1.000
Yankee years		**91**	**204**	**26**	**50**	**6**	**4**	**5**	**21**	**3**	**.245**	**.387**
Career		473	1277	163	313	58	20	50	186	15	.255	.457

BOB TURLEY
New York Finally Got Him

Yankees 1955–1962

*From 1949 through 1953—five straight years—the New York Yankees
were the World Series champions. The team was strong everywhere; such
names as Joe DiMaggio, Yogi Berra, Mickey Mantle, Phil Rizzuto, Johnny
Mize, and Hank Bauer struck fear in the hearts of the rest of the American
League, and indeed in all of baseball.*

*The pitching staff was led by the legendary firm of Raschi, Reynolds, and
Lopat. Those three averaged 17 wins each for those five years. A junior part-
ner was brought in in this period and eventually he would gain the title of
Chairman of the Board. His name was Whitey Ford.*

*And there was a strong cast behind these four, Joe Page, Johnny Sain, Bob
Kuzava, Tom Morgan, Jim McDonald, Tom Gorman, Tom Ferrick, and Fred
Sanford all contributed at one time or another to this greatest of all dynasties.*

*But in 1954, the dynasty ended. The Yankees finished second to the Cleve-
land Indians. Although Raschi was gone, the pitching was still sound, but
Reynolds, who retired at the end of the season, and Lopat were getting old.
There were a few promising arms in the minors, but it did not look as if there
were enough quality arms to return the Yankees to the top.*

*So, as they had done so often in earlier years, the Yankees traded for what
they needed. In what is still the biggest trade in baseball history, New York
acquired what were probably the two best young pitching prospects in the AL
in 1954—Baltimore's Bob Turley and Don Larsen. The amazing thing about
the trade is that the Yankees did not give up a single player who figured in
their plans for 1955.*

*The trade worked. In 1955, the team moved back into first place, for four
more years. Turley and Larsen won at a .676 clip during that time.*

*Bullet Bob Turley, especially, was successful in Yankee pinstripes. In 1955,
his 17 wins were the second best total in the league, and in 1958 he led the
league with 21 wins, a .750 winning percentage, and 19 complete games. He
won the Cy Young Award and the Hickock Belt and finished second to Boston's
Jackie Jensen in the MVP balloting.*

*Against the Milwaukee Braves that October, in one of the outstanding
clutch performances in World Series history, Bob tossed a five-hit shutout in
Game 5, saved Game 6 two days later, and won Game 7 the next day with
six innings of two-hit relief. He ranks in the Top 10 in career World Series
numbers in four categories: games (15, third), starts (8, tenth), bases on balls
(29, fifth), and strikeouts (46, tenth).*

*Bob Turley left baseball after a year as the pitching coach for the Boston
Red Sox and has enjoyed much success in the securities business.*

*As a kid, I was not a Yankees fan but I was a Bob Turley fan. You should
feel honored.*

Bob Turley: I come from St. Louis and the Cardinals were my favorites
and I didn't like the Yankees until they got me.

*Is it true the Yankees thought they had signed you but actually signed your
uncle?*

That's 100 percent right. What happened is, my uncle is one year older than me and we went to high school together and he pitched on the high school team. I didn't pitch on the high school team 'til my senior year, reason being that I went out my freshman year and the coach had his baseball team all fixed. He wanted me to stay on the club to just pitch batting practice all year and not get into a game and I said I wasn't gonna do that. He had his basketball players on the team, so he kept them in shape doing that.

And then I was pitching in the muni league with the kids that were out of school, much older than I was, and I was a star down there. He was the umpire in the summertime, so he kept asking me to come out and finally my senior year I went out for the baseball team.

Then the Yankees had a tryout up in Marion, Illinois, and my uncle and I went up there together. We drove up in the same car. His name was Ralph and, of course, mine was Robert. Both "Rs."

We both signed up. They watched us both pitch and he was a pretty good ballplayer himself, but they wanted to sign me, so they looked in the phone book — they didn't have a phone number — and the only Turley in the phone book was my grandfather because my mother and father were divorced and my mother's name was Hale. So what they did, they called out to my grand- father's home and they said, "Is this the residence of a Turley that went to a tryout camp?" And they said, "Yes." They said, "Well, we'd like to sign him."

In the meantime, the St. Louis Browns had a guy pick up a couple of kids off the Eastside High team and take us over to work out with the Browns. I went over and threw over there, and they wanted to sign me right away but they couldn't because I was still in high school. The night of my graduation, the Yankees' scout went out to my grandfather's house and signed my uncle Ralph, and then a guy came out to my house and signed me up to pitch in the Browns' organization.

About a month later, he was playing for Marion, Illinois, in the Illinois State League in the Yankee organization and I'm pitching for Belleville in the same league in the Browns' organization. I go into Marion and I'm pitching that night and I beat the ballclub real bad. When the game was over, I went around to the clubhouse. My uncle and I were gonna go out and get some- thing to eat and they had his bags packed. I said, "Where are you going?" He said, "They released me. They told me they signed the wrong Turley." (Laughs)

He was a pretty good little hitter. He played second base and shortstop for about a year in that same Class D league, but he never did go on to do anything.

The guy that was responsible for that — missing me — became a good friend of mine with the Yankees. He wouldn't ever admit the story until later on when my career was over. He told me it was true.

In the minor leagues, control was a little problem but it sure didn't slow you down. You won 20 twice down there.

Control wasn't a problem. Control became a problem with me when they kept records. It's like today with the pitchers; they know everything about you, everything you're doing. In the minor leagues [then], nobody paid any attention. The object was to win a ball game and I'd win the ball games. I might give up three or four hits a game and I might walk five or six, but total men on base against me — I was always the lowest. Even in the big leagues with Bob Lemon, who at the time early in my career was one of the best pitchers up there, I ended up — my walks and hits — about 10 percent better than he was. He wasn't a strikeout pitcher; he was a sinkerball pitcher, but you always got a lot of hits off him.

Control, yes, definitely, was always my problem, but I think if you go back and look at any fastball pitcher, control's always a problem. The reason for that is because I can make a good pitch but the guy won't hit it. He swings and misses and I gotta pitch again. Or he foul-tips it and I gotta pitch again. With a guy like Eddie Lopat, sure, he had good control. Hell, when you throw up the stuff *he* was throwing up, they'd jump off their feet trying to hit it. I watched him pitch three innings and I didn't think he threw one strike, but he never walked a guy. The superstars — the Koufaxes, the Ryans — all those guys had problems with control for the reasons I'm telling you. Koufax got control later on.

You joined the Browns at the end of 1951 and pitched one game against the White Sox, then you went in the service.

Two years and two days. What I was, I was a voluntary draft. I was regular army but you had a privilege — and with me it worked out good because as soon as the season was over I wanted to get in the army. I was gonna be drafted and I wanted to go in so that I would save my leave time and then August or September two years later I could join a major league club and that all worked out good for me.

Did you play ball in the service?

Oh yeah. Two years down at Brook Army Medical Center, which was at Fort Sam Houston, Texas, in San Antone. I came out and finished the '53 season with St. Louis and pitched the whole year in '54 in Baltimore.

You were arguably one of the best two or three pitchers in the American League in 1954. There was supposed to be a rebirth of baseball in Baltimore, but it was still the Browns that year.

We just changed uniforms. We still had the same club.

At the end of that season, you were part of the biggest trade in baseball history. What did you think about it?

I was watching television up in Baltimore and I had my young son, Terry, and they flashed my picture on the screen and said, "Bob Turley and 17 other players involved in a trade with New York."

Oh my God! I jumped up and down and screamed! And I don't think the Baltimore Orioles ever called me. I had a lot of friends call me and say, "Don't you hate to go to New York?"

I said, "Yeah, I hate to go to New York. I'll *crawl* to New York." I lived in Baltimore, I liked Baltimore, but with that ballclub I don't know how many games I lost 1-to-nothing, 2-to-1, and all kinds of games like that. But to go to a club like New York that would score four to six runs on an average, that's a pitcher's delight.

Your record in New York in 1955 was 17-13 with a 3.06 ERA. You allowed only about six hits a game; it seems as if you should have maybe won a few more. What happened?

It's hard to say. I can't remember a tremendous amount of it, but you gotta remember, too, those were the years when there were few relievers. You pitched nine innings or whatever took place. I don't really know why I didn't win more ball games, but it seemed like I should have won 20 games that year.

You were used quite a bit less in 1956. Were you hurt?

No, I never got hurt. My arm never got hurt until later in my career. I had it operated on in 1961.

Casey [Stengel] was the type of manager who wouldn't let a pitcher lose a lot of ball games. I wasn't used as much. I think the starts were less, so I didn't start as much and the opportunity wasn't there. I did a little bit of relieving. Actually, all the relieving I did for the Yankees was good.

Those were the days when they weren't afraid to bring a starter in in relief occasionally.

I finished off a *lot* of ball games 'cause he used to put us in the bullpen the third day after you pitched. We'd go down there and warm up and loosen up 'cause you're gonna be pitching shortly. So we'd go down in the bullpen and if they needed you to get one or two men out or pitch an inning, we'd come in and pitch.

Certain pitchers would. Whitey Ford couldn't do that. Allie Reynolds could do it. Vic Raschi couldn't do it, but there was a couple guys who could start and relieve both.

The 1958 season was a fantastic year for you. One of the most amazing stats I've ever seen: that whole year you only gave up one unearned run.

That is unusual. I didn't even know that.

Even on a top fielding team, a starting pitcher will give up a few unearned runs over the course of a season. You must have had great defense behind you.

We did. Also, there's different types of pitchers and I'm not saying I was this type. There's some types of pitcher that when a guy makes an error behind you or something like that, then you get upset. I never got upset when guys made errors behind me, so I bore down twice as much to get us out of a jam. There are certain types of guys that get PO'd and they let more runs in when something like that happens. I'm not saying that's it, but anybody can pitch with nobody on base. It's pitching with men on base that's the true test.

You were clobbered in game two of the World Series that year.

I was knocked out of there in the first inning. I just couldn't get anybody out. I hadn't been very active in September, didn't have much pitching 'cause we'd won the pennant fairly early. I think I won only one game in the whole month of September. I won my 20th game, I know, on August the thirty-first and I only won one game in the whole month of September. I think my record was one and one that month, so I didn't do a lot of pitching.

And, honestly, I was a little rusty. They let me have a little rest and that was a good thing, but I think I was probably a type of guy that had to be pitching a lot.

You certainly came back and redeemed yourself.

In the fifth game, I shut 'em out in New York and we went to Milwaukee. In the sixth game, I came in to relieve Ryne Duren in the tenth inning and got the last out. And then in the seventh game, I came in in the third inning, I believe, and relieved Don Larsen. I gave up one run the rest of the game. Someone [Del Crandall] hit a home run off of me.

Perhaps your biggest claim to fame was your ability to steal signs.

(Laughs) Right. That's true. It is a special knack. I had good eyes and had good concentration. I didn't steal 'em by having me sitting out in the scoreboard or anything like that; I stole 'em right off the mannerisms of the pitcher. I used to look at pitchers and watch 'em 'cause everybody would pretty much have the same habits. When a guy's gonna throw a curveball, they do a variety of different things. We could have a conversation for an hour about all the different ways I would get 'em.

But I was also good at knowing pitchers and what style pitches they would pitch. For example, Mickey [Mantle]—I used to call a lot of pitches for him. I'd say, "Mickey, I feel comfortable I'm gonna call 90 percent right." He said, "Bob, go ahead and call 'em. Me guessing, I'm not as good as you. If you miss it, it ain't gonna kill me."

I used to do that a lot with Mickey and I was pretty accurate with that. Mickey was a great guy for me to give signs to because he wanted a certain pitch and he wouldn't swing until he got his pitch and he would make sure it would be a strike.

A lot of guys I would give signs to. A guy like Bill Skowron — hell, he'd swing at everything. Yogi would swing at everything. Good hitters and everything and they took the signs, too, but I had more luck with Mickey than anybody.

You whistled.

Yeah. Let me just tell you the signs so you'll understand.

Assume that a pitch has already been thrown and assume it's a curveball.

When I whistled, that changes the pitch from a curveball to a fastball, the next pitch. Now if I whistle again on the next pitch, it changes that from a fastball to a curveball. So nobody knew. I would be whistling on fastballs, whistling on curveballs, so nobody ever knew whether we had 'em.

Then Mickey had a sign with me that if I would miss a pitch, he would rub his hat. What would happen then, we'd start all over again. Sometimes he would forget what the last pitch was so he'd give me a sign to start all over again. (Laughs) I had a very shrill whistle so he could hear it because they were always making noise when he came up.

It sure seemed to work well for him.

It did. I can just remember so many games that we won.

There was another thing, too. Mickey was pretty intelligent himself. I would steal signs and I would tell him what was coming, but I would tell him and he would read 'em himself. For example, a guy by the name of Connie Johnson, his foot was on the right side of the rubber when he threw a normal pitch, but when he threw a screwball he would move over to the left. I told Mickey about that and Mickey just waited for him to throw a screwball and every time he did Mickey would like to kill somebody with it. Connie never could figure out why he'd get everybody else with the screwball but he couldn't get Mickey out.

Early Wynn was another one that I told all the guys *exactly* how to get his signs and they did it themselves. I talked to Early later on and he said, "No, I didn't do that," and I said, "Early, you did, partner."

Did this ability help you as a hitter?

Not really. I was just a fair hitter. I wasn't a good hitter. I didn't spend a lot of time at it, probably should've. I got a few hits and a couple home runs — nothing exceptional.

Four home runs — that's more than most pitchers ever hit. Do you remember any of them?

I remember every one of 'em. What do you mean? (Laughs)

The first one I hit was with the St. Louis Browns and I hit it in the left field seats off of the Senators' Sonny Dixon. Of the other three, one came off a left-hander from Baltimore — [Dave] McNally; I was with Los Angeles [Angels] at the end of my career when I hit that one. And then two home runs — I hit one off of Pedro Ramos and then one off of Bud Byerly [both Senators, both in 1958].

Talking about hitting, who was the best hitter?

There's no question. That would be Ted Williams. No question about that. I never saw the guy foul a ball off or break a bat.

How about the best ballplayer?

Well, you know, Mickey — played with him and I played against him and he had so much ability. I mean, the guy could run at the beginning, he

Bob Turley (*courtesy New York Yankees*)

could throw real good — he hurt his shoulder in the World Series sliding or
something like that. I think it was into second base with Milwaukee against
Red Schoendienst. He dislocated his shoulder and that kinda hurt him. And
he could just literally outrun balls in the outfield.

He could win a ball game for us quicker than anybody I've ever known.
I've seen him late in the pennant drives; he'd get on base — they'd walk him,
[or] he'd bunt to get on — he'd steal second, steal third, score on a ground ball
with the infield in. I've seen him do that numerous times.

J. W. Porter said that in 1956, Mantle was the greatest player who ever played the game of baseball.

I agree with him. Nobody could hit a ball further than him, nobody could run faster than him. He's the type of hitter, when he faced the pitcher — you know, some guys will just hit a home run 350 feet — hell, he hit 'em 450 feet! It's an intimidating thing against many pitchers.

Roger Maris —*great* ballplayer, he should get a lot more credit, not only as a hitter bur he was a great defensive ballplayer — but Roger wasn't a real *long* ball hitter. He was kind of a line drive hitter, but he didn't scare people like Mickey did. Look at the infield when Mickey was batting. All the infielders were back on the grass — everywhere —'cause he hit the ball so damned hard. They didn't do that on Roger.

In the beginning years when I was over there —'55, '56, '57, those three were special years, great years — he hit one- and two-hoppers to second base and beat 'em out. They couldn't play back too far, but later on when his knees were a little bad they could. But, still, he could get to first base in plenty of time.

Some say he was faster than Willie Mays in his early days.

There's no question about that. Willie Mays couldn't even carry a candle as far as speed. Now Willie was a great ballplayer. I didn't play against him except in exhibition games. Great defensive ballplayer and nobody could question his ability with a bat and running the bases. I mean, he was outstanding, but he couldn't hit the ball as far as Mantle and he couldn't run as fast as Mantle.

It would have been nice to see 20 years of healthy Mantle.

Ahhh. But he had a lot of years, probably more than he should. (Laughs)

Who was the toughest batter on you?

Nellie Fox. He would do everything. Nellie was one of my best friends and I just couldn't get the little sucker out. He'd get on base. I'd hit him with the ball or he'd bunt or I'd walk him. If he hit two home runs a year, he'd hit one off me. He was just a pesky guy.

Who was the best pitcher?

I'm just talking about a pure pitcher, not the Koufax ability: Whitey Ford. If I had to win a ball game, I'd take Whitey Ford. That little sucker could get out there — now he didn't throw a ball a hundred miles an hour, but he had good speed and he had a good, fast breaking ball and great control. He was really cagey and I've seen him stay in games when I thought he should come out and I've seen him come out when I thought he should stay in, you know. (Laughs) He was a money pitcher; you couldn't find a better guy than that. He just won the big games. They played him in the big games and he would come through.

It's been said if Stengel had pitched him every fifth day instead of holding him for the top teams, he'd have been a 20-game winner four or five more times.

Yeah, that's true. Casey believed in a six- and seven-man rotation and it was tough to win 20 games under Stengel. They didn't have a lot of 20-game winners for as many times as they won the pennant.

This was a very unfair criticism of the Yankees. You don't need a 20-game winner if you have ten guys winning ten apiece. Stengel used his pitchers well.

He sure did.

What was your best game?

I think the best game I ever pitched in the big leagues I lost. That was in a World Series against the Brooklyn Dodgers in 1956, the day after Don Larsen pitched his perfect game. Clem Labine pitched for Brooklyn. It was his first start in ages and he shut us out for ten innings and I lost, one to nothing. I gave up a run in the tenth inning.

In the game, Enos Slaughter misplayed some fly balls. The first fly ball was by Junior Gilliam and he came in, lost it in the sun, turned his back and the ball dropped down, and that was the first hit. The second hit was a ball hit down the left field line by Clem Labine and Enos ran over to the wall in Brooklyn — the wall was close to the foul line — and he hit the wall, fell down, and the ball landed behind him. The third hit was a ball that was hit to [Gil] McDougald and it bounced up real bad on him and it fell down and the guy [Duke Snider] got a base hit.

The fourth and final hit was in the bottom of the tenth with men on first and second and Jackie Robinson was the hitter. He hit a line drive right at Enos Slaughter. All he had to do was just stand still and catch the damned ball, but he came charging in and the ball went over his head and they beat us, one to nothing.

I think he had been in the National League a long time and, of course, he was older and he did a lot of things for us and I didn't try to blame him. Hell, he didn't want to miss the balls, we all knew that. I might have still been pitching today. We may not have scored a run yet.

Johnny Kucks won the next day, nine to nothing. Casey came to the Waldorf-Astoria after the game — I was just sitting over to the side, wasn't saying a lot, and he came over and said, "You know something? Of all the games I've ever seen pitched, the best was not Larsen's. It was the game you pitched and lost. I just want you to always remember that." So that made me feel good when he came up and said that to me.

I was home from school that day — I usually got "sick" at World Series time — and I thought Slaughter should have been given an error on the play, even though he didn't touch the ball.

Yeah, he didn't touch it. I'll tell you, you should have seen me standing on the mound. I said, "Oh, God! Stand still!" But he was old pure hustle, the Pete Rose–type of ballplayer, and he took off and there was no way he could change speeds once he was going.

Did you save souvenirs from your career?

Not a lot. What I did save, I saved all the baseballs that I could get my hands on where I was the winning pitcher, so I have all of those. I drew on all those balls the date, who I beat, how many hits, how many strikeouts. I've got all of those balls. I've got games of the World Series and I've got the first game in Baltimore that was ever played there when I beat the White Sox, 3 to 1. I've got a lot of different things like that.

They're important to me. People say, "Well, how do we know that's what it actually is?" And I say, "You don't, but I know it. They're mine. They're on my wall and you can't have 'em anyway." They aren't going anywhere, they're staying in my family.

In my home down in Marco Island I have two big circles, the shape of big baseballs, and then the seams are all baseballs and in the middle of one I have the Cy Young Award and in the other one I have the Hickock Belt Award.

That was a heck of a year.

Not so much I had a good year, everybody else had a bad year. (Laughs)

Any regrets from your career?

Oh, I don't know. You know, you look back on your career and I'm real happy with it. I tried to keep myself in sound physical shape all those years.

I think I should have been a little bit mentally stronger in changing my style of pitching a little earlier. I changed my style of pitching around 1958 and that's after ten years of pitching. Before that, all it was was just rear back and throw it and strike everybody out, but in '58 I started with the concept of making them hit the ball into the ground, getting my double plays. You know, hitting the ball on the fists, end of the bat, and I really became a pitcher. And I just wish that would have happened to me a little sooner, then maybe my career would have been prolonged a lot longer.

But, you know, it's hard to change. I'm real happy in the fact that I had the opportunity to play with a ballclub like New York and be in those World Series. It gives you something real special that people look up to.

Look at a guy like Robin Roberts — a pretty good pitcher but he never pitched on a championship team. One year they got a pennant — 1950 — and then they lost the World Series.

Would you go back and do it again?

Oh, boy. Comparing against what I do now and then going back and doing it again. If it brought back my youth, hell yes, I'd do it again.

I'm real happy with my life in every aspect. I don't have any regrets. I don't want to go back into baseball, I just want to be a fan and let the guys do it and enjoy themselves. I don't think baseball owes me a damned thing; I think I owe baseball a lot for giving me the name, the reputation. I'm thankful to the Orioles for trading me, I'm thankful to the Yankees for getting me, and all those things.

I enjoyed every moment of it. There's always frustrations in anything you do in life. I think the only thing that frustrated me a little bit is that I was hoping I would stay in baseball in the Yankee organization 'cause I felt like I did more than just pitch ball for them. I did a lot of things, but I understand organizations and what they do, so I don't have any grudges against any of that, either.

When you were with the Angels toward the end, there was talk of the possibility of you becoming a pitching coach.

They talked to me a little bit about it and what they did was release me and nothing happened. Then I went to Boston and then Boston made me pitching coach up there. I coached in '64 — pitching coach for Boston — but I made the mistake of working for a manager that the [front office] management didn't like and so they fired him and I went, too.

It was Johnny Pesky. [Pinky] Higgins was the guy, he's passed on now; his friend was Billy Herman, who was the third base coach, and he wanted Billy Herman to be the manager. Tom Yawkey liked Johnny Pesky 'cause he was everybody's favorite and he wanted him. It was a real conflict.

It was about the saddest year I've ever spent in my life. I saw a lot of talent, a tremendous amount of talent, but I saw an organization that just couldn't get along with each other. It was very frustrating. I've just seen too many people that were — like in the corporate world — everybody watching out for himself and not caring about what the whole thing does.

ROBERT LEE (BULLET BOB) TURLEY
Born September 19, 1930, Troy, Illinois
Ht. 6'2"   Wt. 215   Batted and Threw Right

Year	Team	G	IP	W	L	Pct	BB	SO	H	SHO	SV	ERA
1951	StLA	1	7.1	0	1	.000	3	5	11	0	0	7.36
1953		10	60.1	2	6	.250	44	61	39	1	0	3.28
1954	BalA	35	247.1	14	15	.483	*181	*185	178	0	0	3.46
1955	**NYA**	**36**	**246.2**	**17**	**13**	**.567**	***177**	**210**	**168**	**6**	**1**	**3.06**
1956		27	132	8	4	.667	103	91	138	1	1	5.05
1957		32	176.1	13	6	.684	85	152	120	4	3	2.71
1958		33	245.1	*21	7	*.750	*128	168	178	6	1	2.97
1959		33	154.1	8	11	.421	83	111	141	3	0	4.32
1960		34	173.1	9	3	.750	87	87	138	1	5	3.27
1961		15	72	3	5	.375	51	48	74	0	0	5.75
1962		24	69	3	3	.500	47	42	68	0	1	4.57
1963	LAA	19	87.1	2	7	.222	51	70	71	2	0	3.30
	BosA	11	41.1	1	4	.200	28	35	42	0	0	6.10

*Led league

Year	Team	G	IP	W	L	Pct	BB	SO	H	SHO	SV	ERA
Yankee years		**234**	**1269**	**82**	**52**	**.612**	**761**	**909**	**1025**	**21**	**12**	**3.62**
Career		310	1712.2	101	85	.543	1068	1265	1366	24	12	3.64
				World Series								
1955	**NYA**	3	5.1	0	1	.000	4	7	7	0	0	8.44
1956		3	11	0	1	.000	8	14	4	0	0	0.82
1957		3	11.2	1	0	1.000	6	12	7	0	0	2.31
1958		4	16.1	2	1	.667	7	13	10	1	1	2.76
1960		2	9.1	1	0	1.000	4	0	15	0	0	4.82
5 years		**15**	**53.2**	**4**	**3**	**.571**	**29**	**46**	**43**	**1**	**1**	**3.19**

Courtesy Dooley Womack

DOOLEY WOMACK
The Yankee Saver

Yankees 1966–1968

Dooley Womack was not considered a major league prospect when he won 13 games in 1959 in Class C. He was also not considered a prospect five years later when he won 10 with a 2.32 ERA in Double A, nor a year later when he won 10 again in Triple A, this time with a league-leading 2.17 ERA.

He spent eight years in the minors playing for seven teams in seven leagues. A lot of young men fell by the wayside in that time. Minor league life can be discouraging, year after year.

But Dooley stuck with it and as a reward for his fine season (10-6, 2.17 ERA) in 1965 with Toledo (International League), the parent New York Yankees placed him on their 40-man roster for 1966. Still, he was not expected to be a factor; more than anything, it was a reward for his dedication.

Dooley didn't see it that way, though. He saw it as an opportunity and seized it. He made the team, albeit the worst Yankees team since 1913 and the first since 1912 to finish in the cellar. He and Steve Hamilton were the set-up men for closers Pedro Ramos and Hal Reniff.

Out of the bullpen, Womack went 7-2, with a 2.13 ERA and four saves. An ill-fated start (his only one in the majors) against Washington made his final record 7-3, with 2.64 ERA, but it was still an exceptional season for a non-prospect on a terrible team. The only Yankee pitcher who pitched more than four innings that season who had a lower earned run average than Dooley was Whitey Ford.

The sophomore jinx had no effect on him. He earned the closer's job in 1967 and was one of the American League's top relievers. The Yankees were still not much, climbing one notch out of the cellar only because Kansas City disintegrated. He finished fourth in the league with 18 saves and the three men who finished above him were all on first division clubs. And he lowered his ERA to 2.41. His 65 games pitched equaled the Yankees' all-time record.

Dooley was established, therefore, as one of the AL's top closers. Things were looking pretty good, but in spring training of 1968 he injured his rotator cuff—not while pitching but while batting. A glance at the record book tells the tale. In two seasons before the injury, he went 12-9, with a 2.51 ERA and 22 saves; in two-plus years after the injury, his record was 7-9, with an ERA of 3.53 and two saves. Over his Yankee career, Womack's earned run average was 2.54, a team record for relievers.

His is not the only career ended by injury, of course. Still, every time it happens you have to wonder what would have been had the player stayed healthy.

I remember when you first came up. I assumed your given name was Dooley and I imagine there are a lot of people out there who still think the same thing. Where'd you get the nickname?

Dooley Womack: It's from a friend of the family. His name was Dool and my mom and dad added the "ey". I was a little kid. I went through school as Horace and on the baseball field and basketball court it was Dooley. My senior year in high school I started putting "Dooley Womack" on my class papers. As the teacher was going around, when she got to my name she said,

"We've got an alias in the class." People never did put it together. In fact, now, when people run across me and recognize me, which not many people do, they say "Horace" and I know good and well they haven't seen me in 30 or 40 years. (Laughs)

Were you signed by the Yankees originally?

Yes. It was real strange. I was nine and oh my senior year in high school and my earned run average was less than one. I got a call from one of the coaches over in Columbia and he said, "Dooley, you need to come out here quick. Johnny Neun of the Yankees is here and I'd like you to work out for him." Johnny Neun was vice president and chief of scouts for the Yankees.

So I hustled out there and I threw. I warmed up in front of the mound, on the mound, and went beyond the mound and continued to throw. He [Neun] said, "Why are you doing that?" I said, "Whenever I get up to the mound, home plate looks closer and I feel like I can throw harder." He said, "Logical."

I went on and I worked out for him. He asked was I playing ball anywhere. I said, "I'm playing in the Dutch Fork League for a team called Lexington." He said, "I'll have our scout keep a watch on you."

I played that summer. I was five and oh and I was pitching a game a week and catching the other. I had games where I shut out the other team, I struck out 18 in one game, I was hitting the ball well and then one night he came to a game where I won like 15 to 13. After the game, Ted Petroskey, the scout, said, "I'd like to sign you."

It just blew my mind. I said, "How could you do that? I had 18 strikeouts in one game, shutouts in other games. I don't understand where you're coming from."

He said, "Dooley, I had to see what your 'sticktoitiveness' was. In other words, I wanted to see if you would stick with the game, whether you won, lost, or whatever." That's when I signed.

You began professional ball as a starting pitcher and did well, but over a six or seven year period they gradually started you less and used you in relief more. It was not a sudden change. What did you think of that?

Well, to get to play ball I would do whatever it took to help the team.

The Yankees were always good to me. It seemed like they would call me in and talk to me every year and just tell me, "Dooley, you keep your nose clean, you stay out of trouble, but you gotta come up with that one pitch to help you get to the big leagues." I tried a knuckleball, I tried breaking balls. You try just about everything.

Then a batting instructor by the name of Wally Moses, who passed away not long ago, met my fiancée and me before we got married and liked us so well he just told me one day—the language I'm gonna use here is gonna be a little bit rough—"Dooley, you need to pack your fucking bags and go home because you're too damned hardheaded to listen. If you don't make some changes, just go home!"

I almost cried 'cause it really hurt. That's the first time somebody really said, "Hey! Do it!" I asked him, "What do we need to do?" He said, "Step back a little bit and throw across your body." And that's what I did, and all of a sudden the ball sank. When that happened, I started winning games.

Doc Edwards came down — this was in Triple A [Toledo] — from the big club and he warmed me up that night in the bullpen. He said, "Dooley, you throw just like [Mel] Stottlemyre. Your ball reacts like his, your breaking ball's the same. It's just unbelievable and I don't understand why you can't win."

That was one of those situations where the confidence built and I won like eight games in a row. I won one game in ten innings, one to nothing. The last game of the season, I went 13 innings and got beat either three to two or four to three. I showed them I could last, regardless of being a thin person.

I found out after the season was over that three or four clubs were interested in me and then the Yankees sent me a contract. In fact, my father-in-law came to our apartment and said, "Have you read this morning's paper?" I said, "No," and he said, "Then you haven't heard. You've been added to the 40-man roster for the Yankees." That was a dream come true.

Even though you were on the 40-man roster, you weren't expected to make the club.

Right. When I arrived in spring training, the first guy I went to was Jake Gibbs. He had started out at Toledo and had gone up to the Yankees and he told me, "I want you to know one thing: You can make this ballcub. You have to get out there and bust your fanny, and I mean bust your fanny *hard*, and you can make this team. But if you don't, you're going back to Toledo.

"I'll give you an extra incentive. Since I'll be catching, I'll give you this new MacGregor [fielder's] glove if you make the team." (Laughs) [Gibbs had played third base as well as catcher in the minor leagues.]

You certainly made it. You were one of the top relievers in the American League your first two years. When did you begin having rotator cuff problems?

That happened in '68 in spring training. I had just pitched three outs against the Mets and all [Ralph] Houk asked of a pitcher was he get in shape.

But what happened was, in '67 I had hit .291. They left me in ball games where they wouldn't leave a regular pitcher because I made contact — I put the ball in play.

I was on the bench and the second out was made and I was giving Houk a hard time. He'd already told me to go on in and shower. I said, "Come on, Skip, let me hit!" If I'd kept my big mouth shut — I tore the rotator cuff swinging the bat. It was a freak accident and there was nothing you could do about it.

I learned to live with it. I took cortisone shots like you wouldn't believe, not only in New York but just about everywhere we went I was being popped. I didn't know what it was but every time I extended my arm to really get behind that fastball and make it sink, the shoulder just felt like it was coming apart. It was quite an experience.

You were a different pitcher between '67 and '68.

Oh, yeah. I was oh and 5 so fast in '68 it was unbelievable. Houk called me in and said, "I know something's wrong, Your fastball is that much slower." He held his hands four to six inches apart. "You don't have the movement on it."

At the time, I was trying to make the transition to being a breaking ball pitcher 'cause that took the pressure off my shoulder. Back then, we didn't come in and say, "I hurt." It was a case of going out there and if you hurt, you pitched.

Another thing I did — I came home and had my own arm operated on instead of going to the ballcub. I was finished at like 31. I could have gotten [Dr. Frank] Jobe or one of those that are renowned to examine me.

I can take pain — or I did take pain — 'cause my arm throbbed like a toothache for four years. I finished up in '71 and I came home and talked to Dr. Lunsford here in Columbia. He would put you under a knife in a bat of an eye. I called him on Monday, went in on Tuesday, and on Wednesday he operated on me. He told me the next morning it took eighty stitches to sew it up. He said, "I don't know how in the hell you threw a baseball." That was in February of '72 and I never threw a ball after that.

I was in the Athletics chain at that point. In '71 I was in Des Moines, Iowa. I had gone to spring training with the Triple A club and I had had words with Charlie Finley. I said, "How can you trade for me and I go to the big club and I'm only there for 38 days and then you not even give me an opportunity to try out with the big club the next year? You personally said you gave too much for me for you to give me my release and let me negotiate with another team, yet you can't see well enough of me to let me come to spring training." I just can't understand some logic sometimes. He was just a different owner. I haven't run into [George] Steinbrenner, so I really can't compare. (Laughs)

I went four years where, if I pitched, that night it throbbed. There was just no sleep. The last 30 days before I had it repaired, I didn't sleep at all. Friends would come to me and say, "Dooley, I'm a friend. Are you on drugs?" I had the black lines under my eyes.

You made one start in your rookie year.

Oh, Lord, yes! If I had it to do over again, I'd do everything completely different. Houk told me the day before that I was gonna start. I told my wife that night, "I want you to wake me up in the morning, I want you to make me grits, eggs, a big slab of ham and I'm gonna go back to bed." And I did.

Dooley Womack *(courtesy New York Yankees)*

I got up and ate that big breakfast, crawled back in bed, slept another hour or two, got up, and she had me a big 16-ounce T-bone, medium rare, baked potato, salad. I ate that and I laid back down.

When I went to the ballpark, I was rested. I felt so good, except when I threw the ball it looked like it was coming back to me a heck of a lot faster than I was throwing it. (Laughs) In fact, [coach] Jim Hegan said, "What in the world! You *look* like you're working hard but there's nothing on it!" (Laughs)

When you warm up, things happen but when you go on the field you hope they change. Well, they didn't. Whitey [Ford] summed it up afterwards in the clubhouse. He said, "Dooley, when you jammed Ed Brinkman" — he was one of the weakest hitters in the American League — "and for him to dump the ball over shortstop for a double, I knew you were in trouble." I gave up nine hits and five runs — two home runs — in that three inning period.

Baseball is a psychological game. Physically, you get in condition, but then everything gets to be mental. I psyched myself out of that. What I should have done was gotten up that morning and eaten that big breakfast, but then eat lightly, move around, maybe go work up a sweat, then go out to the ballpark and I would have been ready. I do feel that the way I pitched in Triple A ball, it's no different. You pitch the same way; you try to stay away from that mistake because, in the big leagues, you make the mistake, they kill you. If they foul that ball back, you say, "Phew! Thank goodness!"

It's easier to pitch in the big leagues because if your control is good, you pitch a good game. If it's bad or erratic, get me outta here quick before they kill me! (Laughs)

The conditions up there are so good — when you've got a Clete Boyer at third base, then we had Ruben Amaro [at shortstop], Bobby Richardson at second, [Joe] Pepitone at first. I probably had some of the best infielders.

I used to throw the sinker down and in to right-handed hitters. Clete, in Boston, taught me something one night. It was early in the season. He told me — he's yelling these curse words — "Throw the blankety-blank ball over the blankety-blank plate and let the blankety-blank hitter hit the blankety-blank ball at me!" I looked at him and said, "Okay."

I threw a sinker down and in and the guy hits a *shot* at him. He picks it clean, throws him out. I said, "You know, that wasn't too hard." I threw another one down and in, the guy hits a shot at him, he picks it clean, he throws him out. And this is only a couple of pitches. I threw a sinker that went off the table — occasionally you can do that — and the guy topped it. I saw on the second hop on the grass, this one was gonna take his head off. What happened, he caught the ball behind his head, threw the guy out.

I walked off the field and said, "I'm a believer!" I pitched four innings that night and only gave up one hit. It was Carl Yastrzemski when the umpire called a strike a ball because of who he was and who I was. I threw him the pitch again because Elston [Howard] had some words with the umpire. He got a ground ball single in the hole at first.

After that year, Boyer was gone [traded to Atlanta] and then I really appreciated him — his range. Bobby Cox was our third baseman [in 1968] and anything just a little to his left or right went through for a hit. And Charley Smith played there some, too. We really missed Boyer.

Speaking of umpires, there was Cal Drummond. One night we're in Yankee Stadium and I came in to pitch and I threw the ball down the middle of the plate. "Ball One!" I flinched. I could see Elston back there talking to the umpire. I didn't say anything.

The next pitch was even better. "Ball Two!" Now I'm getting upset and I think I might have yelled something. Next pitch, "Ball Three!" I traipsed around the mound, throwing the resin bag; I'm infuriated. Elston comes running out there, says, "Hey, man. This guy's ready to throw your ass out of the ball game."

I said, "Hell, I'm a rookie! Those are hell of a pitches!"

He said, "He's testing you. He said that."

I said, "Damn, I'm a rookie! You don't test a rookie!"

Next pitch, "Ball Four!" He goes down to first. Next guy comes up, I throw the pitch down the middle, he hits a ground ball, double play, we get out of the inning.

We come to the dugout and, boy, Ralph Houk jumps me! He let me have it right quick. Elston saved me. He said, "Wait a minute, Major. Dooley has been throwing good pitches. He's testing him." And Houk got on Drummond unmercifully after that.

Did he start giving you some pitches?

After that, I didn't have any problems with him.

The thing I used to love is to watch the umpires. If you're around the plate, watch 'em take it two or three inches off the plate, like they're doing now. I watch a lot of games on TV and you can see why the hitter gets highly upset because the ball will come in and maybe come around the plate, but it's where they catch it. The catchers can frame that ball so pretty now. They can get you out of a lot of jams. Plus his [the catcher's] talking to the umpire. He can get a lot out of the umpire. I think Elston Howard played the umpires to the hilt.

He took me under his wing. He told me in Boston, "Dooley, you better get every penny you can. They're gonna use you long relief, middle relief, short relief. You're gonna be warming up every day. For goodness sakes, get everything you can because life's gonna be short-lived here."

They sure did use you. You tied the team record for games in your second year.

Houk had planned for me to break it. He had set it up, and he told me when I was somewhere around 62 or -3, "I will have you in these games." The next-to-last day [of the season], Fred Talbot went in about the first or second inning and he really had one heck of a relief stint going. He shut out Oakland. Houk had me warming up, but the call never came because Fred was sitting 'em up, sitting 'em down. When the game ended, Houk called me into his office and said, "I just wanted you to know the reason I didn't call you in."

I said, "You don't have to say. I understand. Fred's hoping to stay with the ballclub next year." When a guy's got it, don't take him out. Leave him in there. I like the designated hitter. When a guy's got it and he's one run down he can stay in there and pitch all night. Back then, you [the pitcher] had to hit for yourself.

He said, "You *will* be in there tomorrow." And sure enough, the next day I was in. The last hit I got that year I drove in two runs.

Is there one game that stands out in your mind as your biggest thrill?

The biggest thrill was winning the game when [Mickey] Mantle hit his 500th home run. I was tickled to death that day. It was against Baltimore. I came in in the top of the sixth.

Frank Robinson got a double off of me. I've got a picture. Frank is touching home plate as I'm catching the ball from Elston. I'm putting the tag on Frank but he's safe. What happened was I gave up that one run. Robinson was on second, we had one out. Ground ball in the infield, they threw to first, Robinson rounded third and made a fake to home. I yelled to Mick [playing first], "Home!"

Mick had had that shoulder operation and when he came off the bag, he sort of short-armed the ball and he missed Elston by five or ten feet and it went all the way to the screen. Elston was after it and it was a fairly close play at home because he [Robinson] came in standing up instead of sliding.

After Mantle hit his home run, he came in the dugout and he went over in the corner and he said, "Finally it's over."

I got so wrapped up in it that when I started out for the next inning, my stomach did a flip-flop. You mentally get involved in the excitement of his 500th home run, but then all of a sudden it hit me: You so-and-so, you better get your act together because you gotta go get 'em out.

We got 'em out. After the game I was one of the last ones in the dugout and Mantle came over to me and he shook my hand and he said, "Dooley, I just want to thank you for giving me the opportunity to celebrate my 500th with a win." Those are the things that I'll remember for years and years to come.

You pitched 26 consecutive scoreless innings at one point in 1967. You must have been pretty effective over 12 or 13 games. Were you doing anything differently or was everything just going right?

I was loose, the sinker was working, I was putting the ball where I wanted it.

This is where Houk was such an effective manager. I don't know if this [streak] was in the first of the year or later. I just remember halfway in the season: I came in, Baltimore's beating us one to nothing in the stadium. Houk brings me in to sort of hold them down in the top of the ninth to give us a chance at it in the bottom of the ninth.

Before the smoke is all over, we're losing, five to nothing. Houk comes to the mound and says, "Man, you're like a coiled spring. If I cut the rope, you'd spring your ass right out of this stadium." (Laughs) People wonder what the manager says. He laid it on me. "I want you to throw that ball right down the middle of the plate and let him hit the ball out of this park."

I said, "Okay." And I did. I threw the ball down the middle of the plate to Curt Blefary and he hit a dunker over short and it was a double. And I threw Frank Robinson down the middle and he hit a home run in the elevator shaft — it went straight up. He threw his bat and almost threw it into the stands. Ellie pulled that ball in. Before the inning was over, they had scored four. After the game, Houk came up to me and he said, "Dooley, you having any personal problems?"

I said, "No, sir." "Well, something's bothering you and I want you to tell me."

I said, "Skipper, the only thing that's bothering me, and it's in the back of my mind today, is I want to have a second half like the first." I think I had saved nine, won four, earned run average was way down in the two's. I mean, I was really cruising.

He said, "If that's all your problem, I want you to go home tonight, have a couple Bloody Marys, eat a big steak," and the way he put it, "take a good shit and come out and play baseball tomorrow night." (Laughs)

I loved it! I went home and did exactly what he said. The next day I came out, I went out and threw one pitch, got the team out, we won the ball game.

That's why I'm saying it's all psychological. This [John] Smoltz with Atlanta — they go out and get a psychologist to talk to this kid. Hell, all the pitching coach has to do is get into his head and give him confidence.

You mentioned Mel Stottlemyre earlier. Does he belong in the Hall of Fame?

Mel Stottlemyre was one heck of a pitcher. We knew, being on the team with him, that if he got past the second or third inning, we could go eat a pizza. He was steady. If we could score him a few runs, he'd hold the other team down. If you did any work in his behalf, it would have been maybe in the ninth inning. He may run out of steam or if he got a run or two behind he had to be pinch hit for. Houk knew when he put him on the mound he was gonna battle them. He had a career 2.97 earned run average. That's great, especially for a ballclub that finished like we did.

My rookie year we finished tenth [out of ten], second year was ninth, and my third year I was told I figured in about 31 or 32 percent of our wins in '67, with saves and wins. We were a type of ballclub that, if you gave up one run in the late innings, you lost.

The time that you and Stottlemyre were there was probably the worst period in Yankee history to that time.

This is why a lot of writers have said, "Dooley, if you were with any other team, you'd be a shoo-in for the saves [lead]." But then I look at it and say if the Yankees hadn't been in such a bad array at that point, I may never have gotten a chance.

When a pitcher has an ERA under 2.5 he'll get a chance. You saved 25 percent of the team's wins and the rule then made saves a little more difficult to come by.

You had to face the winning or tying run or they had to be on base.

Johnny Keane is the one that gave me my shot. He was fired when the team was out in Anaheim. On the road, one game you're next to someone and the next game you're next to someone else. I happened to be lockering next to Mantle there in Anaheim. We just got the word there in the clubhouse and the guys started lining up at Keane's door and I looked at Mantle and I said, "Mick, what do you say?" He said, "Hell, Dooley, I don't know. This has never happened since I've been here."

I was last. I went in the room and you just don't know what to say. I walked in and I said, "Skipper, I'm sorry to hear what happened but I want to thank you for giving me the opportunity to pitch here."

He said, "Dooley, let me tell you something: If you weren't good enough to be here, you wouldn't be here. You go out and continue to pitch like you're pitching now and you're gonna do well." I came out of that room and he picked me up instead of me picking him up. (Laughs) That was the kind of man he was.

I heard, when he passed away about a year or so later, that he probably died of a broken heart. He probably never had a real chance [with the Yankees]. The ballclub was injured. Mantle got his foot caught under a fence.

[Fritz] Peterson and I, when we first got there as rookies, used to pump Mantle up. We'd say, "Mick, you're gonna hit about 40 this year." And he'd say, "You guys are about ten years too late." We told him if he had sound legs, there's no telling what he would have done. He said if he had sound legs, he may have never played baseball. He said, "I may have never been an athlete." He meant that as, "I don't want this to be an excuse."

I remember one night in Detroit when his hamstring popped. I mean, it sounded like a .22! You saw him bounce that ball back to the mound and he broke out of that box from the left side and I said, "My God! When he was younger, look what he could have done!" I heard he could get down to first in three-something [seconds]. That's like, "Hey, man!" and he's there.

All of a sudden he pulls up lame. He came straight in the dugout, went straight in, showered, hit a plane, and took off for Dallas. Then we were without him for a couple of weeks.

I wonder what would a Mantle, a Mays, an Aaron be paid now? If these guys today can demand five or six million dollars a year and their attitude toward the game is so much different, it would take the National Bank to pay those guys.

Do you get much fan mail?

It comes in spurts. I average a couple a week. I try to get my mail out. I sit down when I get it, do it, and put it right back in the mail.

I had a guy call me from California and he said, "I've got your rookie card with Bobby Murcer on it. If I send it to you, will you autograph it?" I said, "Yeah, as long as that envelope's there. I'll put it right back in the mail."

He asked if I had a second to talk and I said sure. He said, "Being here in San Francisco"— now I'm going back a few years —"Frank Robinson is our manager out here. I happened to catch him one day and I asked him who was the toughest pitcher on him, And he said it was a fairly unknown pitcher by the name of Dooley Womack."

I told him that didn't surprise me because I faced him approximately 17 times, give or take, struck him out 12. He hated me. I mean, we were friends but when we went between the lines, it was Frank against Dooley.

Curt Blefary — I knew him from the Yankees — he got ahold of Frank down in spring training. I'm on the third base line catching the balls [thrown in] from the outfield and Curt said, "Hey, Frank, here's the guy that's sticking that bat up your rear!" He gave him a hard time. He said, "Frank, what did it cost you in income with this guy stuffing you?" Frank said, "At least ten grand." I said, "That's a lot more than I made!" (Laughs) Of course, when the game starts, the joking stops.

Talking about autographs, I did one card show up in New Jersey. I enjoyed it. After it was over, the guy told me, "They loved you. You spoke to them." He asked if I'd do another one and I said, "Anytime. You just say when."

I played in an old-timers game down here, against the guys that played on the old mill teams. I'd like to go to a Yankees old-timers day, but I don't know what you have to do or who you have to impress. I've let 'em know I'm available, but I've never heard anything."

Any regrets from your career, other than the injury?

That's the biggest one. Everything else is plusses.

[Jim] Bouton asked me my rookie year, "What has baseball done for you?" I said, "Jim, I cannot put a dollar figure on my rookie year in the show. I've met people and I've made friends all across the country." He said, "But you're not making any money." I said, "But I still can't put a dollar sign on it."

It's a business now. When I read in the papers that so-and-so has filed bankruptcy and this-and-that-and-the-other, I am awed. I know bad luck hits people, but not when you're making hundreds of thousands of dollars. I just don't understand it.

Would you go back and be a ballplayer again?

In a skinny minute.

HORACE GUY (DOOLEY) WOMACK
Born August 25, 1939, Columbia, South Carolina
Ht. 6'   Wt. 170   Batted and Threw Left

Year	Team	G	IP	W	L	Pct	BB	SO	H	SHO	SV	ERA
1966	**NYA**	**42**	**75**	**7**	**3**	**.700**	**23**	**50**	**52**	**0**	**4**	**2.64**
1967		**65**	**97**	**5**	**6**	**.455**	**35**	**57**	**80**	**0**	**18**	**2.41**
1968		**45**	**61.2**	**3**	**7**	**.300**	**29**	**27**	**53**	**0**	**2**	**3.21**
1969	HouN	30	51.1	2	1	.667	20	32	49	0	0	3.51
	SeaA	9	14.1	2	1	.667	3	8	15	0	0	2.51
1970	OakA	2	3	0	0	.000	1	3	4	0	0	15.00
Yankee years		**152**	**233.2**	**15**	**16**	**.484**	**87**	**134**	**185**	**0**	**24**	**2.72**
Career		193	302.1	19	18	.514	111	177	253	0	24	2.95

YANKEES IN THE HALL OF FAME

Yankees from every position, every decade, and every level of baseball are in the Hall of Fame. Some weren't Yankees long or are not remembered as Yankees, but Yankees they were. Here they are.

Players
Frank "Home Run" Baker, 3b
Yogi Berra, c
Jack Chesbro, p
Earle Combs, of
Bill Dickey, c
Joe DiMaggio, of
Whitey Ford, p
Lou Gehrig, 1b
Lefty Gomez, p
Waite Hoyt, p
Catfish Hunter, p
Reggie Jackson, of
Wee Willie Keeler, of
Tony Lazzeri, 2b
Mickey Mantle, of
Johnny Mize, 1b
Phil Niekro, p
Herb Pennock, p
Gaylord Perry, p
Phil Rizzuto, ss
Red Ruffing, p
Babe Ruth, of
Enos Slaughter, of

Managers
Bucky Harris
Miller Huggins
Bob Lemon
Joe McCarthy
Casey Stengel

Executives
Ed Barrow
Larry MacPhail
George Weiss

BIBLIOGRAPHY

Chadwick, Bruce, and David M. Spindel. *The Bronx Bombers.* New York: Abbeville Press, 1992.

Charlton, James, ed. *The Baseball Chronology.* New York: Macmillan, 1991.

Creamer, Robert W. *Stengel: His Life and Times.* New York: Dell, 1984.

Forker, Dom. *The Men of Autumn.* New York: Signet, 1989.

Gallagher, Mark. *50 Years of Yankee All-Stars.* New York: Leisure Press, 1984.

Golenbock, Peter. *Dynasty: The New York Yankees 1949–1964.* New York: Berkley, 1985.

Johnson, Lloyd, and Brenda Ward. *Who's Who in Baseball History.* New York: Barnes and Noble, 1994.

Marazzi, Rick, and Len Fiorito. *Aaron to Zipfel.* New York: Avon, 1985.

_____. *Aaron to Zuverink.* New York: Avon, 1982.

Reichler, Joe; revised by Ken Samelson. *The Great All-Time Baseball Record Book.* New York: Macmillan, 1993.

Salant, Nathan. *This Date in New York Yankees History.* New York: Scarborough, 1983.

Shatzkin, Mike, ed. *The Ballplayers.* New York: William Morrow, 1990.

The Sporting News Conlon Collection. "Charlie Devens". St. Louis: Megacards, 1994.

Thorn, John, and Pete Palmer. *Total Baseball,* 4th ed. New York: Viking, 1995.

Wolff, Rick, ed. dir. *The Baseball Encyclopedia,* 9th ed. New York: Macmillan, 1993.

Index

*Numbers in **boldface** refer to pages with photographs.*